Religio Duplex

Amicis caris
Martin Mulsow, Sarah and Guy Stroumsa

Religio Duplex

How the Enlightenment Reinvented Egyptian Religion

Jan Assmann

Translated by Robert Savage

polity

First published in German as *Religio Duplex* © Verlag der Weltreligionen im Insel Verlag Berlin 2011. All rights reserved by and controlled through Insel Verlag Berlin.

This English edition © Polity Press, 2014

The translation of this work was funded by Geisteswissenschaften International – Translation Funding for Humanities and Social Sciences from Germany, a joint initiative of the Fritz Thyssen Foundation, the German Federal Foreign Office, the collecting society VG WORT and the Börsenverein des Deutschen Buchhandels (German Publishers & Booksellers Association).

Polity Press
65 Bridge Street
Cambridge CB2 1UR, UK

Polity Press
350 Main Street
Malden, MA 02148, USA

ISBN-13: 978-0-7456-6842-0
ISBN-13: 978-0-7456-6843-7(pb)

A catalogue record for this book is available from the British Library.

Typeset in 10.5 on 12 pt Sabon
by Toppan Best-set Premedia Limited
Printed and bound in Great Britain by Clays Ltd, St Ives plc

The publisher has used its best endeavours to ensure that the URLs for external websites referred to in this book are correct and active at the time of going to press. However, the publisher has no responsibility for the websites and can make no guarantee that a site will remain live or that the content is or will remain appropriate.

Every effort has been made to trace all copyright holders, but if any have been inadvertently overlooked the publisher will be pleased to include any necessary credits in any subsequent reprint or edition.

For further information on Polity, visit our website: www.politybooks.com

Contents

Foreword

This study investigates the differences between public and arcane doctrine, freely available and restricted ideas about the divine, profane and initiated forms of social life, the God of the Fathers and the philosophers' god. My interest in these matters has two roots. Both reach a long way back in my intellectual biography, and they also have something to do with my own 'double life' as Egyptologist and cultural scientist. The first goes back to the project on the topic of 'secrecy' that Aleida Assmann and I (in my role of cultural scientist) investigated in a series of conferences organized some fifteen to twenty years ago by the research group, Archaeology of Literary Communication; the proceedings were subsequently published in three volumes (*Veil and Threshold*, vol. 1: *Secrecy and the Public Sphere*, 1997; vol. 2: *Secrecy and Revelation*, 1998; vol. 3: *Secrecy and Curiosity*, 1999). The second, Egyptological aspect derives from the friendly debate, carried out in the 1980s between Erik Hornung and myself, about the problem of an ancient Egyptian monotheism, a debate in which the question of an esoteric tradition of mono- or pantheistic ideas in the context of ancient Egyptian polytheism also played a role (*Monotheism and Cosmotheism: Ancient Egyptian Forms of 'Thinking the One' and their European Reception History*, 1993). This interest was sustained throughout my research on the reception of Egypt in the seventeenth and eighteenth centuries, documented in *Moses the Egyptian* (1997/98) and *The Magic Flute* (2005). Above all, it was my preoccupation with Mozart's opera and an important aspect of its cultural-historical environment, Viennese freemasonry, which first opened my eyes to the immense importance assigned to Egypt in late eighteenth-century masonic circles as the (supposed) prototype of a culture split between public sphere and mystery cult, exoteric and esoteric religion. I coined the term *religio duplex* to indicate this entire complex of ideas, interpreting *The Magic Flute* as an *opera duplex*. In my book on Mozart's opera, I lacked the space to retrace in any detail the history of this idea from antiquity through to Mozart's lodge and masonic investigations into Egyptian and other mysteries. This study will endeavour to make good that omission.

My work on the study began in early 2004 at the International Research Centre for Culture Sciences (IFK) in Vienna. At the Austrian Grand Lodge, I am deeply indebted to Dr Rüdiger Wolf for placing rare archival materials at my disposal. The study was completed in early 2010 during a two-week stay at the research library in Frieden-stein Castle. The library's director, Prof. Martin Mulsow, kindly placed at my disposal the arcana of his private library as well as the riches of the Gotha collection, drawing my attention to many passages and byways in the labyrinth of baroque erudition that would otherwise have escaped my notice. That is why I dedicate this book to him, alongside my friends in Jerusalem, Sarah and Guy Stroumsa, with whom I proposed some years ago (and subsequently researched) the thesis that the history of religion was discovered in the seventeenth century (ARG 3 [2001]). In April 2010 I was invited to present the most important findings of this study during a short guest professorship at Graz University, and to discuss them with colleagues and students there; for that opportunity, I am deeply grateful to Prof. Irmtraud Fischer. I also extend my heartfelt thanks to Hans-Joachim Simm and Claus-Jürgen Thornton for originally accepting this study for publication in the *Verlag der Weltreligionen*, and especially to Claus-Jürgen for the extraordinary care he took in editing the manuscript. I owe many references and comments in this book to his scrutiny, and it is only at his express wish that they have not been individually acknowledged.

Abbreviations

The following abbreviations have been used in the endnotes:

ARG   Archiv für Religionsgeschichte
JEA   *Journal of Egyptian Archaeology*
JF   *Journal für Freymaurer*
KV   Köchelverzeichnis
RAC   *Reallexikon für Antike und Christentum*

Introduction

To introduce the theme of dual religion, I want to bring two scenes to mind. The first took place in the year 1654. On 11 November of that year, the thirty-one-year-old Blaise Pascal, a mathematician of genius and seeker after God who was suffering from deep depression at the time, and probably tuberculosis as well, had a religious experience that fundamentally changed his life. Wanting to hold fast to this experience under all circumstances, to preserve it from the vicissitudes of memory and fortune, he noted the essentials on a piece of parchment, which he then sewed into his coat so that it would always lie close to his heart. The note was discovered after his death by his manservant. It reads:

In the year of Grace, 1654,

On Monday, 23rd of November, Feast of St. Clement, Pope and Martyr, and of others in the Martyrology,

Vigil of St. Chrysogonis, Martyr, and others,

From around half past ten in the evening until about half past twelve.

FIRE

God of Abraham, God of Isaac, God of Jacob, not of the philosophers and scholars.

Certitude. Certitude. Feeling. Joy. Peace.

God of Jesus Christ

Deum meum et Deum vestrum.

'Thy God shall be my God.' [Ruth 1:16]

Forgetfulness of the world and of everything, except God.

He is to be found only by the ways taught in the Gospel.

Greatness of the human soul.

'Righteous Father, the world hath not known Thee, but I have known Thee.'

Joy, joy, joy, tears of joy.

I have separated myself from Him

Dereliquerunt me fontem aquae vivae [They have abandoned me, the source of the living waters.]

'My God, wilt Thou leave me?'

Let me not be separated from Him eternally.

'That is the eternal life, that they might know Thee, the only true God, and the one whom Thou has sent, Jesus Christ.'

Jesus Christ.

Jesus Christ.

I have separated myself from Him; I have fled from Him, denied Him, crucified Him.

Let me never be separated from Him.

We keep hold of Him only by the ways taught in the Gospel.

Renunciation, total and sweet.

Total submission to Jesus Christ and to my [spiritual] director. Eternally in joy for a day's training on earth.

Non obliviscar sermons tuos. [I shall not forget what you have taught me.] Amen.[2]

In the course of two hours of intense religious turmoil, Pascal thus threw himself into the arms of the God of the Fathers and turned his back on the philosophers' and scholars' god.

The second scene played out 126 years later, in July 1780, in the house of Gotthold Ephraim Lessing in Wolfenbüttel. He had just been paid a visit by the young businessman and writer Friedrich Heinrich Jacobi. Lessing welcomed his fellow freemason as a brother. The following morning, Lessing sought to entertain his guest; Jacobi was still busy and gave his host something to read while he was waiting. It was Goethe's poem 'Prometheus', not yet published at the time. Questioned on it afterwards by Jacobi, Lessing confessed: 'The orthodox concepts of the divine are no longer for me. I cannot stand them. *Hen kai pan!* I know nothing else. That's where this poem is tending, too; and I must confess I like it a lot.' Jacobi: 'Then you would be more or less in agreement with Spinoza.' Lessing: 'If I am to call myself by anybody's name, then I know none better.'[3] Lessing thus rejects the God of the Fathers (if we are permitted to identify 'the orthodox concepts of the divine' with this idea of god), declaring his allegiance to the philosopher's god instead. This split, this tension, this either/or stamped the religious history of the European Enlightenment. Jacobi himself suffered from it throughout his life, and spoke of a *salto mortale* that he had to make in order to be able to think the one God *and* the other god.[4]

The tension between two notions of god – the philosophers' god and the God of the Fathers – was encapsulated in the seventeenth and eighteenth centuries in the opposition between natural religion and revealed (or positive) religion, between reason and faith. What was understood by natural religion was a kind of monotheistically or rather pantheistically conceived primordial religion, a Spinozism *avant la lettre*. The scholars' and philosophers' god, far from having sprung fully formed from a modern, secular age, was thus deemed the most ancient knowledge of humankind; it was certainly anything but a pallid philosophical construct. The formula *hen kai pan* – literally, 'one-and-all' or 'all-one' – is generally traced back to Heraclitus, who reportedly taught that 'all is one'.[5] But another antecedent lay closer to hand in the seventeenth and eighteenth centuries: many scholars thought they could demonstrate this pantheistic primal religion of all-oneness in ancient Egypt, a 'discovery' to which Lessing's *Hen kai pan* possibly alludes.[6] In his imposing work, *The True Intellectual System of the Universe*, the Cambridge Platonist and Hebraist Ralph Cudworth had drawn on hundreds of sources to reconstruct all the theologies of the ancient world, including the theology of ancient Egypt. His aim was to prove that all religions essentially boil down to a monotheism of all-oneness.[7] Although he wrote the work in English, a language that few scholars could understand at the time, it was translated into Latin in 1733 by no less a figure than Johann Lorenz von Mosheim, and so made accessible to the European scholarly world.[8] In this work, Cudworth presented the idea of all-oneness as the quintessence of ancient Egyptian religion and theology, or rather: *one* Egyptian theology, for there were two:

a 'publick' and an 'arcane theology'. According to Cudworth, all ancient religions are two-faced, as it were. They have an outer face, in the form of the official religion, and an inner face, in the form of mysteries, and the original model or prototype of all these dual religions is the religion of the ancient Egyptians. It was from them that Heraclitus borrowed the idea of all-oneness.

Cudworth's may be considered the classic account of the idea of *religio duplex*. The expression itself does not occur in his writings, however. As Martin Mulsow pointed out to me, it was first coined by Theodor Ludwig Lau (1670–1740), who introduced it in his text *Meditationes, Theses, Dubia philosophico-theologica* to refer to the distinction between rational religion (*religio rationis*) and revealed religion (*religio revelationis*).[9] Like Cudworth before him, Lau begins by making clear that there has never been any such thing as atheism; an awareness and veneration of god are basic endowments of humankind. In principle, only *one* religion exists, since there is only *one* reason and only *one* god.[10] There is no end to philosophical and theological statements, however, and these represent modifications of the one truth and theology. They are all more or less true (*plus vel minus veriores*) and differ from each other only in degree, not in kind, insofar as they all bear some relation to the one truth, from which they deviate to a greater or lesser extent. The 'first, oldest, most general and most rational religion is belief in god (*Deismus*).'[11] Religions like 'Judaism, paganism (*Gentilismus*), Christianity, Islam and countless other forms of divine knowledge and religious sects' have emerged from this primordial religion over the course of time. In spite of all their historically conditioned differences, they all concur in affirming: 'Deus est! Deus existit!' (Thesis X); 'God was when no religion yet existed. For god is of eternity, but religion is temporal, historical, and accidental in relation to god' (Thesis XI).[12] And with that, he arrives at Thesis XII: 'Religio duplex: Rationis & Revelationis' – 'Religion is dual: as religion of reason and as religion of revelation'. Reason teaches that god exists and is one in his being. This form of divine knowledge is simple: it satisfies reason. 'Reason worships god as the creator, conserver and governor of the universe through a cult that is as inward as possible. Its book is this universe.'[13] Whoever worships god in this way, reading his signs in the universe, will think and live in peace. 'Here there is no perturbation of the spirit due to sins and eternal fire.'[14] Hell and the devil are equally unknown. Death does not exist, for all things come from god, and since god is eternal, so too are things. Souls migrate from bodies and are united with the world-soul.[15] So much for the religion of reason. The religion of revelation, by contrast, teaches that both Testaments, the Old and the New, are the book of God. God is three-in-one (*triunus*). Adam and Eve, the first humans, fell after they tasted of the forbidden fruit and were exiled from Paradise. That is how sin entered into the world (*Peccatum hinc intrasse Mundum*). God's son, born of a virgin, died on the cross to save us from sin. This Gospel is preached to all. Those who accept it will gain entry into heaven; those who reject it will be consigned to hell (*Recipientibus illud, Coelum: Spernentibus, Infernum*). So much for the religion of revelation. One religion is simple and transparent (*plana et perspicua*), the other more difficult and mysterious (*difficilior et mysteriosa*). Both are true, but they are perfect in varying degrees. The most perfect and excellent religion, however, is the 'Religio quia Dei, & Christi', the religion of God and Christ, which ought by rights to designate the religion of revelation, but which Lau, after everything that has gone before, evidently takes to mean the religion of reason.[16] Thinking back to Pascal's nocturnal epiphany, one could connect the first religion to the philosophers' and savants' god, the second to the God of the Fathers.

The thirteenth thesis further refines the idea of God's two books, an idea which underlies the conception of both religions or of *religio duplex*.[17] God manifests himself in the world in two ways: universally and particularly. Universally in creation: that is the basis of rational religion, and it is common to all peoples. Particularly through 'divine speeches, angels, appearances, visions, inspirations, dreams, oracles, predictions, prophecies, miracles, Holy Scripture: those are the foundations of revealed religion and reserved for particular nations, especially the Jewish and the Christian.'[18] The fourteenth thesis pursues the principle of division into the human world. As God's creatures, all humans are his people. This people, however, can be separated into two categories: the unknown and the known. The unknown people inhabit the visible and invisible spheres of the universes, whereas the known people have our globe as their temporary dwelling place. The known people are split, in turn, between the chosen people and the other nations. The Jews and Christians are the elect. The remaining nations, although not chosen, are still God's people; for they recognize and worship God from creation, whereas the chosen (double) people recognize him from revelation. Knowledge from the book of nature comes earlier, however; the book of scripture appeared later.[19] Natural religion, supported by the book of nature, is thus older and more primordial than revealed religion, which draws from the book of scripture. The latter is twofold as well, being divided into the Old and the New Testaments. 'Now, in a general and abstract sense, all are believers in god (*Deistae*), worshippers and adorers of god, lovers of religion!'[20] This great text from the beginning of the eighteenth century already gives almost exactly the same meaning to the idea of dual religion as that which our investigation, steering a path through Lessing, Mendelssohn, and various more recent positions, will arrive at. It is an idea which still offers a highly topical contribution to peace and understanding between religions.

The _duplex_ in Lau's twelfth thesis is to be understood predicatively, not attributively. He is not talking about a twofold religion, but saying that religion exists in two forms: as (natural) religion of reason and as revealed religion. When Lau typifies one as coming earlier and the other as coming later, he anticipates the distinction between primary and secondary religions introduced by the Heidelberg scholar of religion, Theo Sundermeier.[21] We are dealing here with two different forms of religion, rather than with one religion that has two different faces or two religions coexisting within one and the same culture.

In this latter sense, however, the idea makes an appearance at roughly the same time as Lau's thesis, in a work by the polymath Jacob Friedrich Reimmann, entitled _Idea Systematis Antiquitatis Literariae Specialioris sive Aegyptiacae Adumbrati_.[22] He summarizes his comprehensive enumeration of the various disciplines of ancient Egyptian science in the sentence: 'Suffice it to say that the philosophy of the Egyptians as a whole was twofold (_duplex_): exoteric and esoteric.'[23] Here, too, _duplex_ is predicative, not attributive. But the predicate of duality in this passage refers not to two separate forms of philosophy, but to philosophy in two forms: one public and visible, the other secret and accessible only to the initiated (although here, too, the distinction between reason and faith or nature and revelation always resonates more or less discernibly).

It might be supposed that the God of the Fathers and the philosophers' god could perhaps also be accommodated in such a philosophy or religion – one on the exoteric level, the other on the esoteric. In the context of the _religio duplex_ model, then, the secret or esoteric side of religion does not simply represent one 'heterotope' among other heterotopes segregated from the general, public sphere (such as intimacy, carnival, ritual or masonic lodge), but constitutes the Other of the public and general culture that is defined by this very binary opposition. The model of _religio duplex_ is consequently based not simply on a pluralism internal to a culture, but on a _dualism_. With that, nothing has yet been said about the ideological interpretations, social consequences and political institutionalizations of this dualism; these can vary from epoch to epoch and from society to society.[24]

Where does this idea of a dual religion come from, and how did ancient Egyptian culture come to be seen as the source and inventor of this type of religion? That is the question to which the first chapter of this book is devoted. In the second chapter I investigate how this idea was articulated in the seventeenth century, with a prelude in the twelfth century. The third chapter deals with the political refunctioning of *religio duplex* in the eighteenth century, while the fourth retraces the dialectic of Enlightenment and mystery in late eighteenth-century freemasonry. Taking its cue from Lessing and Mendelssohn, the fifth chapter illuminates the decisive reinterpretation of the idea of dual religion in the sense of an opposition between particularity and universality. We have already seen this process at work in Theodor Lau, and here the idea assumes a form which can claim a certain topicality for us today, as I show by juxtaposing it with more recent positions. The study concludes with a 'prospectus', in which I attempt to follow the idea of *religio duplex* through to the present and demonstrate its continuing relevance, as well as with a 'retrospectus', where I look for traces or foreshadowings of dual religion in the ancient Israelite and ancient Egyptian religions.

Even though the idea of dual religion rests on a misunderstanding, as far as its derivation from Egyptian religious history is concerned, there are still certain features, in the ancient Egyptian as well as in the ancient Israelite religion (and in a wealth of other religions, if this question were to be pursued systematically), which indicate a kind of double-sidedness or complementary dualism within a single religion. To be sure, these phenomena were completely unknown to the seventeenth and eighteenth centuries, when the concept of dual religion was first developed. That is why I have chosen not to deal with them in the first chapter. Instead, I cast a backward glance at the evidence in the Hebrew Bible and the ancient Egyptian tradition which, from today's vantage point, may be interpreted as aspects of dual religion, even though they played no part in the debates of the seventeenth and eighteenth centuries.

I should admit in advance that the term *religio duplex* surfaces only a single time in the sources examined here, in the aforementioned Lau. Unlike the monumental, four-volume work of Ernst Feil, which investigates the incidence and meaning of the word *religio* in a plethora of texts from the sixteenth to the eighteenth centuries, this study is not a contribution to the history of concepts. I follow several stations in the development of an idea that I myself have dubbed *religio duplex*, and which appears under different labels and descriptions in the texts I investigate. The entire discourse on Egypt as *religio duplex* and model for the 'new mysteries' in the absolutist state of the eighteenth century would have remained a marginal phenomenon of merely antiquarian interest, at best, had it not taken a new turn through Reinhold and Schiller – and, in a different way, through Lessing and Mendelssohn – which can also claim relevance for the present and which merits broader public interest. We are dealing, on the one hand, with a reconstruction of European religious history that draws on the idea of *religio duplex* to connect the 'depth current' (Klaus Müller) of ancient – and especially Egyptian – cosmotheism with a Western tradition influenced by Christianity and monotheism; and, on the other hand, with the widening or rechannelling of this 'depth current' into a 'religion of humankind' of concealed truth, which, for Mendelssohn, represents the common goal of all religions. In this form, the model seems pertinent to our own time as well, in which the cultures and therefore religions of this earth have drawn together in such a way that none of them can afford to claim sole possession of absolute and universal truths. Religion has a place in our globalized world only as *religio duplex*, that is, as a religion that understands itself as one among many and has learned to see itself through the eyes of the other, without losing sight of the concealed god or the concealed truth that forms the vanishing point of all religions.

1

Egyptian Foundations
The Dual Meaning of Signs

Religio Duplex and the Endgame of Egyptian Culture

Although the idea of 'dual religion' ultimately derives from ancient sources, it represents a construction of the seventeenth and eighteenth centuries which, so far as ancient Egyptian culture is concerned, rests mainly on misconceptions. Before we turn to address this idea in its own right, three points need to be considered. First, there were certain characteristics of Egyptian culture which sanctioned their interpretation as *religio duplex*. Second, the Greeks – who can ultimately be held responsible for this interpretation – could still experience Egyptian culture in full flower and receive answers to their questions about it. And, third, there is much evidence to suggest that the Egyptians who were interrogated by the Greeks in this way themselves set out to disseminate an image of their culture as a *religio duplex*, a religion split between popular and elite culture. It may therefore have been the Egyptians of this late period who put into circulation many apparent misunderstandings. The idea of Egyptian religion as *religio duplex* would then be a Greco-Roman confabulation, rather than the product of a one-sided Greek projection of native ideas and institutions onto the Egyptian world.[1] We should therefore begin by looking more closely at the interlocutors.

On the Greek side, we find a slew of research into Egyptian culture that almost merits the title of an Egyptology.[2] The second book of the *Histories* of Herodotus, who travelled to Egypt around 450 BCE, offers a comprehensive description of the country, with excurses into its history, religion, customs and mores, geography and chronology.

The four-volume history of Egypt by Hecataeus of Abdera, who lived in Alexandria towards the end of the fourth century BCE, must have been even more wide-ranging. Diodorus of Sicily, a contemporary of Cicero, imported large sections of this book into his *Historical Library (Bibliotheca historica)*.[3] Strabo devoted the seventeenth book of his *Geography* to Egypt.[4] These works deal very extensively with Egypt, shedding light on its state, system of government, religion, culture, history, customs, geography, mythology and much else besides. Despite the occasional expression of bemusement and disapproval, they are all marked by a tone of fascination and admiration. This positive appraisal is perhaps most noticeable in Hecataeus (as cited by Diodorus). It was this representation of ancient Egyptian culture that was to exert by far the greatest influence on the Enlightenment view of Egypt.

Hecataeus of Abdera numbered among the many Greek scholars and philosophers invited to Alexandria by Ptolemy I (367/366–283/282 BCE), with the aim of acquiring intellectual prestige in the Hellenistic world for his newly founded capital. His history of Egypt was meant to provide the Macedonian ruler who commissioned it with an historical past on which he could base his project of a Hellenistic-Egyptian pharaonic dynasty. At the same time, the work was intended to hold up a mirror to Ptolemy, reflecting back the model of an enlightened monarchy. Strikingly, Hecataeus (or Diodorus) fails to mention the divine status which the Egyptians traditionally associated with the office of pharaoh. He depicts the king as a man duty-bound to uphold strict laws and to adhere to a daily routine prescribed right down to the minutiae; a sovereign who excels his subjects through his extraordinary virtues, his extensive education, and the rigorous example of his conduct, at best, but not through any divine attributes.[5] This image of the ideal ruler must be set in the context of contemporary Greek political theory, which distinguished between freedom and despotism and placed the law on the side of freedom and democracy, whereas despots were deplored for ruling without regard for existing laws. Against the background of this alternative, Hecataeus – like Plato, Isocrates and other conservative political theorists before him – recommends Egypt as a third way that unites monarchy and the law.[6] In the heyday of absolutism, this image of Egypt could therefore be advanced as a counter-model to the absolutist state. So it was that, 2,000 years later, Hecataeus's Egypt could once again serve as a mirror for princes. At the behest of Louis XIV, Jean-Bénigne Bossuet wrote his *Discours sur l'histoire universelle* (1681) as a guide- and textbook for the dauphin, hence under conditions comparable to the

Alexandrine Museum. Egypt was described there as the school of wise lawmaking and politics, a land which envisaged the happiness of the people as its supreme goal and strictly committed the king to upholding the law.

With Egypt's annexation by Rome as a crown colony, the country forfeited its political interest for the Greeks. Now religion – and the culture of writing, believed to stand in the closest possible connection to that religion – moved to the forefront of attention. Among the most important works of Greek Egyptology to have survived from this period are Plutarch's treatise, *De Iside et Osiride* (*On Isis and Osiris*),[7] and the text known since the Renaissance by the title *De mysteriis Aegyptiorum* (*On the Egyptian Mysteries*),[8] written by the Neoplatonist Iamblichus and stylized as the reply of an Egyptian priest, Abammon, to Porphyry's *Letter to Anebo*.[9]

To be sure, the Greek 'Egyptologists' had no first-hand knowledge of Egyptian religious affairs. They were ignorant of the language and unable to read the writing. For this reason, modern Egyptology has tended to dismiss this literature as an authentic source on Egyptian religion. What is thereby overlooked, however, is the fact that those who contributed to this Egyptological discourse included Greek-writing Egyptians who were well-versed in Egyptian writing, language and religion: above all, the priests Manetho of Sebennytos[10] (first half of the third century BCE) and Chaeremon of Alexandria (first century CE).[11] While their works are now mostly no longer extant, Plutarch, Iamblichus and others could still consult them, and authentic information may well have found its way into their writings by this route. The image of Egypt that the Greek 'Egyptologists' handed down to us may thus contain more genuinely Egyptian ideas and motifs than we realize.

To this Greco-Egyptian 'Egyptological' canon was added, in late antiquity, a fairly extensive religious Greco-Egyptian primary litera-ture, above all the 'magical papyri'[12] and the treatises of the Corpus Hermeticum.[13] This literature mostly purports to be translated from the Egyptian, but it is so strongly steeped in Neoplatonic terminology and motifs that the Egyptian content has tended to be dismissed as a masquerade.[14] However, Iamblichus expressly points out that the 'Hermetic' writings, in being translated into Greek, were equally brought 'into the language [i.e., conceptual vocabulary] of the phi-losophers'.[15] This means that the situation could be exactly the oppo-site of that assumed by later scholars: the Greek content, not the Egyptian, could be the 'packaging'. At any rate, the Egyptian ele-ments in this discourse, too, are being assessed quite differently today.[16]

The Greek-language literature that flowed from Egyptian quills was unmistakably guided by propagandistic intentions: it was motivated by the desire to present Greeks and others with as impressive an image of Egyptian culture as possible. The authors would have been members of the educated, Greek-speaking former upper class. At the time, these were primarily priests. Under the conditions of foreign rule, beginning with the conquest of Egypt by the Persians in 525 BCE and continuing – and, in many respects, worsening – under the Macedonians and Romans, the native Egyptian elite had been forced to come to terms with the loss of its political power, which had now passed into the hands of the occupying forces. Whereas the Persians had still ruled the land in collaboration with the Egyptians, the Greeks immigrated in vast numbers to Egypt and established themselves as a new ruling class.[17] The Egyptian elite reacted to its loss of political influence and social standing with a process of inner emigration, retreating into the sanctified space of the temple. This led, on the one hand, to a clericalization of Egyptian culture, whose standard-bearers were now to be found above all in the priesthood, and to a structural transformation of religion, on the other hand. The religious traditions now expanded into an immensely complicated system consisting of ritual, learning and grammatology, a kind of arcane glass-bead game which – through the virtuosity with which they played it, the intellectual and spiritual prestige it conferred upon them, even and especially in the eyes of the Greeks, and the magical-spiritual claims to power they asserted through it – could to a certain extent compensate the sacerdotal elite for the political interests they had been forced to relinquish. This transformation most clearly left its mark on the culture of writing, which will be examined more closely in the next chapter. The stock of hieroglyphs increased tenfold; learning to write accordingly meant embarking on a decades-long process of initiation into a highly complex world of knowledge; and mastery of writing came to be regarded as a high art. Shut off in the sanctuary of the temple, the clericalized Egyptian culture for many centuries proved remarkably adept at resisting the pressure to Hellenize, even as it paid for its inner emigration by losing contact with the wider community.

This inner emigration of the elite, its self-imposed isolation from the outside world, finds its clearest expression in temple architecture. In earlier times, temples had formed nodal points in a network of avenues along which the deities, periodically leaving the precincts which sheltered them from their impure surroundings, were drawn through the city. These religious processions transformed the populace into a huge festive crowd, sometimes swollen by pilgrims from abroad.[18] Since the people were forbidden from setting foot in the temples, these festivals provided the only opportunity for more general religious participation; that is why there were so many of them in ancient Egypt. If the traditional religion exhibited any characteristics of a *religio duplex*, then they are to be found in the split between an exclusive everyday cult and communal festive rites. In the Ptolemaic period, however, the temples were transformed into fortress-like precincts, enclosed by high walls, within which the divine processions now took place. Having retreated into the temples, Egyptian culture took on many of the features of an 'enclave culture' (Mary Douglas[19]), which we also see emerging around the same time in sectarian movements in Judaism. These include xenophobia, stricter purity laws, dietary taboos and other forms of self-exclusion from the general culture.[20]

We can easily imagine the Egyptian priests presenting their religion to their Greek visitors as a *religio duplex*. The first questions posed to them by the Greeks would naturally have concerned the more bizarre or even repulsive aspects of Egyptian religion: the holy animals, the theriomorphic gods, and certain cruel or obscene rituals and feast-day customs, such as those described by Herodotus. All that, they would have been told, is put on only for the benefit of the uninitiated; behind it, there stands a deep wisdom which the people know nothing about. The taint of a certain elitist, undemocratic arrogance, which clings to the idea of *religio duplex* from first to last, may be explained by the situation of a politically disqualified and socially degraded elite struggling for status, prestige and recognition. Thomas Mann depicted this problematic aspect of *religio duplex* with unsurpassable pithiness in a scene from the final novel in his Joseph tetralogy. 'I may not think', he has Akhenaten say, 'what I cannot teach.' Tiy, his scheming mother, counters with the principle of *religio duplex*: 'The office of teacher need not darken knowledge. Never have priests taught the multitude all they themselves know. They have told them what was wholesome, and wisely left in the realm of the mysteries what was not beneficial. Thus knowledge and wisdom are together in the world, truth and forbearance.' Akhenaten rejects this as arrogant: 'No, there is no arrogance in the world greater than that of dividing the children of our Father into the initiated and the uninitiated and teaching double words: all-knowingly for the masses, knowingly in the inner circle.'[21] That is the arrogance contained in the idea of *religio duplex*, and it may very well have shaped the mentality of the later Egyptian priesthood.

Sacramental Interpretation: The Dual Meaning of Signs

Transfigurations

In Egyptian religious history, the central importance accorded to secrecy reaches much further back than the problematic split into popular and elite religion. The concepts of the sacred and the mysterious are here closely intertwined.[22] The sacred is held to be the epitome of the occult. Moreover – and this is the phenomenon that I would like to illuminate here in the light of the *religio duplex* idea – we encounter from a very early time in Egypt, at the latest around the middle of the third millennium, a separation and bifurcation of the tradition, although it initially involves rites rather than texts. Behind this development stands a particular group of priests whose office and role was closely linked to texts and writing. In Egyptian, they are called *cheri-hāb(et)*, 'scroll-bearers', which the Greeks translated as *hierogrammateus*, 'priests schooled in writing' or 'priest-scribes'. In the Bible, we meet them as magicians and interpreters of dreams; they vainly compete with Moses in the magic arts and with Joseph and Daniel in the interpretation of dreams.[23]

We see these scroll-bearing hierogrammatists appearing from very early on in depictions of Egyptian rituals, wearing sashes around their chests and sporting long wigs. They are charged with reciting sacred texts in the context of the royal and non-royal death cult. The texts we see these priests reciting in the depictions are called 'transfigurations', *s-akhu* in Egyptian, the causative form of the root *akh*, which means 'to take effect' and, derivatively, 'to be spirit'.[24] The use of the causative form of this generic term alone shows that we are dealing here with powerful texts whose recitation brings about a transformation, specifically, one into the state called *akh*. These texts are not just 'performative', they are 'transformative' in the sense that, if the precisely determined conditions of the rite are observed – if, that is, they are recited with strict accuracy, with the correct intonation and emphasis, at the right time and in the right place, by a ritually prepared ('pure') and authorized speaker – then they have the power to bring about the state to which they refer: the state of transfiguration.[25]

If we cast a glance at the 'transfigurations' which the hierogrammatist was charged with reciting, we notice very quickly that we are dealing here with an ambivalent semantics resting on the distinction between *sensus literalis* and *sensus mysticus*, the level of phenomena and the level of secret meaning. These texts rehearse a procedure that I call 'sacramental explication'. This refers to the rite and the spatial, material and personal circumstances of its enactment, upon which it superimposes a divine layer of meaning. Sacramental explication therefore presupposes the distinction between the 'real world' (or 'cult world') and the 'world of the gods', a distinction which certainly only emerged in the course of the third millennium BCE.

Sacramental explication draws out the occult meaning or *sensus mysticus* of the act, the meaning which, for the uninitiated spectator, remains hidden from view. Ritual cloaking (*sensus literalis*), for example, is explicated as an 'embrace' (*sensus mysticus*), ritual cleansing with a jet of water (*sensus literalis*) is interpreted as 'rebirth' (*sensus mysticus*), while the ritual 'feeding' of the dead (*sensus literalis*) becomes an 'ascent into heaven' (*sensus mysticus*).[26] In several respects, the procedure of sacramental explication appears to bear an affinity to allegory. The divine meaning of objects, people and ritual acts constitutes a higher, concealed, secret layer of meaning, a covert knowledge.

We are dealing here not just with explication, however, but with an actual process of transformation. By establishing a link between the cult world and the divine world, a liturgical procedure is transformed into an event in the world of the gods. As the cloak is donned, for example, a mystical embrace of god and priest or dead father and surviving son is not just indicated, but ritually enacted. This transformative function of the spoken word is expressed in the word *s-ākh* ('transfigure'). The recitation of the text, along with its sacramental explication, has a transformative effect which presumes the linguistic complexion of two spheres of meaning.[27] The things of this world become transparent to those of the next, which in turn shines through in the here and now.

Initiatory interrogations

The divine level of meaning is the subject of an occult knowledge that can only be attained through initiation. This emerges from a second group of sources to which we now turn. We are dealing here with dialogues in which one speaker is interrogated by the other about the divine or mythic significance of particular objects. Such dialogues have come down to us in coffin texts thematizing the transition to the afterlife. The motif of transition appears to be constitutive here: the dialogues take the form of 'initiatory interrogations'.[28] Two complexes of objects which are subject to mythic explication in the dialogues are particularly associated with this transition: the boat that ferries the dead man to the next world and the fishing net in which he wants to avoid getting caught. The fishing net is spread out between heaven and earth, threatening the dead man as he braves the passage in the form of a bird.

In the ferry texts, the deceased is interrogated by the ferryman. The interview typically proceeds in the following way. First, the dead man is asked who he is, where he wants to go and what he intends to do when he gets there; then, who will bring him the ferry which, disassembled into its individual parts, lies in the shipyard and must now be put together again through language. The ferry is reassembled piece by piece and identified for the world of the gods. The fishing-net texts, by contrast, are not written as a dialogue. Here, only the dead man speaks, listing the elements of the fishing net along with their divine meanings. In other texts, the objects themselves are allocated speaking parts and quiz the dead man about their names. The principle is always the same. A list of things in this world is correlated with a list of things, persons and events in the world beyond. What connects the two worlds is language, in which references and meanings are preserved.

Dino Bidoli, who researched the fishing-net sayings and ferryman texts in his doctoral dissertation, very convincingly reconstructed the real-life basis of these interrogations by drawing parallels with the Islamic and European guild systems. The ferry text, for example, could allude to a ceremony

> that was actually performed with assigned roles in a shipyard of the Old Kingdom, presumably when a new member was inducted into the guild of shipwrights. We would then have here an ancient Egyptian example of an initiation into the 'mysteries' of a vocation, in the typical form of an examination in a prescribed question-and-answer format, such as can often be found among artisan groups in quite different epochs and cultural settings; indeed, until quite recently it was still practised among guilds in Egypt. Such examinations were not meant to test the candidate's knowledge of his chosen craft. Instead, they were primarily a means of justifying his induction by demonstrating his command of a richly figurative idiom. This idiom was typically guarded as a secret for members of that particular guild, and it consisted largely of a symbolic or mythical transcription of the most important parts of the object to be built – in our case, the ship referred to as a 'ferry' – and the tools and instruments used to build it.[29]

We encounter here the social function of secrecy, to which Georg Simmel, above all, drew our attention. As Simmel showed, secrecy represents the most effective means of group cohesion, the strongest social putty.[30] Guild secrets are a typical phenomenon of the ancient and modern world, and the freemasons, amongst whom ancient

Egypt and the idea of dual religion were to play a quite exceptional role, built on the fraternal mysteries of the construction industry. In societies without writing, all initiations and fellowships rest on secrecy and concealment. It would be difficult to identify any groups or collective traditions which have eschewed secrets of this kind. In the everyday world, such initiatory interrogations signify and seal induction into a professional organization. In ancient Egyptian beliefs about the dead, they induct the candidate for initiation into a community of other-worldly, immortal beings, likewise imagined as a kind of fraternity or 'community of care'. Initiatory interrogations effect the transition from this world to the next. The deceased qualifies for entry into the afterlife by showing that he has mastered the knowledge and language which connect the two worlds. The bifurcation of the world, its separation into *sensus phaenomenalis* and *sensus mysticus*, is overcome through language. In these interrogations, the candidate for initiation demonstrates his credentials through his command of an occult language: whoever understands this occult language belongs in the secret world to which it refers, and therefore gains access to that world. The cult commentaries, for their part, provide sacramental explication of the rite, ensuring that everything that happens in the world of the cult is transposed into a divine, other-worldly context.

What we are witnessing here is the confluence of writing, secrecy and power. In the case of the initiatory interrogations, power is expressed in the control that the initiate gains over the ferry, the fishing net, and the things of the divine world in general; in the case of the cult commentaries, power is expressed in the transformative force of sacramental explication. The decisive point is the presumed efficacy of a spoken language which touches on the mysteries of the divine world. The Egyptians gave the term *ākh* to this peculiar efficacy, from which the word *s-ākh*, 'to transfigure', is derived. The hierogrammatists are the real custodians of this efficacy. They invoke it whenever they recite the sacred texts from their scrolls in the context of cult ceremony.

Iamblichus and the Egyptian mysteries

In this tradition lies the kernel of truth in Greek notions about the Egyptian mysteries, and here the Greeks once again prove to have been remarkably well informed. At the time when they first encountered Egyptian culture, an Egyptian generic name for these sacred texts for recitation had already established itself. To our ears, at least, it sounds quite strange: 'the power of the sun god', or, in an alternative translation, 'solar energy'.[31] The Egyptians assumed that sacred and magical texts were able to promote cosmic harmony and balance and keep chaos at bay, in cult usage, just as they could heal the sick and keep domestic evils at bay, in magical usage. According to the Egyptians, the impact of these texts was powerful enough to assume cosmic dimensions, and their misuse could wreak havoc on a similar scale. The Neoplatonist Porphyry alludes to this in his letter to the Egyptian priest Anebo, known to us from the reply of Iamblichus. Porphyry expresses his outrage that a priest would seek to influence the universe through his recitation: the reciter threatens 'that he will assail the sky, that he will reveal to view the arcana of Isis, that he will expose to public gaze the ineffable symbol in the innermost sanctuary, that he will stop the Baris; that, like Typhon, he will scatter the limbs of Osiris, or do something of a similar character'.[32] In fact, many such texts set out to do just that. It would be impossible to convey the Egyptians' ideas about the power of cultic language more precisely. The threats which Porphyry has in mind appear by the dozen in Egyptian magical texts. Much more generally, however, he is sketching the performative force of cultic language as such. Sacred texts are quite capable of unleashing such effects – and similar effects must be feared if they are profaned, if they end up in the wrong hands, or if their secrets should ever see the light of day. 'Power of Ra' is, as mentioned, the collective name for such 'holy texts'. They must be protected and kept secret, because they contain the cosmogonic knowledge which, when read aloud in the rite, maintains the world by attuning it to the cosmic work of the sun's course. In Egypt, a holy text was considered a linguistic vessel of the sacred, and it was subject to access restrictions and protective measures that were no less stringent than those applied to the cult image itself. The recitation of a sacred text was just as effective as the sacred image in making present, or 'presentifying', the divine.[33] This literature was kept secret because it belonged to the cult mysteries, which were to be protected from profanation and degradation by the outside world. A sacred text that had been desecrated was believed to have lost its power to make present the divine.

In his efforts to counter Porphyry's accusation that the Egyptian priests sought to threaten the gods, compel them, or otherwise influence them to do their bidding, Iamblichus used arguments which likewise betray an intimate knowledge of Egyptian cult worship. His argument rests on the idea that the priest approaches the gods not as a human being, but in a divine role. The priest does not draw the gods down to his level, but is raised up to theirs:

For such invocation does not draw down beings that are impassive and pure, to that which is susceptible and impure. On the contrary, it makes us who had become impressionable through the generated life, pure and steadfast. (I.12)

That is why Iamblichus insists

that divine works are not effected through the contrariety of two distinct parties (human and divine), but every such work is accomplished through sameness, union and consent. (IV.3)

The theurgist, through the power of arcane symbols, commands cosmic forces no longer as a man, nor as employing a human soul; but as existing superior to them in the order of the Gods, he makes use of greater mandates than pertain to himself, so far as he is human. (VI.6)

The basic idea behind ancient Egyptian ritual beliefs could not be more trenchantly expressed. This 'theurgic' principle applies to the ritual act, and particularly to the language with which it is inseparably linked. The recitations accompanying the acts exert a transformative, transfiguring influence; that is why the priest is always there with his scroll. He administers the linguistic side of the operation, the recitation, which becomes divine speech in his mouth and in the moment of the cult act. When the priest speaks, one god speaks to another, and the words unleash their transformative, performative and 'presentifying' force. The words he intones may be likened to a musical performance or recital, while the scroll he holds in his hand corresponds to the score. In its meaning and essence, the sacred recitation is thus divine speech, stored up in the medium of writing and realized in the context of cultic role-play. The priest does not express it for his own sake; he does not appear before the divine image as a human being. Rather, he slips into a role in the context of an other-worldly 'constellation'. Cult language is the language of the gods.[34]

The *language* of the gods is also, however, their *writing*. The Egyptian term for hieroglyphics is 'divine word'. This lack of differentiation between writing and language speaks volumes for the close connection between writing and cult worship in Egyptian thought. The priest's scrolls store up the divine words which keep the world in order, but which can also wreak havoc upon it. The divine words reveal the secret meaning of what is clearly visible in the Egyptian cult: the acts of the priest and the sacred objects. The alliance between writing and mystery in Egyptian cult worship had been anchored in this form for millennia, before giving rise – in the context of the Neoplatonic epistemology of veiled truth and the penchant for allegorical interpretation characteristic of the late period – to the idea of Egyptian mysteries as the paradigmatic manifestation of a *religio duplex*.

The Two or Three Scripts of the Ancient Egyptian Culture of Writing

The most important cue for the emergence, in the seventeenth and eighteenth centuries, of the image of ancient Egyptian culture and religion as *religio duplex* was provided by commonly held ideas about the ancient Egyptian script, or rather, the various Egyptian scripts. These ideas, in turn, owed much to the fact that, although the hieroglyphs had not yet been decoded, the Greek and Latin literature concerning the hieroglyphs was sufficiently copious to foster the impression that a great deal (if not everything) was already known about them, and to sanction the formulation of the most far-reaching theories.

It would therefore be untrue to say that scientific research into ancient Egyptian culture dates from Champollion's decoding of the hieroglyphs in 1822. It had already been pursued by the ancient Greeks, who (as I stated earlier and must continually re-emphasize) could still encounter Egyptian culture in a living condition. So what exactly did the Greeks know about the hieroglyphs? Two characteristics of the ancient Egyptian culture of writing, in particular, fascinated the Greeks: the existence of several scripts of utterly different appearance and the pictographic quality of one of these scripts, the hieroglyphs. A third characteristic that intrigued scholars was only discovered during the seventeenth and eighteenth centuries. This was the evolutionary history which scholars thought they could infer from the Egyptian culture of writing, and which can be summed up in the phrase 'from pictures to letters'. I will discuss these three sources of fascination in turn.

Digraphy

It is commonly assumed that the alliance between writing and secrecy is as old as the invention of writing itself, a direct result of the exclusiveness of the command of writing in early cultures. From the very outset, it is claimed, writing 'stands under the banner of the rare and the arcane'; it is a 'secret technology, an esoteric, specialized knowledge accessible only to the few'.[35] 'In its earliest stages,' states Niklas Luhmann, 'the function of [writing] was to establish relations with deities, and the only ones who could manage these relations, from the human side, were priests.'[36] Only with the invention of the alphabet by the proto-Hebrews[37] or the Greeks[38] – so the story goes – was mastery of writing 'democratized' and the alliance between writing and secrecy broken. This view represents a complete misunderstanding that must be refuted from the outset. The earliest forms of writing were invented in Mesopotamia and Egypt towards the end of the fourth millennium BCE, and arose in the context of state formation; far from being designed to safeguard secrets, they served the needs of the economy, administration and public representation.[39] As a successor institution to village and tribal communities, the early state required writing as an artificial memory enabling it to master the unending data stream generated by economic and administrative activity, but also as an artificial voice to broadcast royal decrees to every corner of the empire, and thereby visibly represent the king's power to all his subjects.

Writing makes possible new forms of control and administration. Without writing, everything upon which more complex communities and early states are based – account-keeping, record-keeping, census-taking, tax assessment – becomes impossible. There were no free markets in these states, only an economic system based on careful planning and stockpiling against future scarcity, such as that described in the context of the Joseph story in the Bible. The murals in ancient Egyptian tombs present us with a world dominated by writing and scribes. There was hardly a single area of life that was not, in some way, touched by writing. Although only relatively few people were able to write, no Egyptian could fail to understand what 'writing' meant. Far from being an esoteric art-form about which the common populace had not the faintest inkling, writing was an everyday cultural technology that formed the basis of the entire state, with all its economic sub-branches and institutions. Everyone was affected by it in some way, even if they were illiterate themselves. The infrequency with which writing was actively practised stood in inverse relation to the all-encompassing, pervasive extent of its influence.

While the primary function of writing was not to preserve secrets, it did stand in the service of bureaucracy and hence, as in classical China, the formation of elites. During the classical periods of Egyptian writing history, writing functioned as the central dispositive of power. Those who were trained to write could typically expect to be appointed to an administrative or cultic position. Learning to write was thus inseparably linked to a future career as an official or priest. No other path led to high office in religion or politics, and writing, for its part, led nowhere else: there were no freelance writers and autonomous intellectuals in ancient Egypt. When the Persians and subsequently the Greeks and Romans came to rule Egypt, however, the Egyptian elites found themselves excluded from positions of political influence and reduced to holding sacerdotal positions in the temple cult.

Accustomed to associating the acquisition of literacy with ideas of power and prestige, they now invested the complicated route to hieroglyph writing, whose different varieties so impressed the Greeks (as we will see below), with all the glamour befitting initiation into sacred mysteries and the attainment of supreme religious power. This route held out to adepts the prospect of an important position close to the gods, both in this life and, above all, in the next. In a certain sense, the Egyptian mysteries functioned both as a successor institution to the pharaonic state and as a compensation for its loss. Having been deprived of its political influence, the elite could still cling to the idea that mastery of writing would gain it access to the highest goals, those reserved for the select few. According to both Plutarch and Clement of Alexandria, the highest stages of initiation were reserved for those called to rulership. Under the new dispensation, as under the old one, writing equalled power. Religious power now took the place of political power, while the mysteries stood in for the state. Even if this power reposed solely on memory and imagination, and no longer on political and historical reality, what mattered was that these were the memory and imagination of the Egyptians themselves – and hence not a Greek misinterpretation of the hieroglyphs. The alliance between writing and secrecy arose in Egypt itself and had already been established there.

By the time the Greeks came into contact with Egyptian culture, with the founding of the colony Naukratis and as mercenaries in the service of the pharaoh, three types of writing were in use: hieroglyphs for inscriptions; hieratic script, a cursive form of writing for manuscripts on papyrus and other materials; and, third, a far more polished cursive writing for notating colloquial language, demotic script. The peculiarity of this situation must have struck the Greeks. Whereas older reports only distinguished between two scripts, probably conflating both cursive scripts into one, later accounts correctly identified three and then introduced further distinctions within these three systems of writing. Today we know that these were simply three versions of a single writing system; but the Greeks concluded that the handwritten script was accessible to everyone ('demotic' script, from the Greek *dēmos*, 'people', means 'popular writing'), while the monumental script was intended only for priests (hence *hiero*glyphs, from *hieros*, 'holy', *hiereus*, 'priest'). Herodotus, visiting Egypt around 450

BCE, already notes that they 'use two kinds of written characters, one called "holy", the other called "demotic"'.[40] This point is also expressed very clearly in the Kyme Aretology of Isis, a list of her own merits recited by the goddess herself:

> I am Isis, the mistress of every land,
>
> I was taught by Hermes and with Hermes I devised letters (*grammata*), both the sacred and the demotic, so that all things might not be written with the same (letters).
>
> I gave and ordained laws (*nomous*) for men, which no one is able to change.[41]

Diodorus of Sicily (first century BCE) gives a similar, albeit more extensive account, one that here (as presumably elsewhere) draws heavily on Hecataeus of Abdera, a source from the late fourth century BCE:

> The Egyptians use two different scripts: one, called 'demotic', is learned by all; the other one is called 'sacred'. This one is understood among the Egyptians exclusively by the priests, who learn them from their fathers in the mysteries.[42]

In the eyes of Diodorus, demotic writing is thus a general system of writing learned by all, whereas sacred writing is a special script used only by priests and passed down from fathers to sons in the 'mysteries'. The mysteries appear here as an educational institution through which the sacred script (that is, hieratic and hieroglyphic writing) is taught to the next generation.

The idea of a dual culture derives from this theory of Egyptian literate culture as a digraphy. A culture so strictly split between the exoteric and the esoteric needs two forms of writing, or, conversely, a culture needing two forms of writing can only be a divided one, a dual culture. With Linda Simonis, I make a distinction between the secret (or occult) and the esoteric: what is *secret* can only be communicated in the dark, even as signs; what is *esoteric*, on the other hand, is publicly communicated as signs, but the (real) meaning of these signs can only be deciphered by the initiated.[43] In this sense, the hieroglyphs are to be understood as an esoteric form of writing, whereas cursive script is an exoteric form. It was always obvious that the hieroglyphs were displayed in public, as monumental writing for stone inscriptions – indeed, such inscriptions were available for inspection by Early Modern scholars in the form of Roman obelisks removed from Egypt – but it was also assumed that these could only be understood by the initiated. Hieroglyphs only functioned as the medium of a *secret* communication when they were inscribed in places to which the profane were denied access – for example, in the subterranean burial chambers of the Egyptians, widely believed in the eighteenth century to have been sites of occult worship and study.[44]

As previously mentioned, however, not two but three forms of writing were in use among the Egyptians of the Greco-Roman period: hieroglyphic, hieratic and demotic. The Church Father Clement of Alexandria, writing two centuries after Diodorus, describes these three forms much more precisely.[45] He describes learning to write as a path of initiation from simple scribe through to fully initiated scholar (*hierogrammateus*). The student first learns the epistolary script ('letter writing'), then the priestly or hieratic script and finally the hieroglyphic script. Clement calls the hieroglyphic script *hystatēn kai teleutaian*, the 'last learned and final' script. The writing culture of the priests, raised to a high art and practised with the utmost virtuosity, reaches its apogee in this script. The expression *teleutaian* alludes unmistakably to *teletē* ('mysteries, initiation'). Like Diodorus before him, Clement considers learning the hieroglyphs to be the highest stage of initiation into the Egyptian mysteries. The border between the outside and the inside, the exoteric and the esoteric level of Egyptian culture, runs between 'letter writing' (a literal translation of the Egyptian term for demotic script) and the two priestly scripts, which for their part mark a distinction within the mysteries. The bipartite opposition within literate culture, upon which the idea of dual religion is based, is thus maintained, as shown in figure 1.

Clement not only distinguishes between three different forms of writing, but also identifies different modes within hieroglyphic script.[46] Hieroglyphic writing, he asserts, signifies in two ways: first,

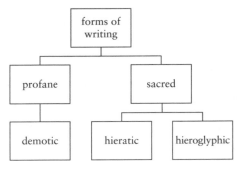

Figure 1

in a simple and straightforward manner ('kyriologically'), 'by means of elementary letters' (*dia tōn prōtōn stoicheiōn*), and, second, through symbols. The symbols, for their part, come in three varieties: (a) simple or pictographic ('kyriological'); (b) figurative or 'tropic' (whereby one sign is transferred to a different area); and finally (c) allegorical or enigmatic (figure 2).

We thus encounter in figure 2 the 'kyriological' mode twice within hieroglyphic writing: once in signs that function like letters (III.1), and again in signs which directly represent what they refer to (III.2a). The verb *kyriologeisthai* stands opposed to *allēgoreisthai*. The former designates a direct, simple, and authentic connection between signifier and signified, the latter a transposed, indirect and figurative relation. The distinction between 'kyriological' and 'symbolic' (III.1 and 2) can really only refer to the two levels of linguistic articulation: the phonetic level (to which writing in the 'kyriological' mode refers 'by means of the elementary letters') and the semantic level, to which it refers through depiction of the signified object, metaphorical symbolization or allegorical encryption. By *prōta stoicheia*, Clement understands either 'letters', hence the single-consonant signs under the hieroglyphs,[47] or 'phonemes', as defined by Plato in the *Philebus*.[48]

Porphyry, too, discusses Egyptian forms of writing in the context of initiation into the Egyptian mysteries, in this case the initiation of Pythagoras, who supposedly spent decades under the tutelage of Egyptian priests. Like Clement, he distinguishes between three types of script, which he calls 'epistolographic', 'hieroglyphic' and 'symbolic'.[49] Within the symbolic script type, he makes a further distinction between 'kyriological' and 'allegorical' references. By the former,

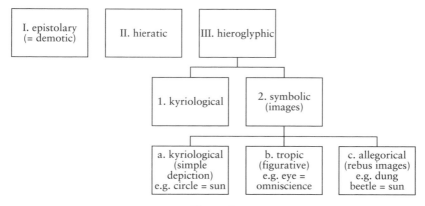

Figure 2

he means the straightforward designation of the referent *kata mimēsin*, hence according to the same principle of simple depiction identified by Clement (III.2a in figure 2); by the latter, he means the transferred designation *kata ainigmous*, hence through figurative encryption. Clement and Porphyry thus both associate writing in hieroglyphs with the idea of an arcane cryptography linked to its function in the mysteries.

We conclude that the fascinating spectacle of different systems of writing operating within a *single* culture and society was associated by the Greeks with the structure of a dual religion and culture. Whereas one system of writing served the needs of everyday communication, the other was reserved solely for the temple mysteries, in which the Greeks again distinguished between different levels of secrecy or encryption.

Pictography

The second aspect of Egyptian literate culture that intrigued the Greeks was the vividly pictographic appearance of the hieroglyphs, the (presumed) medium of esoteric communication. The Greeks drew two conclusions from this, both of which were as false as they were influential in the subsequent history of ideas: first, that this writing referred directly to things rather than to articulated sounds, and, second, that the image-signs represented a form of 'compact communication', to borrow Niklas Luhmann's term.[50]

The theory that hieroglyphic writing was purely referential and bore no relation to the sounds of a particular language is based on a work from late antiquity, the *Hieroglyphika*, by Horapollo Nilotes.[51] Horapollo was an Egyptian living at the beginning of the fifth century, when knowledge of the hieroglyphs had already died out in Egypt. We should not forget, however, that he could draw on older works that still assumed living knowledge of the hieroglyphs but have since been lost – above all, the *Hieroglyphika* of Chaeremon.[52]

Horapollo claims that his book was translated from the Egyptian; this is surely a fiction, even if Egyptian, or rather Coptic, was his mother tongue. The first book – the second is a later, inauthentic addition – discusses approximately seventy hieroglyphs, most of which, judged by our knowledge today, are read correctly but wrongly explained. Thus, Horapollo writes quite accurately that the Egyptians draw the picture of a hare when they want to denote the concept 'to open'; yet the explanation he gives is not that the word *w-n* ('to open') is pronounced the same way as the word *w-n* ('hare'), but that this animal never closes its eyes. Another example is the image of a duck: Horapollo rightly informs his readers that it is used to write the word 'son', but he adds that this meaning derives from the particularly well-developed family feelings of waterfowl. This, needless to say, is utter nonsense. Here, too, the correct explanation is that the Egyptian word for 'son' is pronounced the same way as the word for 'duck' (or 'goose'). The principle is clear. Horapollo completely disregards the phonetic aspect of the characters, presumably because he no longer understands it. He replaces this lost complex of knowledge with another body of knowledge that played no role in the classical Egyptian system of writing: a popular zoology which ascribed to animals all manner of characteristics and behavioural norms, and which is familiar to us from many ancient works of natural history such as Aelianus, Pliny the Elder and the *Physiologus* (whose roots go back to antiquity, but which first grew in the Middle Ages into the manuscript tradition we know today). This popular zoology dictates that the hare never closes its eyes, that the duck has a highly developed sense of family loyalty, that the lion is a royal animal, that the snake is immortal since it constantly rejuvenates itself, and so on. Through this moral zoology, concrete images can be used to represent or 'write' abstract ideas like 'open', 'family', 'care', 'rule', 'immortality' and so forth. For Horapollo, anyone who aspires to understand hieroglyphs must be initiated into this kind of knowledge.[53] Whoever masters the hieroglyphs knows the characteristics of the things they represent: the being of animals, the effects of nature, the natural order of the world. Phonology is replaced by physiology, linguistic knowledge by knowledge of the universe.

Hieroglyphic writing is already described in similar fashion by Diodorus (or rather his source, Hecataeus of Abdera), at a time when knowledge of it could still be assumed. According to Diodorus, hieroglyphic writing uses images of animals such as falcons, crocodiles and snakes. The falcon connotes speed, the crocodile malice, and so on. The characters do not refer to speech as the stringing together of syllables – the phonetic aspect is thus explicitly denied – but refer metaphorically to the significance of the represented objects, which are preserved in memory. (Metaphorical writing draws on the mnemonically encoded significance of things: the crocodile's malice must be known in order for the character to be understood.) 'By straining to uncover the meanings concealed within these forms, they learn through years of practice and memory training to read everything that has been written.'[54]

This connection between knowledge of writing, memory and knowledge of the universe fascinated scholars during the Renaissance. For example, Giordano Bruno writes:

> [. . .] the sacred letters used among the Egyptians were called hiero-
> glyphs, which, in place of referential signs (*designanda*), were images
> taken from the things of nature, or their parts. By using such writings
> and voices (*voces*), the Egyptians strove to capture with marvellous
> skill the language of the gods. Afterwards when letters of the kind
> which we use now with another kind of industry were invented by
> Theuth or some other, this brought about a great rift both in memory
> and in the divine and magical sciences.[55]

What particularly interested Renaissance scholars was the fact that
the hieroglyphs referred not to language, but directly to the things
and ideas themselves; Aleida Assmann calls this the principle of
'immediate signification'.[56] With that, a debate was reopened that
Plato had initiated in his dialogue *Cratylus* and that Aristotle seemed
to have settled once and for all. The crux of the debate was the relationship between language and reality. Is the relationship between
spoken words (*verba*) or written signs (*signa*) and the real things to
which they refer a natural one (*physei*, 'by nature'), or merely conventional (*thesei*, 'posited')? In deciding this question, Aristotle came
down on the side of conventionality. He first categorically distinguished between language and writing, subordinating writing to
spoken language. Language, Aristotle says, relates to *ta en psychē*,
'that which is in the soul [i.e., in consciousness]', whereas writing
relates to *ta en phonē*, 'that which is in the voice'. Writing encodes
spoken sounds, which in turn encode ideas and thoughts. To use
Aleida Assmann's terminology, the principle of 'mediate signification'
prevails in Aristotelian semantics. The relationship between written
signs and spoken sounds is no less arbitrary or conventional than the
relationship between spoken sounds and thoughts. The same spoken
sound can be notated in many different forms of writing, just as the
same idea can be expressed in many different languages. So long as
Western alphabetic scripts – Greek, Latin, perhaps also Hebrew and
later Arabic – were the only ones known, the evidence in support of
this interpretation seemed overwhelming. The case appeared to be
closed. With the rediscovery of Horapollo in 1419, however, this
question appeared in a completely new light. Hieroglyphs, as
explained by Horapollo, should now be understood as signs that
referred directly to things rather than to spoken sounds. Moreover,
they did so not on the basis of conventional agreement but of natural
(or iconic) relation.

According to the Early Modern grammatologists, hieroglyphs
referred not only to the things they directly represented (this would
be the 'kyriological' mode of signification) but also to abstract con-

cepts, which had to be inferred from images in the allegorical or enigmatic mode. This (supposed) function of hieroglyphs subsequently led to the flourishing of the emblem, conceived by its Early Modern practitioners as a continuation or revival of ancient Egyptian hieroglyphics.

In this connection, a passage from Plotinus, the third-century Neoplatonic philosopher, was commonly cited:

> The wise of Egypt [. . .] indicated the truth where, in their effort towards philosophical statement, they left aside the writing-forms that take in the detail of words and sentences – those characters that represent sounds and convey the propositions of reasoning – and drew pictures instead, engraving in the temple-inscriptions a separate image for every separate item: thus they exhibited the absence of discursiveness in the Intellectual Realm. For each manifestation of knowledge and wisdom is a distinct image, an object in itself, an immediate unity, not an aggregate of discursive reasoning and detailed willing.[57]

In this form the passage is fairly obscure, but we have Marsilio Ficino to thank for a commentary that immediately makes clear what is at stake here. He elucidated the principle of Egyptian hieroglyphic writing intended by Plotinus with reference to the concept of time:

> You have a discursive knowledge of time that is complex and flexible, as when you say, for example, that time passes and that after a particular passage of time the end reconnects to the beginning. [. . .] The Egyptians, however, condense an entire discourse of this kind into the image of a winged snake swallowing its own tail.[58]

According to Plotinus, the written meaning may be defined as the discourse that the image symbolizes in condensed form, and which can be read off the image by the initiated. The Egyptians were in fact familiar with the symbol of the Ouroboros, the snake swallowing its own tail, albeit without wings. But the Ouroboros is not a hieroglyph and has nothing to do with writing.

Iamblichus, a student of Plotinus, adduces two further examples from the realm of this sacral iconography, which he likewise mistakes for written signs: the child on the lotus blossom, and the god in the solar barge.[59] The first 'hieroglyph' is interpreted by Iamblichus as symbolizing the relationship between the divine and material worlds. The child stands for god, mud for matter, while the lotus flower – which rises from the mud without being in the least sullied by it – represents the majesty of the divine and the categorical separation of god and matter. Iamblichus interprets the god in the barge as a symbol of the divine energy that steers the cosmos. Both symbols are indeed richly attested, but as motifs in painting (or what might be called 'iconograms') rather than as written signs. This is true of both the 'sun god on the flower', an image of cosmogonic myth common from the Amarna period (mid-fourteenth century BCE) onwards,[60] and the sun god in the barge. Ficino's example, the Ouroboros snake, belongs in the same repertoire of images; from the time of Tutankhamen it is frequently encountered as a motif in painting, but never as a written sign. To an astonishing and perhaps unique extent, all Egyptian art is 'ideogrammatically' organized.[61] The same things are represented in the same way, strict formulas regulate the composition of the scene, and most of these formulas are handed down almost unchanged through the millennia.

Even if, following on from the rediscovery of Horapollo and the grammatological debates, the principle of iconic compact communication reached a high point in emblematic art of the sixteenth and seventeenth centuries,[62] in this context one thinks also, and above all, of Romanesque art. Artists of this period endeavoured to express highly complex theological matters, such as the relationship between the Old and the New Testaments, in images which were meant to be read and translated back into discourse, just as Plotinus had postulated for hieroglyphic writing. Two examples may serve as illustration. The first, from the twelfth century, comes from Vézelay and renders the relationship between the two Testaments in the image of the 'mystic mill'. We see Moses pouring the grains of the law into a mill while Paul stands below receiving the flour of faith. The New Testament is thus understood to be a sublimated, refined, processed version of the Old. This idea is here brought into the form of a condensed image that can, in turn, be translated at will into various discourses. The second example, dating from the thirteenth century, comes from one of the famous windows at Chartres and represents the four evangelists sitting perched on the shoulders of four Old Testament prophets: Luke on Jeremiah, Matthew on Isaiah, John on Ezekiel and Mark on Daniel. The prophets foretold the Messiah whom the evangelists and their contemporaries beheld in the flesh, but they could only recognize him as such because they stood on the shoulders of the prophets, knew their writings and were thus able to read the signs of their times. With the Neoplatonic principle of the condensed image – somewhat akin to data compression in its visual representation of highly complex theological and philosophical ideas – Christian art develops a didactic-argumentative function that aims at precisely what Plotinus describes as the achievement of the Egyptian hieroglyphs. This supplements its pre-existing narrative function, dating back to antiquity, of illustrating biblical history.

What is important, for our purposes, is that the interpretation of the hieroglyphs as a symbolic script independent of language, and as a form of iconic compact communication, links up with the function of esoteric communication in the context of the mysteries. This medium is not intended for everyday use. Reading these signs requires comprehensive knowledge of nature and of the relationship between microcosm and macrocosm, the moral and the natural world.

The idea of the hieroglyphs functioning as a form of compact communication and 'immediate signification' was a misunderstanding that for a long time stood in the way of efforts to decipher them. It was a misunderstanding that was suggested, however, by several characteristics of hieroglyphic writing itself. The first is the distinctly pictorial quality of hieroglyphs. Insofar as they represent something recognizable, these are not arbitrary signs, like alphabetic writing, but a kind of language of things. It was easy to conclude that they referred not just to the objects they represented, but equally (through a process of metaphorical transference) to all sorts of other ideas. That conclusion is not entirely false, only the principle of transference actually operates by way of homophony rather than metaphor. Second, there are in fact hieroglyphs which have only a semantic value and no phonic value, the so-called determinatives. This name is given to signs referring to semantic categories such as 'gods', 'people', 'movement', 'space', 'time', 'liquid', 'plants' and so on. These signs not only cannot be pronounced, but mostly have a meaning for which there is no corresponding word in the Egyptian language.[63] In Egyptian, the corresponding concept is thus realized only graphically, not lexically. This can be illustrated by the case of a sign that appears as the determinative for a class of words like malice, aggressiveness, attack and rapacity: the sign of the crocodile. It signifies a trait that is demonstrated in exemplary fashion in the behaviour of crocodiles, and which we might call 'crocodileness'. But this concept of crocodileness is only articulated in writing, not in the spoken language. We thus have here, in the written system, an example of a condensed image in Plotinus's sense; yet this sign refers, not to a word, but to a complex of ideas which would have to be articulated in a more or less comprehensive discourse on malice and aggressiveness. With that, we have arrived at Diodorus's (or Hecataeus's) understanding of hieroglyphs as a moral and allegorical zoography.

The idea of the hieroglyphs' pure referentiality rests above all on an opinion that the Egyptians themselves had already formed about their writing. It is expressed in a process that might, by analogy to etymology, be called 'etymography'.[64] When the Egyptians reflected on the meaning of a word, they mostly began by considering how it was written. In the demotic myth of the solar eye, there can be found many explanations which follow the etymographical method of Horapollo: 'If you want to write the word "honey", draw a picture of Nut holding a reed in her hand; for she is the one who purifies the temples of Lower and Upper Egypt when they are first established.'[65] 'If you want to write the word "year", draw the picture of a vulture, because she [the goddess written with the vulture] causes the months to rise and fall. The primal goddess is the one who lets everything [on] Earth rise and fall: everything came out of her.'[66] The expression, 'the bee is also called "queen"', recalls that the royal title *bjt* was written with the bee. Further such explanations are found in the Decree of Canopus[67] and the Jumilhac papyrus. It is written there, in relation to the three single-consonant signs used to write the divine name 'Anubis': 'As far as the "J" is concerned, it is the wind; the "N" is the water; the "P" is the mountain.'[68] Another passage describes how the enemy of the gods, Baba, killed himself with an axe blow, upon which the gods remarked: ' "His weapon is in his head", and so arose the word *khefti* ("enemy")': it is written with the sign of a dead man who split his own skull with an axe (*heauton timōroumenos*).[69] What 'arose' here was not the word but the written sign – compelling evidence for etymographical thinking. When they pondered the word *khefti* ('enemy'), the Egyptians did not think of its etymology (from *kheft*, 'opposite', as in the English 'opponent', Greek *enantios*, French *adversaire*). Instead, they considered how it was written.

The idea of a symbolic language, and the discourse on hieroglyphics that went with it, must have emerged in the final phase of Egyptian culture, when hieroglyphs and cursive script had moved far apart from each other and the demotic had developed alongside the hieratic cursive script. In my opinion, the Western discourse on hieroglyphics – which, as we have seen, rests on precisely this distinction between pictographic writing and abstract writing – was therefore born in Egypt, not in Greece. We are the inheritors of Egypt when we reflect on questions of pictography and writing, motivated and arbitrary signs, immediate and mediate signification. They were the ones who first practised these distinctions in their two and then three different systems of writing; the Greeks theorized them; and the West discussed them all the way to our current reflections on a turn or return from words to images. Accordingly, my thesis is that it is in late Egyptian culture we find the germs of the grammatological debate that was then theoretically developed by the Greeks and that, following its resumption in the Renaissance, has continued to influence Western art and philosophy right down to the present day.

From pictures to letters: the history of writing as history of religion

The third aspect of the Egyptian culture of writing to fascinate posterity was the process of evolution that seemed to take place over the course of its long history, although this aspect intrigued scholars of the eighteenth century, with its ideas of development, far more than it did the Greeks. Evidence for this process was culled from statements made by Clement and Porphyry about how the different Egyptian forms of writing were learned in a step-by-step process. This gave rise to a theory of scriptural evolution that reversed the curriculum offered to the apprentice scribe. The scribe began by learning the abstract, aniconic 'epistolary writing', considered to be an alphabetic script, before proceeding through hieratic writing to hieroglyphics, the summit of his training; the path thus led from letters to pictures. The theory of evolution inferred from this curriculum proceeded in the opposite direction: it traced the development of writing from pictures (i.e., hieroglyphs) to letters, via various intermediate stages. Since writing and language were considered indistinguishable at the time, this phase of the discourse on hieroglyphs also bore on the origin and development of language as such. Just as our forebears first wrote in images before availing themselves of letters, so they first spoke in images before learning to connect their sentences through logical argumentation. As early as 1610, Francis Bacon wrote in his essay 'The Advancement of Learning': 'As hieroglyphics were before letters, so parables were before arguments; and nevertheless now and at all times they do retain much life and vigour, because reason cannot be so sensible, nor examples so fit.'[70]

In the eighteenth century, Giambattista Vico added a historical and poetological dimension to this grammatological theory of evolution. In Manetho, Herodotus and other ancient writers, he found evidence to suggest that the Egyptians not only distinguished between three forms of writing but also between three epochs, in which first gods, then half-gods or heroes, and lastly mortals, exercised sovereignty. This account finds support in the Egyptian king-lists, which reach all the way back to the middle of the second millennium BCE. For Vico, the gods presided over an age of poetry and hieroglyphics, which he too understands as a simultaneously written and spoken language: a motivated medium translated directly from natural experience, notated in images which unambiguously and immediately bring the signified to living presence. The heroic age corresponds to the epic and to hieratic writing, which Vico takes to mean emblems and symbols resting on arbitrary and conventional designation rather than on natural inspiration; he primarily had in mind the heraldic emblems of the medieval aristocracy, whence his association of hieratic writing with the heroic. The age of mortals, finally, corresponds to prose and to alphabetic writing.[71]

At the same time, working independently in England, the learned bishop William Warburton supplemented the grammatological theory of evolution with a religious-historical dimension. In his monumental work on the divine legation of Moses, he associated the transition from images to letters with the shift from idolatry to imageless monotheism. Warburton introduced an evolutionary perspective to the idea of an Egyptian dual culture. Against Athanasius Kircher, who had emphatically supported the interpretation of the hieroglyphs as a cryptographic script reserved solely for the initiated, Warburton argued that, to begin with, the hieroglyphs were a perfectly normal and everyday system of writing. They only evolved into a secret code in the course of Egyptian history, as the priesthood was transformed into a specialized profession whose members, duly initiated into this occult language, thereby segregated themselves from the rest of society. Therein lies the origin of the Egyptian double culture, which for Warburton then became the model for all other ancient cultures apart from the Israelites.

Forty-five years later, this theory was taken up by the Jewish philosopher and Enlightenment figurehead, Moses Mendelssohn. In his text, *Jerusalem oder über religiöse Macht und Judentum* (*Jerusalem, or, On Religious Power and Judaism*, 1783), he wrote:

> I think the changes that have taken place in writing characters, at different periods of civilization, have had, from the beginning, a very considerable share in the revolutions of human knowledge in general, and in the various modifications of men's ideas and opinions about religious matters, in particular.[72]

Mendelssohn, too, associates the evolution of writing 'from images to letters' with a shift from the cult of images to the cult of the word, which coincides with the transition from polytheism to monotheism. God (or Moses) could never have inscribed the tables of the law in hieroglyphs; for this purpose, an abstract, alphabetic writing had to be invented.

This theory even has a kernel of truth, albeit one which neither Warburton nor Mendelssohn could have known anything about.

Alphabetic writing was in fact invented by Egypt's nomadic neigh-
bours. In contrast to the vividly pictographic appearance of the
hieroglyphs, both hieratic and demotic writing are aniconic but they
are not alphabetic. The only alphabetic script is Protosinaitic, which
Semitic nomads pieced together from Egyptian written characters
towards the beginning of the second millennium BCE.[73] Alphabetic
writing, this truly world-changing invention, initially represented
nothing more than a simplification of Egyptian hieroglyphics, which
semi-literate tribes-people modified to suit their own limited purposes
(and certainly not in order to codify divine revelations). Nevertheless,
if God (or Moses) had appeared on Mount Sinai in the fourteenth or
thirteenth century BCE to set down divine laws in writing, he would
have used the purely alphabetic script of Protosinaitic.

2

From the Dual Meaning of Signs to Dual Religion

Verba Duplicata: Moses Maimonides

In his *Guide to the Perplexed* (*Dalâlat al-ha'irîn*, Hebrew *Moreh Nevukhim*, 1190), the Jewish philosopher Rabbi Moses ben Maimon, known as Maimonides (1135/38–1204), paints a picture of Jewish religion as a *religio duplex* with an outside and an inside. Rather than two different scripts, this religion uses *divre kefilajim*, 'double-words', or *verba duplicata* in John Spencer's translation – that is, an ambiguous mode of expression.[1] In contrast to the fourfold method of scriptural interpretation advanced by Scholasticism, we are dealing here not with a step-by-step ascent from the literal meaning to ever more spiritual levels of meaning, but with the distinction between exoteric and esoteric communication.

Maimonides arrives at this interpretation in the context of his interpretation of Jewish ritual law. There are three types of laws: moral, juristic and ritual (*mitsvôt, mishpatim* and *hukkîm*, or *moralia, iudicialia* and *caeremonialia*, as Thomas Aquinas calls them; his treatise *De legibus* in the *Summa Theologica* draws extensively on the *Guide to the Perplexed*). Moral and juristic precepts can be justified on rational grounds; they are ethically or politically reasonable. Ritual laws, by contrast, cannot be justified, which is why it is forbidden to question their validity. Maimonides refused to accept these fetters on inquiry, for how could God ordain laws that were completely unjustified and irrational? Wherever rational reasons cannot be found, historical causes must be adduced. Maimonides found the historical validation he was looking for in the principle of the normative inversion of paganism. In both graciously and cunningly making allowances for the customs and limited mental capacity of humans who were already accustomed to a multitude of pagan rites, God decided not to confront his people directly with the full truth of his religion, but instead gave them ritual laws which turned pagan practice on its head. If the pagans worshipped the bull and the ram, these animals were now to be slaughtered. If the pagans cooked kids in their mothers' milk and then sprinkled this milk on their fields, plants and trees to promote fecundity, milk and meat were now to be kept strictly separate. In this way the Jews would come to forget pagan religion while imperceptibly moving closer to the truth.

The law, or rather the entire biblical religion as a complex praxis of cultic customs, rites and maxims, receives a twofold justification in the light of this theory. It appears as the historical, temporally conditioned vessel for a timeless truth that lies concealed within it, and which will only gradually come to light through a long process by which the Jews are purified, weaned off idolatry, and directed to a pure knowledge of God. Maimonides speaks in this context of God's cunning.[2] With this cunning, an esoteric dimension and a historical perspective, completely absent from the pagan or 'Sabian' religion,[3] enter into biblical religion. Paganism was pure idol-worship, unenlightened by any glimmer of truth. In the biblical religion, this worship (with all its accompanying rites) is directed away from the idols and towards God. It is reduced to the temporally conditioned packaging for a truth that the heathen know nothing about and that cannot be directly communicated, even to the chosen people.

Maimonides may thus be considered an early representative of the *religio duplex* theory. Yet for him, as we have seen, only the biblical religion is distinguished by such depth; pagan religion is shallow and simple. In the seventeenth and eighteenth centuries, by contrast, pagan and especially Egyptian religion was imagined as *religio duplex*. Leaving this to one side, the key elements of the *religio duplex* theory are already to be found in Maimonides. To quote the summary provided by Moshe Halbertal:

> Maimonides' idea of the necessity of esotericism is grounded in the deep cleavage between the enlightened elite and the ignorant masses. The noncorporeal abstract conception of God could not be disclosed to the masses exoterically, since they cannot grasp a nonmaterial existence. Furthermore, such a conception of God and a naturalistic theology accompanying it would endanger the social order, which depends upon belief in Divine Providence and retribution. A widespread belief in a personal God who rewards the righteous and punishes the wicked is the main motivation for maintaining the basic norms necessary for

social stability. An Aristotelian naturalistic theology would be danger-
ous to the uninitiated.[4]

According to Halbertal's account of Maimonides, we already see
before us here the theory of *religio duplex* in the full sense given it
by the Enlightenment. A more precise correspondence could hardly
be imagined, particularly to the views of the English deists. It seems
clear to me that the theory of dual religion, with its distinction
between an exoteric political theology and an esoteric philosophical
theology, goes back to Maimonides.

Maimonides distinguished between two different objectives of the
law: the first is the establishment of a just social order; the second is
the abolition of idolatry and the triumph of the true religion. Maimonides treats the first, political goal as a short-term goal and the
literal meaning of the law; the second, theological goal is the long-
term goal and the mystical meaning of the law.[5] The establishment
of a just social order was attained with the lawfully instituted Constitution of Israel. The eradication of idolatry, however, is still a long
way off.

Even more striking than the historicization of the law, in the sense
of a divine concession to the ideas and customs of his people, is the
temporalization of revelation. According to Maimonides, this is not
accomplished once and for all but proceeds in small, nearly imper-
ceptible steps. One could almost speak of an evolutionary process of
revelation here, and Maimonides does in fact refer to God's workings
in nature as the model for his workings in history. Abrupt contrasts,
sudden reversals and irrational phenomena have no place in nature.
All elements are organically attuned to each other, and the new
emerges smoothly and continuously from the old. *Natura non facit
saltus*: nature makes no leaps. The passage from one extreme to
another necessitates a sequence of infinitely delicate transitions and
lengthy detours. Revelation should be understood in the same way,
as a process of subtle transformation and natural growth.[6] The logic
of smooth transitions is manifested in all 'works of God (*pe'ulot ha-
elohijot*) or of nature (*tiw'ijôt*).' Therein are to be found the 'cunning',
'wisdom' and 'strategy' of God's actions, his accommodation to conditions here on Earth.[7] With that, Maimonides destroys the conventional distinction between nature and revelation. As an historical
phenomenon, revelation is also a quasi-organic product. For Maimonides, the divine will is revealed in both natural and religious
evolution. The formula of 'God's divine or natural works' anticipates
Spinoza's *deus sive natura*. From this evolutionary perspective,
the structure of *religio duplex* is only a transitional phase between

paganism and an enlightened humanity. The philosophers' god began by revealing himself to his people as the God of the Fathers, making allowances for their limited rational, emotional and imaginative capabilities, but he also provided enough hints for the wise to intimate the truth behind this mask.

Egyptian Hieroglyphs and Mosaic Laws: John Spencer

Although Maimonides' work, written in Arabic and Hebrew, was not completely ignored in the Christian West, the most significant phase in the history of its reception did not get under way until the seventeenth century, initiated by Johann Buxtorf the Younger's translation into Latin of *More Nevuchim* (Basel, 1629). The 'Christian Hebraists', above all in England and Holland, henceforth leaned on Maimonides as a kind of Protestant counter-weight to the Catholic Thomas of Aquinas.[8] The first name that should be mentioned here is John Spencer (1630–93). Spencer explicitly presents his monumental interpretation of Hebrew ritual law (*De legibus Hebraeorum ritualibus et eadem rationibus libri tres*, London, 1685) as the renewal, in a Christian context,[9] of Maimonides' project to explicate the 'meaning of the laws' (*ta'ame ha-mitsvôt*).[10] From Maimonides, Spencer adopts the theory of a double goal. At the very beginning of his work, he introduces the distinction between the primary and secondary meaning of laws. In his view, the primary basis is the therapeutic or educational function of overcoming idolatry, equivalent to Maimonides' 'long-term goal'. However, for Spencer, this goal was attained with the eradication of paganism. That is why he considers it a short-term goal. Standing on the ground of Christian tradition, he identifies the secondary meaning – equivalent to the second, long-term goal – with the prefiguration (*adumbratio*) of Christianity,[11] referring in this context to Maimonides, whose notion of 'double-words' (*verba duplicata*) distinguished between the *sensus literalis* and the *sensus mysticus*.[12] God wished to conceal certain more sacred things (*sacratiora quaedam*) in the law beneath the veil of symbols and signs (*symbolorum et typorum velis obducta*). This principle of double coding was what Moses and the Hebrews supposedly learned and adopted from the Egyptians. In Spencer's presentation, the law appears in this context as the 'veil' (*velum*), 'covering' (*involucrum*) or 'protective guise' (*cortex*) that allows the truth to be passed down through its very concealment. This hieroglyphic function of the law represents its 'secondary' basis or goal in Spencer's system. He glimpses the literal meaning of the law in its drawing the believer towards God, whereas the mystical meaning consists in its drawing the believer towards Christ and the Gospel: '[. . .] so that the law of Moses, taken in its literal meaning, should educate to God, whereas the same law, regarded in its true mystical meaning, not infrequently educates to Christ and the gospel'.[13]

Maimonides had drawn his image of heathen religion, which he identified with the Sabaeans, from the book *The Nabataean Agriculture* by the tenth-century author Ibn Wahshiyya.[14] Spencer, on the other hand, identified heathen religion with ancient Egypt, finding support for this view in the inexhaustible plenitude of Latin, Arabic and rabbinical sources that seventeenth-century scholarship had placed at his disposal.[15] The image of heathen religion he found in Maimonides compelled Spencer to abandon the polemical image of Egypt which had hitherto defined theological and historical engagement with the book of Exodus and the Moses tradition, and to replace the model of normative inversion with the concept of appropriation (*translatio*). He found the impression of concord to be far stronger than that of discord. Theologically, what was the sense in God first bringing his people to Egypt, only to have to arduously purge them of the idolatrous habits they had acquired there upon their escape? Why would God – and this is Spencer's strongest argument – have called on to lead his people a man who had been brought up at pharaoh's court and who, as it says in Acts 7:22, 'was learned in all the wisdom of the Egyptians', if not because his background made him uniquely qualified for the task? For this purpose and no other, God made his people tarry in Egypt for centuries and then sent them a leader whose knowledge of the Egyptian mysteries was unsurpassed. In Spencer's words, God chose as his first prophet a man 'steeped in the hieroglyphical literature of Egypt' (*hieroglyphicis Aegyptiis literis innutrium*): 'God wanted Moses to write the mystical images of the more sublime things.' Nothing was more suited to this goal than the hieroglyphical literature in which Moses had been trained.[16] For Spencer, too, the meaning of the Israelites' Egyptian sojourn and their leader's hieroglyphical education lay in the principle of *religio duplex*.[17]

Maimonides had not only invoked God's benevolent deference to man's limited mental capacity to explain the split in Jewish religion between an exoteric and an esoteric side; he had also characterized this split as a cunning strategy (*talattuf*,[18] Hebrew *'ormah* and *tahbulah*) on God's part.[19] Spencer adopts this expression in a form that almost suggests a pious deception. He believes that God used *methodis honeste fallacibus et sinuis gradibus*, 'honourably deceitful methods and crooked paths',[20] when making allowances for human weaknesses and customs. For Spencer, God's cunning consists above all in the fact 'that God gave the Jews a religion that was carnal only on the outside, but divine and wonderful on the inside, accommodating his institutions to the taste and usage of the age so that nothing ordained in the name of truth would appear to be missing from his law and his cult'.[21] The Jewish religion of revelation is thus just as much a mystery religion as the Egyptian. In support of this view, Spencer cites a passage from Eusebius, who believed that the Torah was also a doubly encoded text, one which offered the common people a multitude of concrete regulations while giving the wise even more to think about:

> Moses commanded the Jewish people to follow all the rites set out in the words of their law. But he wanted those whose spirit and virtue were stronger, because they were free of this external layer, to grow accustomed to a more divine philosophy surpassing the understanding of the common man, and to penetrate with the eyes of the mind into the higher meaning of the laws.[22]

Admittedly, this is a very free translation of Eusebius. The passage in question reads as follows:

> Now since we have gone through the commandments of the Sacred Laws, and the nature of the idea allegorically expressed in them, it would be next in order to indicate the following point. The *logos*[23] divided the whole Jewish nation into two sections. And while it meant to lead the multitude on gently by the precepts of the laws as enjoined according to the literal sense (*kata tēn rhētēn dianoian*), the other class, consisting of those who had acquired a habit of virtue, it meant to exempt from this literal sense, and required them to give attention to a philosophy of a diviner kind too highly exalted for the multitude, and to contemplation of the things signified in the meaning of the laws.[24]

There is no word of Moses here, only the *logos*. Here too, however, the principle of *religio duplex*, with its sharp division between the profane and the initiate, is expressed with the utmost clarity.

God's well-meaning deception is to have adopted from the Egyptians the principle of mystery religion (*ainigmata*) or dual religion. In countless passages, Spencer traces back this idea of God's cunning to the doctrine of accommodation expounded by the Church Fathers. He places the following motto at the head of his work, a quotation from a letter of the Egyptian monk, Isidore of Pelusium (*c*.400):[25]

hōsper tēs men selēnēs kalēs ousēs, ou tou Hēliou kreittonos, heis estin
ho dēmiourgos; houtō kai palaias kai kainēs diathēkēs heis nomothetēs,
ho sophos, [kai prosphoros] kai katallēlōs tois kairois, nomothetēsas.

Quemadmodum et pulchrae Lunae, et pulchrioris Solis, unus
idemque effector est; eodem modo et Veteris et Novi Testamenti unus
atque idem est Legislator, qui sapienter, et ad tempora accomodate,
leges tulit.

Just as there is only one single creator of both the beautiful moon
and the even more beautiful sun, there is also only one single legislator
of both the Old and the New Testaments, who gave the laws wisely,
[fittingly] and with respect to temporal circumstances.

Christianity accounts for the law by referring to God's wisdom and
benevolence. God adapted or 'accommodated' himself to the people
by giving them the rites to which they had grown accustomed, rather
than imposing on them a religion for which they were not yet ready,
one resting solely on faith, justice and worship. It may take them
millennia to prepare themselves to receive the truth; yet this truth
already lies concealed in the hieroglyphic form of the laws. The idea
of dual or mystery religion therefore logically flows from the doctrine
of accommodation, and it develops over the course of the seventeenth
century within the parameters of a research movement that might be
termed 'paganology' or 'heathen studies': the science of paganism,
the study of heathen history, cultures and religions. The goal of paganology was to investigate the historical context to which God tailored
his revelation. That is why paganology is originally a theological
project, however secular its later scientific and speculative offshoots
may have been. It is certainly not to be confused with the studies
pursued by the Humanists, who researched the pagans for their own
sake and for the sake of the classical status accorded their civilizational legacies. With the Christian doctrine of accommodation, an
evolutionistic perspective enters into the history of religion, a theological counterpart to the grammatological evolution discussed in the
previous chapter. Spencer turns to ancient Egypt as a theologian, not
as a historian; he enquires into the historical conditions and grounds
of the Mosaic laws, with the aim of descrying what God intended
when he led his people into Egypt and then decreed them a multitude
of 'Egyptian' laws.

In the light of this evolutionistic perspective, which looks backward to the Church Fathers even as it looks forward to Herder's and
Lessing's idea of an education of the human race, the structure of
religio duplex also appears as an interim solution. The truth, whose
time has not yet come, is nonetheless stored up in rites and images
which communicate it esoterically to those who know how to read

them. Only at the end of a long educational process involving the entire human race will the truth become the common property of a truly enlightened humankind.

The Platonic Construction of Dual Religion: Ralph Cudworth

In the same place and at the same time, and certainly not independently of John Spencer, his colleague Ralph Cudworth was developing a similar image of ancient Egyptian religion as a *religio duplex*, only this time on a Platonic basis. He presented his findings in *The True Intellectual System of the Universe*, completed in 1671 but not published until 1678.[26] Together with Henry More and Benjamin Whichcote, Cudworth was one of the Cambridge Platonists, who transplanted the Platonism of the Florentine Renaissance to English soil.[27] Renowned for his immense philosophical, literary and antiquarian learning in the field of classical antiquity, he was also, like Spencer, a theologian, Regius Professor for Hebrew and Master of Christ's College. No less a figure than Isaac Newton, who studied Hebrew and read Maimonides with Spencer,[28] compiled lengthy excerpts from Cudworth's *True Intellectual System*.[29]

Spencer and Cudworth were pursuing quite different objectives in their studies of Egyptian religion, however. Spencer was interested in the *structure* of Egyptian religion as a *religio duplex*. He wanted to prove it to have been a model for the religion of the Old Testament. He showed no further interest in the *content* of the Egyptian mysteries; yet precisely this aspect was to assume central importance for Cudworth. Accordingly, the model of *religio duplex* is contoured differently in Cudworth. For Maimonides and Spencer, religion's constitutive ambiguity was a matter of semiotics: religious meaning was doubly encoded, meaning that religious signs could be read in two different ways. In Cudworth, by contrast, religion is split into two distinct theologies: a popular religion for the masses and an occult theology for the elite. His presentation may be considered the *locus classicus* for the idea of an Egyptian *religio duplex*, even if this term does not appear in his writing.

With his *True Intellectual System of the Universe*, Cudworth pursues the polemical objective of refuting atheism. He sets out to prove two things: that all known religions, including polytheistic paganism, believe in a single god,[30] and that this one god was always understood as a spiritual rather than a material being. His book is graced by a frontispiece showing two groups of three philosophers standing opposite each other before the altar of 'religion'. On the left-hand side, beneath a wreath labelled 'victory', stand the 'theists': Socrates, Pythagoras and Aristotle; on the right-hand side, beneath a wreath labelled 'confusion', we see the 'atheists': Strato, Epicurus and Anaximander. Atheism refers here to a monism or materialism which recognizes nothing other than visible nature, in contrast to 'theism' (which corresponds more closely, however, to what the eighteenth century would call deism), which distinguishes between matter and spirit. The entire work is structured around this opposition. For Cudworth, 'atheism' is an invention of certain strands of Greek philosophy, whereas the idea of a supreme unity underlying all religions in some form or other must be understood as theist. For his argument to succeed, it is vitally important that he defend ancient Egyptian theology against the charge that it ultimately only worshipped the cosmos or the stars.

Porphyry and Iamblichus had already corresponded on this question. It subsequently became one of the main bones of contention in the theological controversies of the seventeenth and (especially) eighteenth centuries. At stake is the distinction, on the one hand, between the personal, biblical God, the 'God of the Fathers', and the philosophers' god, the *causa prima*, and, on the other hand, between a transcendentalist position that differentiates between God and the world and an immanentist position that identifies them. It is therefore worth examining more closely the relevant passages in Iamblichus's 'Reply of Abammon', widely circulated under the title *On the Egyptian Mysteries*. Rather than drawing on Cudworth's summary, I will refer back to the Greek text itself and occasionally comment on it from an Egyptological point of view, since here three layers emerge with particular clarity: (1) authentic late Egyptian ideas; (2) their Greek translation into Neoplatonic categories; and (3) their uptake and resonance in the context of the theological controversies of the seventeenth and eighteenth centuries.[31]

Porphyry inquires about the Egyptian idea of a *causa prima* (*prōton aition*): whether it is spirit or something higher than spirit; whether it is One or linked with others; whether it is corporeal or incorporeal; whether it is identical with the creator or comes before the creator; whether everything arose from the One or the Many; whether the Egyptians posit a primal matter or physical beings with particular properties; and whether the primal matter is created or uncreated (VIII.1). In his answer, Iamblichus runs through a number of different positions (referring to the 20,000 books of Hermes – according to Seleucus; according to Manetho, there are some 36,525). One god exists before everything else, 'unmoved in the aloneness of his unity' (*akinētos en monotēti tēs heautou henotētos*), self-engendered, his own father and son; from this god shone (*exēlampē*) the god who suffices unto himself (*autarkēs theos*), origin and god of gods, prior to all Being (*proousios*) and source of all Being. (Although this concept of the divine undoubtedly has parallels in Neoplatonism,[32] it coheres remarkably precisely with Egyptian cosmology, according to which the pre-existing god Atum [nothingness = the universe] arose as the sun and so set in train the creation of the world.[33]) So much for first principles, which Hermes sets out even before the ether, fire and sky gods. Hermes elsewhere posits 'Emeph' (i.e., Kmeph or Kneph = *Kem'atef*, 'he whose time has come'). This is the mind (*nous*) that thinks itself. According to late Egyptian theology, Kneph is the primal form of the god who, as Amun, becomes the origin and creator of the world emerging from him, and, as Amenemope (Amun-in-Luxor), his filial form, observes the rites for his primal form Kneph. He is thus a god who exists in three generations – once again, a conception that bears remarkable similarities to the triadic or trinitarian ideas about god advanced by Neoplatonism. Iamblichus goes on to speak about the creator, 'the creative mind (*dēmiourgikos nous*) and fount of truth and wisdom, who, by bringing to light the power of secret words, is called "Amun" [the concealed one], as the true and ingenious creator of all things is called "Phthà", and as the creator of the good is called "Osiris"' (VIII.3, Part 1).

In Jablonski we find very interesting entries on Kneph and Ptah, which relate directly to the distinction between atheism and theism. In his article on Ptah, he cites Eusebius, who writes that Orpheus borrowed his entire theology from Egypt when he equated god and the world (*Mundum utique Deum esse voluit*).[34] 'Should we not say that Spinoza took his [doctrine] from the Egyptians?' In another passage, Eusebius writes that the Phoenicians and Egyptians worshipped the sun, moon and stars as gods and believed them to be the origin of all things.[35] For Jablonski, that clearly speaks for the Spinozism – that is, the monism, materialism and atheism – of Egyptian theology.[36] In his article on 'Cnephus vel Cnuphi', however, he asserts that, although the wise men of Egypt gave the sun and moon control over the sublunary world, they ascribed the entire force, motions and operations of these heavenly bodies to an 'eternal divine spirit'. Introducing Vulcanus (=Ptah) with the Virgil quotation *mens agitat molem* ('the mind moves matter'), Jablonski describes the god in unmistakably hymnic language as 'highest ether, finest and purest flame, immutably shining forth in eternal, unchanging light, all-embracing, all-powerful, he suffuses, animates and enlivens the entire universe'.[37] That amounts to an unambiguous acquittal from the same charge of atheism which the other article had levelled against the Egyptian idea of Ptah. Jablonski illustrates this Egyptian idea of a *spiritus aethereus divinus* by referring to the veiled image at Sais, whose inscription he translates as 'Quae sunt, quae erunt, quaeque fuerunt, ego sum. Tunicam meam nemo revelavit' ('I am what is, was and shall be. No mortal ever lifted my veil'). In his interpretation, this infers that everything that befalls humans, whether for good or for ill, derives from a single source, a *numen duplex* whose benevolent side is called 'Cneph' and whose malevolent side is called 'Tithrambo'.[38] These two entries bespeak, on the one hand, the great ambivalence of Egyptian theology in the eyes of scholars at the time, with their oscillation between materialism and deism, and, on the other, the cardinal importance of this distinction for the study of pagan religions.

But let us return to Iamblichus:

> In addition there is a supreme authority (*hēgemonia*) ruling over the elements of creation (four female, four male), which they ascribe to the sun-god,[39] and another ruling over perishable nature, which they associate with the moon.[40] They then divide the heavens into two, four, twelve, thirty-six and twice as many sections, allot a ruler to each [the decans and 'chronocrators' of late Egyptian astronomy], and again appoint the One to rule over them all. In Egyptian cosmology, everything thus commences with the One and trickles down to the fullness of the Many, which in turn is governed by the One, and limitless nature is everywhere bounded by a strict measure and ruled by the supreme, all-unifying cause (VIII.3, Part 2).

Iamblichus explicitly adds that his writings, in being translated into Greek, have also been brought 'into the language of the philosophers', but none of the details in his presentation is incompatible with ancient Egyptian ideas.

Hermes evidently is no atheist, materialist or monist. 'The Egyptians do not say that everything is nature. They distinguish between nature and mental and spiritual life, and not only in relation to the universe, but also in relation to humans.' For him, the spiritual always takes precedence over the material and the existent, and within what exists there is a guiding intelligence in the form of the sun, the moon and the stars which rule over time.[41]

The rule of the stars represents the next problem, however. Porphyry claimed that 'most Egyptians consider our free will to depend on the stellar movements'. Iamblichus's response to this, while certainly ingenious, no longer has anything to do with Egyptian ideas. He refers here to the two souls doctrine we find in Numenius of Apamea, Plotinus, Gnosticism and Manichaeism:[42]

Man has two souls – one is from the First Mind (*apo tou prōtou noētou*) and shares in the power of the demiurge, the other has been put in from the revolutions of the heavenly bodies. The soul that has descended to us from the spheres follows along with the revolutions of the spheres; but the soul present in us as mind from the Mind is superior to the revolutions that work becoming,[43] and it is through it that liberation from the dominion of fate (*heimarmene*) and the ascent to the intelligible gods comes about. (VIII.6)

The universe, split into a spiritual (or extra-cosmic) and a material (or cosmic) order, thus has a counterpart in the two souls of man, one belonging to the extra-cosmic sphere, the other subjected to the cosmic order: *mundus duplex* and *homo duplex*. So much for Iamblichus's remarks on Egyptian theology, which I have explored in some detail here because they enjoyed almost canonic status among scholars prior to the decipherment of the hieroglyphs.

Cudworth's thesis that even polytheistic religions rested on the oneness of God led him to posit *religio duplex* as the form taken by a religion that was at once polytheistic and monotheistic. Cudworth divided Egyptian theology into a 'Vulgar and Fabulous Theology' and an '*aporrhetos theologia, Arcane and Recondite Theology*, that was concealed from the Vulgar and communicated only to the Kings, and such Priests and others as were thought capable thereof'.[44] This double structure was by no means unique to the Egyptians: all religions had such an outside and an inside, a secret doctrine accessible only to the initiated. Cudworth draws on a wealth of ancient quotations to support this thesis. The central passage stands in Origen's text *Contra Celsum*. Celsus had claimed in his polemic against the Christians (*Alēthēs logos*) to have thoroughly understood all matters pertaining to Christianity. Origen has this to say in response:

[Celsus] appears to me to act very much as a person would do who had visited Egypt (where the Egyptian savants, learned in their country's literature, are greatly given to philosophizing about those things which are regarded among them as divine, but where the vulgar, hearing certain myths, the reasons of which they do not understand, are greatly elated because of their fancied knowledge), and who should imagine that he is acquainted with the whole circle of Egyptian knowledge, after having been a disciple of the ignorant alone, and without having associated with any of the priests, or having learned the mysteries of the Egyptians from any other source. And what I have said regarding the learned and ignorant among the Egyptians, I might have said also of the Persians; among whom there are mysteries, conducted on rational principles by the learned among them, but understood in a symbolical sense by the more superficial of the multitude. And the same remark applies to the Syrians, and Indians, and to all those who have a literature and a mythology.[45]

Origen is saying two things here: he is asserting that all religions known to him have an esoteric dimension to which only the wise are privy, and he is claiming that the same is true of Christianity, so that an outsider like Celsus could only have glimpsed the exoteric outer layer. In this respect, Clement of Alexandria compares the Egyptian religion with the religion of the Israelites:

> The truly secret Word, deposited in the shrine of truth, was by the Egyptians indicated by what they called 'adyta', and by the Hebrews by the curtain [in the temple]. In respect to concealment, the mysteries (*ainigmata*) of the Hebrews and the Egyptians are very similar.[46]

According to Cudworth, the secret teaching shared by all religions consists in the knowledge that God is All and that All is One. This theology of all-oneness first arose in Egypt as an occult doctrine before being disseminated elsewhere by suitably initiated travellers. Insofar as it is shared by all peoples and common to all religions, the doctrine of all-oneness constitutes the 'True Intellectual System of the Universe'.

Cudworth maintains that the Egyptians used two means of transmitting this doctrine to the knowledgeable while concealing it from the common folk: allegories and hieroglyphs. Cudworth accepted the common explanation of hieroglyphs as 'Figures not answering to sounds or Words, but immediately representing the Objects and Conceptions of the Mind', chiefly used 'to express the Mysteries of their Religion and Theology, so that they might be concealed from the prophane Vulgar'.[47] This was the 'Hieroglyphick Learning and Metaphysical Theory' Moses had been instructed in. According to Cudworth, there can be no doubt that it consisted in the 'Doctrine of *One Supreme and Universal Deity the Maker of the Whole World*'.[48]

Like his fifteenth-century predecessors Marsilio Ficino and Pico della Mirandola, Cudworth leaned on the *Corpus Hermeticum* in support of this claim. This compendium of Greek-language philosophical and theological texts, purportedly written by the Egyptian arch-sage Hermes Trismegistus, had arrived in Florence in 1463 from Byzantium, creating a furor in the West besides which the rediscovery of Horapollo paled in comparison. Whereas Ficino, the texts' translator into Latin, believed the *Corpus Hermeticum* to be a repository of age-old wisdom that reached back to the days of Moses, and possibly even earlier, Cudworth heeded the criticism of Isaac Casaubon (1559–1614), who had proved beyond reasonable doubt that the *Corpus Hermeticum* dated from late antiquity.[49] For Cudworth, the *Corpus* testified not to the age but to the longevity of the Egyptian theological tradition, which had not yet been extinguished at the time these texts were written.[50] The arcane theology of the *Corpus Hermeticum*, distilled by Cudworth from dozens of quotations, essentially amounts to a theology of all-oneness. For the Egyptians, the One (*to hen*) manifests or 'conceals' itself in the All (*to pan*), as its invisible origin. *Pan* is the external manifestation or extension of *to hen*. Cudworth marshals an extremely impressive array of passages from the sixteen treatises of the *Corpus Hermeticum* to illustrate this theology of *to hen kai to pan* (the One and the All). He quotes these passages both in their original Greek or Latin and in his own beautifully hymnic translation. Historical reconstruction here shades into full-blown confession. The Anglican theologian no doubt rediscovered his own credo in the hermetic texts: 'All ye powers that are within me, praise the One and All.'[51]

Cudworth moves beyond the idea of all-oneness, however, to trace back the negative theology of the Hidden God to Egyptian arcane theology as well. In Plutarch's treatise *On Isis and Osiris*, the best source on Egyptian religion available to him at the time, he found that Manetho of Sebennytos 'conceives the word Ammon to signify that which is hidden'.[52] The current state of Egyptological research confirms that the name does in fact mean 'the concealed one', something also constantly alluded to in the Egyptian texts. Cudworth associates this divine name with popular religion and philosophy. For the corresponding idea in arcane theology, he refers to Damascius, the last pagan scholarch of the School of Athens:

> The Egyptian Philosophers that have been in our times, have declared the hidden truth of their Theology, having found in certain Egyptian Writings, that there was according to them, One Principle of all things, praised under the name of the Unknown Darkness, and that thrice repeated: Which Unknown Darkness is a Description of that Supreme Deity, that is Incomprehensible.[53]

For Cudworth, the arcane theology of the Hidden God finds its most sublime expression in the inscription on the veiled image at Sais. He appears to have been the first to accord Plutarch's and Proclus's famous description a central place in Egyptian theology. He renders Plutarch's version of the inscription 'on the temple at Sais' with the words: '*I am all that Hath been, Is, and Shall be, and my* Peplum *or*

Veil, no mortal hath yet uncovered.' According to Cudworth, Isis is the voice of divine nature in this inscription. Berkeley summarized Cudworth's argument very aptly:

> Plato and Aristotle considered God as abstracted or distinct from the natural world. But the Aegyptians considered God and nature as making one whole, or all things together as making one universe. In doing which they did not exclude the intelligent mind, but considered it as containing all things. Therefore, whatever was wrong in their way of thinking, it doth not, nevertheless, imply or lead to Atheism.[54]

With that, Berkeley put Cudworth's construction of Egyptian arcane theology in a nutshell. God was equated with nature, but not in such a way that God was reduced to nature. Rather, nature was conceived as the all-encompassing, invisible godhead, the spiritual principle which manifests or conceals itself as visible nature (*natura naturans*).

Can Cudworth be considered the discoverer or inventor of dual religion? As Peter Miller and Martin Mulsow have pointed out, Cudworth's distinction between a vulgar polytheism and an elite monotheism had already been introduced by John Selden in his book *De Diis Syris* (1617). Selden distinguished there between the false doctrine of multiple deities, widespread among the pagans – in Greek, *tēs polytheou planēs* – and the 'healthier insight' vouchsafed to the more learned philosophers and 'hierophants' (initiated priests) among the pagans (*gentium*), and taught by them in mystical manner (*mysticè docebant*). The latter preached 'that ONE was the supreme cause of everything, ONE the governor of the world, and worshipped in many forms'.[55] Selden elaborated the distinction between popular and learned views about the divine with reference to the gods' gender. In some religions or languages, revered heavenly bodies like the sun, the moon and Venus appear as masculine, whereas in others they are considered to be feminine. Among the Greeks, the Romans and even, 'if I am not mistaken' (*ni fallor*), the Egyptians, a more abstract idea of god arose, a 'transcendent and broadly monotheistic consciousness shared by the educated elite'.[56] The example he goes on to cite for the abstract monotheism of the Egyptians is particularly informative, since in this case the genesis of the misunderstanding can be more clearly demonstrated than elsewhere. From the earliest times in ancient Egypt, the 'attendants of Horus' would precede the king in festive processions. These consisted of four divine standards: two jackals, the Upper and Lower Egyptian Upuaut ('opener of the ways'), a falcon (Horus), and the throne cushion, often replaced in the Late

Period by an ibis (Thoth). Clement of Alexandria describes this procession as follows:

> They carry about golden images – two dogs, one hawk, and one ibis; and the four figures of the images they call four letters.[57] For the dogs are symbols of the two hemispheres, which, as it were, go round and keep watch; the hawk, of the sun, for it is fiery and destructive (so they attribute pestilential diseases to the sun);[58] the ibis, of the moon, likening the shady parts to that which is dark in plumage, and the luminous to the light.[59] And some will have it that by the dogs are meant the tropics, which guard and watch the sun's passage to the south and north. The hawk signifies the equinoctial line, which is high and parched with heat, as the ibis the ecliptic. For the ibis seems, above other animals, to have furnished the Egyptians the first rudiments of the invention of number and measure, as the oblique line did of circles.[60]

Much in this account is correct. The two dogs, or rather jackals, do indeed refer to the south and north, although less in the sense of hemispheres than of the two kingdoms of Upper and Lower Egypt; the falcon undoubtedly has to do with the sun, just as the ibis is associated with the moon. The significance of the Egyptian divine symbols has not yet been entirely lost. However, the cosmological meaning that is read into these signs here is quite new.

Synesius, the Platonist and Bishop of Cyrene, comes to speak of this passage in his *Praise of Baldness* because the hemispheres mentioned by Clement apparently give a meaningful cosmological explanation for the baldness of the Egyptian clergy. While the sense he makes of Clement's description of the Egyptian processions represents an extreme example of misreading, it also offers very clear ancient evidence for the idea of dual religion.

Among the Egyptians, Synesius asserts, the priests expressly forbid those who make useless and profane things from producing images of the divine, lest they go beyond their area of competence. The priests delude the common people with the hawk and ibis beaks they carve on the entrance halls (*vestibula*) to their temples. They themselves, however, go down to the sacred caves (*sacra antra*) to conduct their business there in secret. They keep there *komastēria*, certain chests said to contain spheres (*sphaeras*). If they saw these spheres, the common folk would take offence, since they disdain what is easiest for them to understand and require made-up miracles instead.[61]

Here Clement's *komasia* ('processions') have become *komastēria*, a word not found in Greek and obviously unknown to Synesius as well. He imagines these to be containers in the sense of a *cista mystica* (the lidded basket used particularly in the Eleusinian Mysteries). The spheres they contain are all that remain of Clement's divine images, the hemispheres symbolized by dogs. What Synesius wants to illustrate with this scene is the *religio duplex* of the Egyptian priests, who performed all manner of hocus pocus for the populace but themselves descended to their hidden crypts to worship the cosmic god in spherical form. This is also the aspect of the story that interests John Selden:

> The Egyptian prophets took a different approach, I believe, but among them there was also to be found a wholly concealed symbol of unity. For they showed the profane crowds the ridiculous figures, extraordinary and beyond number, playing particularly on the superstition of the inexperienced; others they used as mysteries, enclosing them in sacred shrines: to wit, certain spheres were apparently symbols of the ONE DIRECTOR of the entire universe. For just as the sphere shows the form of the world, so also – and not badly – does it show the unity of the supreme cause. There was thus also an immense difference between the secret shrines of the prophets and what was invented for the populace.[62]

Seldom can the emergence of a misunderstanding be traced so clearly. There is method to this misreading, however: it stands in the service of a construction of ancient Egyptian religion in the sense of a *religio duplex*. One should perhaps therefore not speak of a 'discovery' in Cudworth. At any rate, he has the merit of having broadly elaborated, and illustrated with a wealth of ancient sources, a thought which had already been expressed by John Selden, and presumably by many other authors of the seventeenth century.

Leaving aside the question of whether Cudworth was right to reconstruct the religion of the ancient Egyptians in the sense of this theory of 'dual religion', split into an official political theology and a secret philosophical theology, we must recognize that his derivation of this principle from a great many ancient sources is of considerable interest. While Cudworth did not discover the ancient Egyptian religion, which naturally remained inaccessible to him owing to his ignorance of the original sources, he did discover a late antique – above all, middle- and Neoplatonic – theory of religion which is significant in itself, and which through his mediation was to gain an importance in the century of secret societies that cannot be overestimated. According to this theory, there is a secret tradition, a 'kabbalah', behind every official religion. Every tradition has two sides. Knowledge is unequally distributed in the world, and truth can only ever be had in veiled form. This conception is informed by middle- and Neoplatonic epistemology, according to which truth in this world is always hinted at in riddles, fables and allegories, never directly known and apprehended. The phenomenal world is the veil in which truth at once reveals and conceals itself. The truth is difficult to attain, and only the wise can even dare approach it. The ancient theory of Egyptian occult religion, as we encounter it in Plutarch and Diodorus, Philo, Origen and Clement of Alexandria, as well as in Porphyry and Iamblichus, finds its most beautiful expression in the Gospel of Philip, a Coptic-language Gnostic text from Egypt: 'Truth did not come into the world naked; rather it came in types and images. The world will not accept it in any other form.'[63] Just as the words 'I am what was, is and shall be' on the inscription at Sais may be interpreted as the refusal of a name, but also as the revelation of the nameless god, so the veil mentioned in the following words – 'no mortal ever lifted my veil' – signifies as much a concealment as a manifestation of the deity. Goethe pithily expressed this dual aspect of mystery as both conceal-ment and manifestation of truth: 'The true is godlike: we do not see it itself; we must guess at it through its manifestations.'[64]

Cudworth's importance for European religious and intellectual history lies above all in the fact that, through his influence, the 'monistic depth current of the Christian discourse on God',[65] which had swollen mightily in the Renaissance and then ebbed away with the condemnation of *Prisca Theologia*,[66] underwent an enormous resurgence that carried all the way through to the pantheism debates of the late eighteenth and early nineteenth centuries. With the concept of arcane theology, he not only located this depth current in ancient religions, he also pre-assigned it a place in the contemporary world that the secret societies of the eighteenth century were eager to fill. Since the early fifteenth century, monism (or cosmotheism) has been the arcane theology of Christianity.

3

Religio Duplex and Political Theology

John Toland and the Critique of Political Theology

All the theories of dual religion discussed so far, from Maimonides to Cudworth, attribute the splitting of religion or culture into an exoteric and an esoteric side to the unequal intellectual capacity of humans. They are thus rooted in the Platonic idea that the truth is concealed or hard to grasp. Only the philosopher or initiate can directly approach it, whereas ordinary people must make do with myths, allegories and images. Alongside this philosophical interpretation, however, a political line of reasoning becomes increasingly prominent in the course of the seventeenth century. Political considerations demand that the truth be kept secret. Exoteric and esoteric doctrines now diverge into 'political theology' and 'natural theology'.[1]

In the seventeenth century, the concept of 'political theology' has two different meanings. On the one hand, it appears in conjunction with the sacral functionalization and intensification of political authority, as exemplified by the miracle-working kings of the medieval English and French traditions, and in the contemporary context by Louis XIV. It is in this sense, as Martin Mulsow has shown, that the concept is used by Georg Morhof, for example.[2] On the other hand, and conversely, 'political theology' can refer to the political functionalization of religion,[3] and in this sense it forms the basis of the deist and atheist critiques of institutionalized religion in the seventeenth and eighteenth centuries. The chief protagonists of this reinterpretation are atheists, who unmask religion as priestly charlatanry in the service of politics,[4] and deists, who present revealed religion from the perspective of a natural or philosophical religion, exposing it as a construct invented for political purposes. This reproach was most trenchantly expressed in a blasphemous treatise with the title *De tribus impostoribus* – its author and historical context were finally identified by Winfried Schröder – in which Moses, Jesus and Mohammed are denounced as the three arch-deceivers of the human race,[5] as well as in the similarly named French treatise, *L'Esprit de Monsieur Benoit de Spinosa: Traité des Trois Imposteurs*, which already flags its affiliation to Spinoza in the title.[6] Both texts achieved notoriety at the time and circulated in numerous handwritten copies, but they are only the tip of the iceberg; we are dealing here with a widespread, passionately conducted debate. Spinoza plays a significant role in this tradition. It was he who, in his *Tractatus theologico-politicus*, encapsulated this critical view of positive religion in the concept of the 'theological-political' or 'political theology'.

For their part, the atheists argued almost exclusively with recourse to texts from classical antiquity. The critical thought is that belief in god was invented by rulers or legislators to lend authority to their laws and to instil in their subjects a fear of divine punishment, so deterring them from committing crimes in secret. This thesis can be found in Polybius, for example.[7] For that author, one of the principal causes of Rome's historical success was the paramountcy which the Romans accorded religion in their Constitution. 'The quality in which the Roman commonwealth is most distinctly superior', he writes, 'is in my opinion the nature of their religious convictions (*peri theōn dialēpsei*).' The Romans prioritized religion 'for the sake of the common people' (*dia plēthous charin*), as the opiate of the masses, to speak with Marx. 'For this reason I think not that the ancients acted rashly and haphazardly in introducing among the people notions concerning the gods (*peri theōn ennoias*) and beliefs in the terrors of hell.' They further kept the masses docile by exposing them to spectacles which filled their minds with terror: 'every multitude is fickle, full of lawless desires [. . .], therefore the multitude must be held in check by invisible terrors (*adēlois phobois*) and suchlike pageantry (*tragōdia*)'. While religion – more precisely, popular religion – may be fictitious, as a fiction that promotes order, peace and justice, it is a legitimate, useful and even indispensable civilizational achievement. Polybius emphasizes that 'the moderns are most rash and foolish in banishing such beliefs'. Popular religion ought not to be tampered with, even if it is a fiction that is binding only for the great majority.

The so-called 'Fragment of Critias', generally held to be the *locus classicus* of the ancient critique of religion, gives even more radical expression to the idea that the gods were invented to ensure law and order.[8] According to this text, 'some shrewd man, a man in judgment wise, found for mortals the fear of gods, thereby to frighten the wicked should they even act or speak or scheme in secret. Hence it was that he introduced the divine.'[9] Not just popular religion but belief in the divine as such is presented here as a fiction concocted for political purposes. The idea of an omniscient deity was devised to induce humans to obey the law even when there are no witnesses and no public authorities to prevent them committing an offence. This deity could not only police their acts and deeds but their unspoken thoughts as well. The motif of wicked thoughts and secret crimes plays a central role in the entire debate. The use of this text in the critical discourse of the early Modern Age presumably runs counter to its original meaning. The fragment is an excerpt from the satyr play *Sisyphus*, now attributed to Euripides.[10] The blasphemous ideas are thus voiced by a stage figure, and a notorious god-denier at that, rather than by the author speaking in his own voice. But such considerations were of scant interest to the authors of the seventeenth and eighteenth centuries.

Cicero further accentuates this position in a statement placed in the mouth of the neo-Academician Cotta. According to Cotta, this position not only presents belief in the gods in general (*tota de dis opinio*) as a fiction invented by clever statesmen, but in doing so eradicates religion as such.[11] The cleverest such statesman was Numa Pompilius,[12] who all but appears as a *doppelgänger* of Moses. Just as Moses attributed authorship of the Ten Commandments to Yahweh, so Numa claimed the nymph Egeria as the source of the laws he handed down to his people. Like Moses, Numa also codified these laws in a book. In contrast to Moses, however, he preferred to take this book with him to the grave rather than bequeath it to a posterity that would only subject his laws to further manipulation. The earliest version of the French *Traité des trois imposteurs* devotes an entire chapter to Numa.[13]

The passage most frequently cited in the seventeenth and eighteenth centuries, from Diodorus's *Historical Library* (I.94.1–2), deals with the six great lawgivers of human history. Of all the Greek and Latin texts on political theology cited at the time, this is the only one to mention Moses by name. The first of these lawgivers was the founder of the Egyptian Empire, whom Diodorus variously calls Menas, Menes and Mnevis. He 'claimed that Hermes gave him the laws.' Among the Cretans, similar claims were made by Minos about

Zeus; among the Spartans, by Lycurgus about Apollo; among the 'Arians' (*arianoi*), by Zoroaster about Agathos Daimon (Ahura Mazda); among the Getae, by Zalmoxis about Hestia; and among the Jews by Moyses about Iao (Yahweh).[14] Diodorus – or rather his source, perhaps Hecataeus of Abdera – is by no means out to attack religion, describing this strategy as a legitimate and successful ploy to found a constitution and proclaim laws by means of political theology. In the fifteenth century, Ficino, for example, could derive the model for his 'old theology' from this passage by interpreting the concept of 'legislation' in the sense of 'establishing a religion'. Ficino replaces the great lawgivers with the 'wise old men' – Zoroaster, Hermes Trismegistos, Orpheus and so on – who brought religion to humankind, and with it the laws of civil coexistence. It was not until the seventeenth century, with its critique of political theology, that this passage was used to denounce the unholy alliance of sovereignty and salvation.

In these texts, Diodorus is mostly paraphrased without acknowledgement rather than cited by name, and his list of six pre-eminent lawgivers is considerably expanded.[15] The standard, continually transcribed and modified quotation was taken from a work which, far from circulating underground, belonged to the officially printed, scholarly discourse of the time: the *Considérations politiques sur les coups d'État* by Gabriel Naudé (1600–52), first published in 1639 and reprinted in 1667. Naudé writes:

> All ancient legislators, wanting to authorize, consolidate and secure the laws they gave to their people, knew no better means than to proclaim and make the people believe [. . .] that they had received them from some divinity: Zoroaster from Oromasis [Ahura Mazda], Trismegistos from Mercury, Zalmoxis from Vesta, Charondas from Saturn, Minos from Jupiter, Lycurgus from Apollo, Draco and Solon from Minerva, Numa from the nymph Egeria, Mohammed from the angel Gabriel; and Moses, who was the wisest of them all, describes in Exodus how he received his laws directly from God.[16]

This passage is reproduced at the beginning of chapter 17 of the *Traité des trois imposteurs*.[17]

The English deist, John Toland, dedicated several writings to this debate. They included the treatise *Adeisidaemon*, which deals particularly with Numa Pompilius (in Livy's account) and with Cicero's summary of the ancient critique of religion;[18] the *Origines Judaicae*, published alongside *Adeisidaemon* in 1709, which discusses Moses and takes Diodorus's passage on the six lawgivers as its point of departure; and the treatise *Clidophorus*, which appeared in 1720 as

part of his *Tetradymos*. In his *Origines Judaicae*, Toland contrasts
the Moses of the Bible, who follows the general principle of 'invent-
ing' (*finxisse*) God as the author of his legislation, with the Moses of
Strabo, who does the exact opposite, radically rejecting the principle
of political theology.[19]

Strabo describes Moses as an Egyptian priest who left his land out
of 'dissatisfaction' with the Egyptian religion and moved to Palestine
to start a new religion with a group of like-minded followers.[20]
Toland reconstructs the Egyptian religion rejected by Moses as a
political polytheism. Each province had its own deity, since –
according to Diodorus – 'a certain very wise ruler', wanting to ensure
harmony in his kingdom, introduced 'a pluralistic and polytheistic
religion' to prevent a conspiracy arising among the Egyptians. According to Tacitus, the Egyptians worshipped many animals and mon-
strous images. Moses could stand this no more. In Toland's view,
Strabo's Moses was not an atheist but a 'pantheist or, to speak in the
new terminology, a Spinozist'. Once again we encounter Spinoza in
the context of the critique of political theology. For the (proto-)
Spinozist Moses, God is 'nature or cosmic matter, arranged mechani-
cally and acting without consciousness and intelligence'. The name
Moses gave to his God means nothing other than 'necessary being'
(*necessarium solummodo existentiam*) or 'that which exists through
itself' (*quod per se existit*), in much the same way that the Greek
word for Being (*to on*) designates the intransient, eternal and infinite
universe. The cult founded by 'Moses Strabonicus' did away with
extravagant sacrifices, ecstatic inspirations and other 'absurd deeds'.[21]
For Strabo, the complicated ritual laws which the Bible ascribes to
Moses are a later symptom of decadence. Moses established a cult of
the utmost purity and simplicity. The only feast was the Sabbath, the
only law was the law of nature (*lex naturae*), consisting of the Ten
Commandments, and the only cult was the worship of the two stone
tables on which those commandments were inscribed. Everything else
– the distinction between pure and impure foods, circumcision, ritual
sacrifice, and so on – is the result of a subsequent relapse into idolatry
on the part of the Jews. In this way, religion degenerated into
superstition.

Toland draws the same distinction between religion and superstition in *Adeisidaemon*. There is no religion other than the religion of
reason, whereas superstition is a man-made and irrational pseudo-
religion devised solely to buttress the existing political order (in the
sense of a political theology). Political theology itself is the signature
of false religion and a telltale sign of decline. More orthodox authors
availed themselves of precisely the same argument, but in their hands

it was used to diagnose pagan religions. Thus Alexander Ross writes in the second edition of his work *Pansebeia* (1653): 'All false religions are grounded upon Policy', this being the 'humane Policy to keep people in obedience and awe of their superiours [sic].'[22]

In his *Clidophorus* (1720), Toland locates this development in the context of *religio duplex*. The full title of Toland's treatise already states his thesis with the utmost clarity: *Clidophorus, or, Of the Exoteric and Esoteric Philosophy; that is, Of the External and Internal Doctrine of the Ancients: The one open and public, accommodated to popular prejudices and the RELIGIONS establish'd by Law; the other private and secret, wherein, to the few capable and discrete, was taught the real* TRUTH *stript of all disguises.*[23]

Toland begins his treatise by deploring the mendacity of humankind: 'To know the TRUTH is one thing, to tell it to others is another thing: and as all men profess to admire the first, so few men practise the last as they ought.' The truth is known, but it is not communicated. Thus knowledge is split between an exoteric and an esoteric philosophy. This split began when 'some cunning persons' hit upon the idea of appealing to 'a superior and supernatural knowledge, not subject to the rules of Criticism', openly contending 'that it was lawful to lie for the public good' so that the common people would 'be deluded by agreeable fables into obedience to their Governor'. Toland illustrates this strategy by revisiting the topos of the great lawgivers: Mnevis in Egypt, Zoroaster in Bactria, Pythagoras in Crotona, Zalmoxis among the Scythians, Minos and Epimenides on Crete and Numa among the Romans. All these legislators went about 'feigning an extraordinary communication with heaven'. Diodorus and several other ancient authors even had the audacity to include Moses in this list; 'but as this incomparable Legislator ought to want no apology among Christians', Toland limits himself to the pagan deceivers, 'who perceiving that what was built upon fraud, cou'd only be supported by force, they made it capital to question their dictates'.

> Hence no room was left for the propagating of TRUTH, except at the expense of a man's life, or at least of his honor and imployments, whereof numerous examples may be alledg'd. The Philosophers therefore, and other well-wishers to mankind in most nations, were constrain'd by this holy tyranny to make use of a twofold doctrine; the one *Popular*, accommodated to the PREJUDICES of the vulgar, and to the receiv'd CUSTOMS or RELIGIONS: the other *Philosophical*, conformable to the nature of things, and consequently to TRUTH; which, with doors fast shut and under all other precautions, they communicated only to friends of known probity, prudence, and capacity. These they generally

call'd the *Exoteric* and *Esoteric,* or the *External* and *Internal Doctrines.*[24]

In what follows, Toland collates a number of examples from ancient authors and finally comes to speak of the Egyptians:

> The Egyptians, who were the wisest of mortals, had a twofold doctrine: the one secret and in every respect sacred; the other popular and consequently vulgar. Who is there, that is ignorant of their sacred Letters, Hieroglyphics, Forms, Symbols, Enigmas, and Fables? Far and near was spread the fame of the Egyptian Philosophy, *concealing things under the appearance of Fables* (says PLUTARCH) *and in speeches that contain'd obscure indications and arguments of the truth: which they themselves expressly declare, by placing Sphynxes before most of their Temples; thus insinuating, that their doctrine concerning sacred things, consists in a sort of wisdom which is designedly perplext, and lying hid under study'd veils.*[25] That we may give a specimen of such things as they conceal'd, *the fame of Minerva* (says PLUTARCH again) *whom they think to be the same with ISIS, has this Inscription at Sais:* I AM ALL THAT WAS, IS, AND SHALL BE: NOR HAS ANY MORTAL DISCOVER'D WHAT'S UNDER MY HOOD.[26]
>
> ISIS therefore, whom the vulgar believ'd to have been a *Queen,* and of whom they had a thousand different fables; was the *Nature of all things,* according to the Philosophers, *who held the* UNIVERSE *to be the principal* GOD, or the supreme being, and consequently abstruse or obscure, none seeing beyond the surface of Nature. But this they only discover'd to the initiated. To that of Sais corresponds another Inscription still remaining at Capua; TO THEE, WHO ALONE ART ALL THINGS, O GODDESS ISIS.[27]

Toland further demonstrates the philosophical idea of Isis as nature – in the sense of *natura naturans* – by citing the goddess's words of self-introduction in Apuleius's *Golden Ass*:

> Moved by thy prayers, O LUCIUS, behold NATURE, the parent of all things, standing before thee; the mistress of all the elements, the initial stock of ages, the highest of the higher and queen of the lower powers, the uniform appearance of God and Goddesses, who govern by my motions the luminous heights of the sky, the salutary breezes of the sea, and the melancholy silence of the nether parts: whose one only Deity under numerous forms, various rites, and different names, is ador'd by the whole world.[28]

For Toland, it is clear that the exoteric doctrine (or popular religion) stands in the service of the state, its laws and institutions. As political theology, it rests on the 'lies' peddled by wilfully deceiving priests. In this respect, all that separates Toland from the atheist critique of religion – the priestly fraud thesis of Bernard Le Bovier de Fontenelle and Van Dale, and the two treatises on the 'Three Imposters' – is that he excludes Moses from the club of pious fraudsters. His Moses, however, as little resembles the biblical Moses as, say, the Moses in Schoenberg's *Moses and Aaron*: both are concerned with the philosophers' god, not the God of the Fathers. For Toland, the real fall from grace in the history of religion is the invention of political theology, which accompanied the foundation and consolidation of states. The 'history of the original religion's corruption' (Martin Mulsow[29]) flows directly from religion's political instrumentalization. From a twenty-first-century perspective, it has this in common with the much discussed 'return of religion'.

William Warburton and the Redemption of Political Theology

By far the most important and influential eighteenth-century work on questions of revelation and political theology, the Anglican bishop William Warburton's *The Divine Legation of Moses*, likewise stands in this tradition.[30] For Warburton (1698–1779), politically instrumentalized religion is the hallmark of pagan religion.[31] Belief in the gods was invented as a useful fiction to provide a foundation for the law. Warburton was a trained lawyer and philologist who edited the works of Alexander Pope and Shakespeare and advanced in his ecclesiastical career from a country parsonage to the bishopric of Gloucester. Like Toland, he gave the structure of dual religion a political interpretation in his magnum opus, which appeared in three volumes between 1738 and 1741.

Like Cudworth's *True Intellectual System*, planned as a refutation of atheism, Warburton's *Divine Legation* springs from a polemical, apologetical intention. While his work is dedicated to 'Free-thinkers' and his title alludes to deism, his real opponent is Pierre Bayle, whose name he mentions again and again. In particular, Warburton seeks to demolish the thesis advanced in Bayle's *Pensées diverses sur la comète*: that atheists were capable of founding a well-ordered state and leading virtuous lives. That is the position his entire work is directed against, and from this hostile stance its political and theological orientation is derived. Warburton aims to demonstrate that a religious foundation is indispensable if political and social order are to be maintained.

In refuting Bayle's thesis, Warburton pursues exactly the same strategy as Cudworth some sixty years earlier. Just as Cudworth wanted to show that belief in one God is shared by all the world's peoples and religions, so Warburton sets out to prove that there has never been a polity or civil society which dispensed entirely with religion. He starts out by revisiting the debate on the problem of the political functionalization of religion, which we discussed earlier in connection with John Toland. Displaying his characteristic erudition, Warburton adds several names to Diodorus's classic list of lawgivers who called on a divine authority to sacralize their laws, arriving at the conclusion that every act of legislation is necessarily founded on such a connection to the divine – a problem that still occupies us today in the context of the European Constitution. Incidentally, Warburton fails to mention that Diodorus also included Moses among the great lawgivers who pursued this strategy. The verb used by Diodorus in this context, *prospoiein* ('pretend', 'presume'), leaves no doubt about his estimation of the fictive character of such an appeal to divine legitimation; yet far from criticizing this strategy, Diodorus praises it as a particular sign of political wisdom. Warburton sees eye to eye with him on this. Since the pagan civilizations had not received the blessing of divine revelations, they had to invent religions to give the necessary sacral framework to their Constitution and civic laws. Pagan religion is thus a fiction in the service of political order, justice and social peace. As such, it is not a conspiracy of prelates but a great civilizational achievement. It is at bottom, however, a political institution: pagan religion rests on political theology and is the work of monarchs and legislators, just as the gods of this religion are nothing other than deified monarchs and legislators.

According to Warburton, the religious doctrine essential for maintaining political and social order is belief in 'a future state of reward and punishment', a judgement from beyond the grave on one's earthly existence. In order to 'inculcate' this doctrine among the people, religion was founded alongside the law, and as a twofold religion at that, split between 'public' and 'private' (137). Warburton imagines the 'public religion' as a sacrificial cult, replete with rites and feasts celebrating communion with the (invented) deities. Because he considers it to be morally indifferent and therefore of no use for his assault on Bayle, he does not discuss it any further. What interests him is 'private' religion. He does not have in mind an internalized and individualized religion of a 'God of one's own' (Ulrich Beck) but a different, no less political institution: the mysteries. In this context, 'private' simply means 'not public'. The real moral instruction about life after death underpinning political order and civil society takes place here.

But is there not a contradiction here? How can the doctrine that needs to be 'inculcated' in the entire populace be kept secret? Precisely this dilemma leads to a further distinction within the mysteries, that between greater and lesser mysteries. In the lesser mysteries, secrecy functions as an 'attractor', luring as many people as possible into learning about the doctrine of the 'future state'. Hieroglyphic riddles and allegories arouse the initiate's curiosity, seducing him into wanting to find out more. The lesser mysteries are primarily a pedagogical institution, an aspect that also played a key role in many secret societies, particularly the Jesuits and the Illuminati. Only when presented within a framework of tests and theatrical spectacles can religious teachings be branded ineradicably into the initiate's mind. In the greater mysteries, however, secrecy has exactly the opposite function: its purpose is to exclude the masses and reveal the truth only to those deemed capable of enduring it and passing it on. To be precise, we are thus dealing with a *religio triplex*, separated into popular religion, lesser mysteries and greater mysteries. Popular religion offers nothing but fictions and illusions; the lesser mysteries do not contest these fictions, but they do teach the moral doctrine ignored by popular religion and the ideas about the afterlife associated with that doctrine; finally, the greater, highly exclusive mysteries destroy the fictions left unchallenged by the lesser mysteries and lead the initiate to 'epopty', or contemplation of the truth. The truth glimpsed at this level is no less morally indifferent than the sacrificial ceremonies prescribed by popular religion and therefore cannot function as the basis for civic order; indeed, it threatens to destroy the state.

The lesser mysteries are concerned with the hereafter. The prospect they offer of a blissful life after death is the basis for the laws of the state, civic society and general morality. Warburton illustrates this connection of the mysteries to a fate beyond the grave with an impressive bouquet of citations culled from ancient writers. His evaluation of the evidence is confirmed by numerous more recent sources, particularly the inscribed Orphic gold-leaf tablets and other mystery texts.[32]

In a somewhat far-fetched interpretation of the sixth book of Virgil's *Aeneid*, Warburton argues that the reports of journeys into the underworld contained in ancient writings in fact represent initiations into the Eleusinian Mysteries. The initiation was thus dramatized as a descent into the realm of the dead.[33] In this context, he also analyses Apuleius's report on his initiation into the mysteries of Isis, interpreting the voyage through the elements as a journey to the underworld. Above all, he places the famous Plutarch fragment from Stobaeus in this setting, in which near-death experiences are compared with experiences of initiation into the great mysteries:

> The mind is affected and agitated in death, just as it is in initiation into the grand mysteries. And word answers to word as well as thing to thing: for *teleutan* is to die; and *teleisthai*, to be initiated. The first stage is nothing but errors and uncertainties; laborious wanderings; a rude and fearful march through night and darkness. And now arrived on the verge of death and initiation, every thing wears a dreadful aspect: it is all horror, trembling, sweating, and affrightment. But this scene once over, a miraculous and divine light displays itself; and shining plains and flowery meadows open on all hands before them. Here they are entertained with hymns, and dances, with the sublime doctrines of sacred knowledge, and with reverend and holy visions. And now become perfect and initiated, they are free, and no longer under restraints; but crowned and triumphant, they walk up and down the regions of the blessed; converse with pure and holy men; and celebrate the sacred mysteries at pleasure.[34]

Warburton prints this text – which Plutarch explicitly relates to the *greater* mysteries – in capital letters so as to emphasize its extraordinary importance.[35] In the greater mysteries, as mentioned, secrecy has the function of exclusion rather than attraction. Under no circumstances is the truth at stake in these mysteries to be made known, since it would expose the fictitiousness of the gods and thereby bring about the downfall of the state. To quote a contemporary summary:

> According to the Bishop of Gloucester, the lesser [mysteries] taught, by certain secret rites and shews, the origin of society, and the doctrine of a future state; they were preparatory to the greater, and might be safely communicated to all the initiated, without exception. The Arcana of the greater mysteries were the doctrine of the Unity, and the detection of the errors of the vulgar Polytheism; these were not communicated to all the aspirants, without exception, but only to a small and select number, who were judged capable of the secret.[36]

The exclusiveness of the (greater) mysteries is emphasized by Clement of Alexandria, for example:

> The Egyptians did not entrust the mysteries they possessed to all and sundry, and did not divulge the knowledge of divine things to the profane; but only to those destined to ascend the throne, and those of

the priests that were judged the worthiest, from their nurture, culture, and birth.[37]

Plutarch also writes about the initiated kings in his text *On Isis and Osiris*, in a passage that may be considered a *locus classicus* for the interpretation of the Egyptian religion as a *religio duplex*:

> When amongst the Egyptians there is any King chosen out of the Military Order, he is forthwith brought to the Priests, and by them instructed in that Arcane Theology, which conceals Mysterious Truths under obscure Fables and Allegories. Therefore do the Egyptians place Sphinges before their Temples, to declare thereby, that the Doctrine concerning God is Enigmatical and Obscure.[38]

For Warburton, both passages are of central importance since they emphasize the connection between politics and religion. In the first instance, the greater mysteries are the prerogative of those called upon to rule. As Warburton understands them, these mysteries were made up of two stages. In the first stage, the neophyte was freed from his previous errors. The gods now stood revealed as what they always had been: figments of the imagination. Initiation was thus essentially a process of disillusionment. In crossing the threshold from the lesser to the greater mysteries, the initiate was called upon to abandon his previous faith, recognize its false and fictitious character, and 'see things as they are'.[39] The disillusionment of the initiate was attained by explaining to him that the gods are nothing other than deified mortals.

But that is not all. The second stage consists in 'epopty', the contemplation of truth. At this point Warburton seems to have forgotten that he is writing about 'pagan' religion. For what truth is there to contemplate here? From an orthodox point of view only darkness ought to prevail, since the light of divine revelation never shone upon these religions. With Clement of Alexandria, however, Warburton takes a different view of things: at the final stage of the greater mysteries, 'nothing remains to be learned of the universe, but only to contemplate (*epopteuein*) and comprehend (*perinoein*) nature and things (*pragmata*)'.[40] What the initiate ultimately gazes upon is 'the UNIVERSAL NATURE, or the first cause' (222): 'HE IS ONE, AND OF HIMSELF ALONE; AND TO THAT ONE ALL THINGS OWE THEIR BEING.' This sentence is taken from an Orphic *hieros logos* ('sacred legend') encountered in many patristic and older authors, and quoted by Warburton in the version cited by Clement of Alexandria in his *Protrepticus*. Warburton interprets this text as the speech given by the hierophant in the Eleusinian Mysteries to the initiate. In Warburton's translation, it reads:

> I will declare a SECRET to the Initiated; but let the doors be shut against the profane. But thou, O Musaeus, the offspring of bright Selene, attend carefully to my song; for I shall deliver the truth without disguise. Suffer not, therefore, thy former prejudices to debar thee of that happy life, which the knowledge of these sublime truths will procure unto thee: but carefully contemplate this divine Oracle, and preserve it in purity of mind and heart. Go on, in the right way, and contemplate THE SOLE GOVERNOR OF THE WORLD: HE THAT IS ONE, AND OF HIMSELF ALONE; AND TO THAT ONE ALL THINGS OWE THEIR BEING. HE OPERATES THROUGH ALL, WAS NEVER SEEN BY MORTAL EYES, BUT DOES HIMSELF SEE EVERY ONE.[41]

'Suffer not, therefore, thy former prejudices to debar thee of that happy life' – for Warburton, this sentence disavows the old, familiar religion in favour of the All-One. Everything that exists came from the One. Only with this step is the transition from the official, fictitious religion to the secret, true religion actually effected. Both religions are mutually exclusive, and it is only by maintaining the strictest secrecy that their coexistence within one and the same society can be ensured.

With this political reconstruction of *religio duplex*, Warburton brought the ancient mysteries to the attention of the secret societies of his own time, transforming a subject of antiquarian interest into a theme of the utmost topicality. On the other hand, however, it cannot be said that his construction is very plausible, historically speaking. How is a culture that promotes two mutually exclusive religions supposed to survive and flourish? There was no shortage of criticism along these lines. Perhaps the most damaging assault was launched by Baron de Sainte-Croix, whose *Mémoires pour servir à l'Histoire de la religion secrète des anciens Peuples, ou Recherches historiques et critiques sur les mystères du paganisme* (Paris 1784) must be considered one of the best-informed contemporary accounts of the ancient mystery cults. His criticism is of sufficient interest to be summarized here. Warburton, the Baron writes, 'flattered himself [. . .] to have made a very important discovery, that of the secret doctrine of the initiated. But he only created a system supported by great erudition, built with infinite artistry, and expounded with marvellous ingenuity.'[42] Furthermore:

In confining the doctrine of God's unity to the sanctuary and only teaching it to the initiated, the lawgivers and mystagogues would have smashed polytheism even as they sought to establish it through a multitude of laws and rites. What then would have become of the public religion, which relied on their sanction? Such a contradiction could not exist: it would not only have finished by overturning the altars, it would have ruined the peace of society itself. What confusion, what disorder would not have resulted from creating with one hand and destroying with the other! To deceive publicly and enlighten in secret; to punish sacrilege with all firmness while clandestinely encouraging the unbelieving – what a strange system of legislation! It is nonetheless the one that Warburton supposes the wisest peoples of antiquity to have practised when he adopts the opinion of the Epicureans without reflecting on its consequences. These tended to further the spread of atheism by making God's unity seem a political invention of the priesthood rather than a natural truth. According to them, this unity was revealed only in the inner sanctum of the temples reserved for celebrating the mysteries. For my part, I think that if this doctrine ever penetrated into the mysteries, then it did so when the light of faith [footnote: Tertull. de baptism. 226] besieged it, so to speak, from all sides. This great truth could never have entered there earlier; strong barriers stood in its way, those of superstition, government and sacerdotal interest. The proofs that the Bishop of Gloucester adduces for his argument are even weaker than the argument itself. He produces the palinody ascribed to Orpheus, an obviously misattributed work, the speech of Isis invented by Apuleius, in which nothing but pure pantheism is to be found. Finally, he quotes these famous verses from the *Aeneid* [footnote: Aen. 6.726–7], in which Virgil so clearly explicates the system of the world soul that anyone with the least knowledge of ancient philosophy could not possibly misconstrue him.[43]

Far from revealing God's unity, the Eleusinian Mysteries commemorated the introduction of agriculture and the 'age-old belief in general Providence' – which, however, was hardly a mystery.

Baron de Sainte-Croix's objections to Warburton's construction of the mysteries in the context of *religio duplex* are only too justified. It goes without saying that the mysteries had nothing to do with the philosophers' god, the religion of reason and natural theology. It is interesting to note that this critique was voiced at the same time that Warburton's theory began to make headway among the German freemasons, as we will see below.

Of the remaining books of the *Divine Legation*, only the third is important in our context. While the second book is devoted to religion, split into 'public' and 'private' cults (with the latter further divided into lesser and greater mysteries), the third deals with philosophy and its division into an 'external and internal' doctrine. Warburton frequently refers in this context to a 'double' or 'twofold doctrine'. Just as the Egyptians preside over religion, so the Greeks preside over philosophy. Warburton thus draws a sharp line between religion and philosophy, something which his predecessors and many of his contemporaries and successors failed to do. For Warburton, this failure to distinguish between the two led to a crucial slip. The Egyptians taught as a great mystery 'that God was all things, a spirit diffusing itself through the world and intimately pervading all things' (126).[44] The Greeks made this to mean 'that all things were god, *hen ti ta panta*, and so ran headlong into what we now call Spinozism'. They then ascribed this view to the Egyptians, however; Warburton refers here to the hermetic treatise 'Asclepius', which states on several occasions: *omnia unus esse et unum esse omnia* (126–7). The Greeks, it might be said, transformed Egyptian theology into a henology. For Warburton, however, henology is tantamount to atheism: *To hen* is 'rankest Spinozism' (131). Within this framework there can be no Providence, no 'future state'. If the Greek philosophers nonetheless taught such a doctrine, they cannot have believed in it themselves. That is the reason for their 'twofold doctrine'. The twofold religion of the Egyptians appears among the Greeks as twofold philosophy: one side exoteric, the other esoteric.

Book IV returns to Egypt, using the most painstaking grammatological analysis ever devoted to Egyptian texts prior to their decipherment to demonstrate the age and developmental history of the Egyptian mysteries. Here, again, Warburton shows great ingenuity in deriving the Egyptian culture of mysteries from the Egyptian culture of writing. I will not go any further into this here and refer the interested reader to the relevant chapter of my book, *Moses the Egyptian*.[45]

Warburton originally planned that this reconstruction of the pagan world would be followed in Books V to IX by his presentation of a religion that had no need for such duplicity: the great counter-example of the *religio simplex* founded by Moses and based on divine revelation. This plan was never realized. Books V and VI did appear. In Book V he sets out to prove that the doctrine of a 'future state' was alien to 'Jewish theocracy' (even the biblical religion is conceived by Warburton as a political system), and in Book VI he demonstrates, above all with reference to Job ('I know that my redeemer liveth'), that this idea was probably known but not publicly preached by virtue of its self-evidence. Having entangled himself in such contradictions, it is understandable that Warburton no longer found the strength to see his plan through to its conclusion. Books VII to IX remained unwritten; the initial stages of Book IX were later published as Book VII.

Warburton was particularly discouraged by the criticism which greeted the publication of the first volume, containing Books I to III. The most concentrated attacks came not from deists and other free-thinkers, whom he had sought to refute by demonstrating the divine legation of Moses, but from the ranks of Anglican orthodoxy. In his lengthy introduction to Book IV, the second volume of his work, he took up the cudgels against his critics, drawing parallels between his own hostile reception and that of Ralph Cudworth. I find his comments so revealing for both works that I will quote them here:

> The philosopher of Malmesbury [Thomas Hobbes] was the terror of the last age, as Tindal and Collins have been of this. The press swet with controversy; and every young Church-man-militant would needs try his arms in thundering upon Hobbes's steel cap. The mischief his writings had done to Religion set Cudworth upon projecting its defence. Of this he published one immortal volume; with a boldness uncommon indeed, but very becoming a man conscious of his own integrity and strength. For instead of amusing himself with Hobbes's peculiar whimsies, which in a little time were to vanish of themselves, and their answers with them; which are all now forgotten, from the Curate's to the Archbishop's [Tenison]; he launched out into the immensity of the Intellectual System; and, at his first essay, penetrated the very darkest recesses of Antiquity, to strip Atheism of its disguises, and drag up the lurking monster into day. Where though few readers could follow him, yet the very slowest were able to overtake his purpose. And there wanted not country Clergymen to lead the cry, and tell the world, – That, under pretence of defending Revelation, he wrote in the very manner that an artful Infidel might naturally be supposed to use in writing against it; that he had given us all the filthy stuff that he could scrape together out of the sink of Atheism, as a natural introduction to a demonstration of the truth of Revelation: that with incredible industry and reading he had rummaged all antiquity for atheistical arguments, which he neither knew, nor intended to answer. In a word, that he was an Atheist in his heart, and an Arian in his book. But the worst is behind. These silly calumnies were believed. The much injured author grew disgusted. His ardour slackened: and the rest, and far greatest part of the Defence, never appeared. (295–6)

These lines fittingly describe the problem and the reception accorded to both Cudworth and Warburton. No one who has read Cudworth will dispute the legitimacy of the criticisms levelled against him from the side of orthodoxy. The enthusiasm with which he informs his readers about the hermetic truth of all-oneness is unmistakable. The same holds true of Warburton's presentation of the mysteries. Every reader must come away with the impression that Warburton is divulging his own credo here and that, like the Greek philosophers before him, he upholds a 'twofold doctrine'. He shared the fate of Cudworth and subsequently Jacobi, who sparked off the so-called Spinoza renaissance through his exposition of a doctrine he purported to disavow.

Warburton's interpretation of popular religion as political theology can be understood as an attempt to redeem it from the deception theory, which discovers in it nothing other than a cynical Machiavellian strategy. The personal deities may be fictions, but they are indispensable, salutary fictions which give humans what they need in order to live together as a community. Looking forward to Durkheim, Voegelin and others, one could argue that the community symbolizes itself as a 'realm of religious order' in the fictions of popular religions.[46] With that, political theology would receive a kind of natural foundation, a *fundamentum in re*; it would represent a structural category grounded in the nature of the matter itself rather than a purely strategic one. Necessarily and inevitably, it could be argued, the process of political organization and the institutionalization of community results in the formation of a *religio duplex*. Not only the religious forces of society as 'elementary forms of religious life' (Durkheim[47]), but also the religious forces of nature as the epitome of the cosmic foundations of life find expression here as 'political' and 'natural' theology.

It should not be forgotten that Warburton's theory of dual religion understands itself (or at least presents itself) as a theory of paganism, that is, as a theory of false religion, from which it seeks to glean as much truth as possible – far too much, in the eyes of his orthodox critics. This theory may be summarized in two theses: first, even the pagans had knowledge of God's oneness, which they attained by following the path of natural theology; but, second, they were forced to keep this knowledge a secret, since it would otherwise have caused the fictitious popular religion, the mainstay of social and political order, to come crashing down. Building on this, Warburton proceeds to his main argument, likewise split into two theses. First, in instituting the Israelite religion, Moses superseded the structure of *religio duplex*. He relied neither on the fiction of a political theology, nor on natural theology, but could instead find support in a revealed law which was binding for everyone and accessible to all. Second, the very lack of a doctrine concerning the 'future state' with which Deists reproached the Hebrew Bible proved its divinity. Under divine guidance, the Israelites had no need to contemplate immortality and retribution in the hereafter since, for them, unlike for other nations, all accounts were already settled in this life. The law functioned as a mechanism that already linked action and consequence, doing and suffering, in this life rather than the next. No one was willing to follow him in this argument, brilliantly summarized by Lessing in several paragraphs of his *Education of the Human Race*.[48] Warburton's monumental work owed its considerable influence to two of its nine books only: the second, on the mysteries, and the fourth, on hieroglyphs. These were the two books in which he elaborated the political function and grammatological foundations of Egyptian culture as the paradigmatic dual religion.

Oddly enough, almost a hundred years after Warburton, we come across a similar theory of mysteries where we would least expect to find it: in the late Schelling. In his *Philosophy of Revelation*, Schelling comes to speak of the mysteries and the secrecy in which they were shrouded, remarking that the publication of the mysteries was 'seen as an attack on the state itself'. I cite Ernst Feil's summary of Schelling's chain of argument:

> Towards the end of this discussion, he says of the 'mysteries' that they are conceived as a 'universal religion' transcending the realm of the Hellenes. The content of this religion was therefore regarded as 'truly universal, as world religion'.[49] He nonetheless considers this intended religion to be not yet given; of the triune Dionysus, he sees the last as the 'third world-ruler' and speaks of a 'spiritual religion that will be ushered in by him' (508). He thus paradigmatically assumes that the Hellene found himself 'placed between a sensuous religion, to which he is subjected in the present, and a purely spiritual religion, which would only be shown to him in the future' (512). Yet with an eye to the 'still presiding and present gods, the future, absolutely liberating religion could not be proclaimed'. This was because the entire 'existence of the state' rested on the 'inviolable reality of the supposed gods'. The 'mysteries' thus point towards a 'religion to come', a 'universal religion that will unite, bind and bring together the whole human race, currently divided and disunited through polytheism'. (522)[50]

Schelling thus interprets the mysteries as the religion of the future, which must be kept secret under current conditions lest the existence of the state be jeopardized. This idea can be applied to Christianity, which appears from a pagan perspective as the religion of the future; but we can also relate it to a religion that is still to come and will encompass the entire human race, perhaps resembling what Lichtenberg imagined as 'purified Spinozism'.[51]

The mysteries 'play an important role', not only in the late Schelling, but 'in early Idealism' as a whole, according to Manfred Frank.[52] Thus, 'the opposition of mystery to revealed religion' appears as a 'leitmotif' that already 'pervades the mythological-political reflections in Schelling's early work'.[53] In both early and late Schelling, what is worshipped in the mysteries is nature. 'The divine is esoteric in nature and exoteric in the popular religion, where it visibly (communicably, symbolically) reveals its truth.'[54] In a letter to Jakob Hermann Obereit from 12 March 1796, the young Schelling is still arguing within the bounds of the paradigm that saw in the mysteries an institution for the enlightenment and education of the human race: 'I believe that mysteries have a part to play in a national education in which the youth is initiated in stages. The new philosophy is to be taught in these mysteries. It should be the final disclosure vouchsafed to the tested student of wisdom.'[55]

The opposition between the public and the secret is preserved, but it loses the antagonistic, almost dualistic character that Warburton had given it when he set fiction against disillusionment. The poles are now differently occupied and both are positively appraised. They are no longer called popular and arcane religion, but mythology and mystery. In mythology, the truth or the divine announces itself in a universally communicable, symbolic manner; in the mysteries, as an abstract idea perceptible only to the mind. We are no longer dealing here with two religions existing side by side within one and the same culture. In keeping with the Platonic model, we instead have a single religion permitting different forms of participation.

Schelling's conception of the mysteries finds its clearest expression in the early essay 'Philosophy and Religion' (1804).[56] Here, starting out from the original unity of religion and philosophy, Schelling sketches the utopia of their future reunion. In between lies the epoch of *religio duplex*, bifurcated into the esotericism of the mysteries (philosophy) and the exotericism of popular religion (mythology). For Schelling, both have an equally legitimate place within that 'monotheism of reason and the heart, polytheism of the imagination and of art' which Schelling, together with his student friends Hölderlin and Hegel, had called for in the so-called 'Oldest System Program of German Idealism':

> Monotheism of reason and the heart, polytheism of imagination and art, this is what we need. Here I will first speak of an idea which, as far as I know, has never occurred to anyone else – we must have a new mythology, but this mythology must be in the service of ideas, it must be a mythology of *Reason*. Until we render the ideas aesthetic, i.e.

mythological, they are of no interest to the *people*, and, vice versa, until mythology is rational the philosopher has to be ashamed of it. Thus, in the end, enlightened and unenlightened must extend their hands to one another; mythology must become philosophical and the people rational, while philosophy must become mythological, in order to make the philosophers sensuous [*sinnlich*].[57]

Behind this demand stands the idea of a *religio duplex*, whose division into mythology and philosophy is yet to be overcome.

Secrecy under the Banner of Morality and Politics

With the political turn taken by the discourse on mysteries with Toland and Warburton, the Platonic-philosophical distinction between 'common folk' and 'wise men' is transformed into the distinction between the state, founded in (popular) religion, and the secret religion of truth. The priestly fraud detected by atheist critics of religion makes way for princely deception, even if, as Warburton never tires of emphasizing, this 'deception' – the fictions of a political theology – is perpetrated with the best of intentions and precisely for the sake of public morality. Without religion there can be no morality, Warburton had argued against Bayle, and there can likewise be no religion without a state, just as, most importantly of all, there can be no state without religion. Warburton's model relied on a threefold distinction: between politics (the popular religion underpinning the state), morality (the lesser mysteries) and nature or truth (the greater mysteries). In this model, the freemasons, particularly the Illuminati, were to find their place and their task in society. By withdrawing from politics into the protected zone of their lodge mysteries, they effectively arrogated to themselves responsibility for matters pertaining to morality and truth.

It was not Warburton but the Göttingen philosopher Christoph Meiners, however, who with his 1776 text on the Eleusinian Mysteries first gave this model a broader resonance and, in doing so, unleashed a true mania for mysteries.[58] Meiners adopted Warburton's political concept of dual religion, if anything deepening the antagonism between popular and elite religion. In his eyes, the mysteries of the Egyptians concerned knowledge 'which they necessarily had to keep secret, since it posed a threat to the general faith of the people, and through its dissemination would have overturned state and religion, put down the gods from their seats and toppled the altars'.[59] While Meiners already spoke in relation to the lesser mysteries of a

'powerful shift in understanding',[60] the real moment of disillusionment for the neophyte came with his initiation into the greater mysteries. Here he 'was instructed in principles which threw the entire
popular religion on to the heap'. Now 'the veil of superstition, which
the fables of the poets and popular religion had woven before the
aspirant's eyes, was lifted from the eyes of the epopt.'[61] Appropriating
Warburton's political-theological perspective, Meiners emphasized
that the priests who presided over the greater mysteries 'dethroned
the gods, and in the inner sanctuary of the temple divested the epopt
of the self-same errors which they sought to encourage or foster
among the common people'. Yet they 'not only tore down an old
building of errors, they also built in its place a new, magnificent
temple of salutary truths, which all antiquity believed the great crowd
to be too feeble-minded to comprehend. They [the initiates] had
proclaimed to them the doctrine of a single god, were taught the true
nature and character of the spirits, or demons, and were shown at
the same time the nobility, blissfulness and future destiny of our
human souls.'[62]

Adam Weishaupt, professor for canon law in Ingolstadt, drew
heavily on this text when he founded the Order of Illuminati in the
very year of its publication.[63] The Order stipulated that society was
to be remade in the image of Enlightenment values such as the abolition of class barriers, freedom of thought, freedom of the press,
fraternity, human rights, education, justice and charity, and especially
care for the poor and the sick. 'Through the formation of a new elite
of the virtuous', the Order strove for 'the complete transformation
of all social and political structures, the dawning of a world republic'.[64] The goal was not political revolution but the 'ennoblement' of
mankind, starting out with the individual, who was to be guided
towards a higher state of perfection with the aid of his brothers.
Through his subsequent activity in public office and, if possible, close
to or even on the throne, society at large would be ennobled in such
a way that the state and its instruments of control would eventually
become superfluous. Then, as we are told twice in *The Magic Flute*,
'earth will be a realm of heaven / and mortals will be like gods'. The
proximity of these ideals to the catchcries of the French Revolution
was obvious, and after 1789 it led the Order, already outlawed in
Bavaria since 1784, to come under increasing persecution in other
places as well, culminating in the Jacobin trials under Franz II.

The seven degrees of the Illuminati were separated into three
classes of three, two and two. The lowest class, called the 'nursery',
corresponded to the three degrees of 'blue' freemasonry (Apprentice,
Fellowcraft and Master mason). The second class corresponded to a

certain extent to the upper degrees of 'red' freemasonry (*Illuminatus major* and *Illuminatus regens* or *dirigens*). The highest class – the unique selling point of the Order, so to speak – were the 'mysteries', divided into 'lesser' and 'greater' mysteries. Here Weishaupt drew directly on the Eleusinian Mysteries and the account of them he found in Meiners. Each degree was to be marked by initiation into a particular category of secrets, in the form of a previously withheld body of knowledge. Weishaupt and Knigge spent years feverishly elaborating this knowledge and its hierarchical distribution across the individual degrees. As hordes of aspirants streamed into the lower degrees and impatiently awaited advancement, and with it the disclosure of further mysteries, the research associated with the upper degrees was still far from complete. Deciding which areas of knowledge were to be assigned to the mysteries class (or sacerdotal class) proved particularly challenging. The Order's priests, it was said, are 'the guardians of the accumulated scientific treasures, allocated into classes according to subject'. They 'bring the higher philosophical systems into order, and elaborate a popular religion which the order intends to reveal to the world soon.'[65] We thus have here a system that faithfully reproduces the structure of *religio duplex* in Warburton's sense: split into popular religion and mysteries (lesser and greater), with an intervening phase of learning and purification (the lower degrees) that prepares the initiate to receive the real mysteries (the higher degrees). *The Magic Flute* alludes to this progression: 'Enlightened, he will *then* be able / to devote himself wholly to the mysteries of Isis.' The research activities of the Viennese lodge 'Zur wahren Eintracht' ('True Concord'), which I will discuss in the next chapter, subscribe to the same programme.

If the Illuminati, along with other secret societies dedicated to upholding Enlightenment values, identified themselves with the Egyptian model of *religio duplex*, it must at the same time be emphasized that they viewed the alliance between Enlightenment and secrecy as a temporary measure dictated by the adverse temper of the times. This idea can be found, for example, in Ignaz von Born's treatise *On the Mysteries of the Egyptians*, which I will return to later. In that work, Born offers his brothers the dazzling image of the Egyptian priesthood as the model for a 'scientific' freemasonry, founded on the contemplative study of nature rather than on revelation. According to Born, the Egyptian priests were the standard-bearers of an enlightenment which they had to keep secret only because the time was not yet ripe for the truth to be made known to all. Secrecy was a strategy necessitated by the still imperfect state of social and political relations, not a condition intrinsic to the matter itself. He sees in this a

parallel between ancient Egypt and his own time: 'We too reveal to
the initiate, as soon as he has seen the light, that we are not destined
to remain a secret and concealed society, but that we gathered behind
closed doors, when tyranny and vice carried all before them, in order
to oppose them all the more resolutely.'[66]

Reinhart Koselleck has identified the distinction between politics
and morality as the crucial semantic distinction in the century of
secret societies. 'Secrecy, this element apparently so at odds with the
spirit of the age, [. . .] leads to the heart of the dialectic of morality
and politics. Secrecy covers up in ambivalent fashion the political
underside of enlightenment.'[67] Masonic secrecy draws a sharp line
between insiders and outsiders. This distinction is no longer (just)
determined in the old Platonic way, however, as the crowd versus the
elite, the profane mob versus the initiated; it is also, if Koselleck is
right, semantically invested as an opposition between politics and
morality. By declaring the masonic lodge to be an apolitical space,
this distinction constructs politics as an amoral space. Therein lie its
dialectic and its subversive, critical force. The absolutist state is
guided solely by *raison d'état*, an amoral Machiavellian logic which
has its goal not in the 'happiness' of all citizens but in the mainte-
nance and expansion of power. The lodge, by contrast, establishes
itself on the basis of an apolitical morality. From its perspective, the
absolutist state appears as 'tyranny'.

Yet the masons did not set themselves the revolutionary goal of
overthrowing the state; rather, they sought to establish in the lodge
a small-scale alternative state grounded in morality – and the claim
that they were forming a *statum in statu* was to become a recurring
motif in the accusations and suspicions directed against them. The
ideals of this micro-state were virtue and justice, active philanthropy,
friendship and equality. That sounds harmless and desirable enough,
and it might be asked why it was thought necessary to make a secret
of it all. The compulsion to secrecy stems from the utopian character
of these ideals. Mozart and Schikaneder placed the following verses
in a very prominent position[68] in *The Magic Flute*: 'When virtue and
justice / strew with fame the path of the great, / then earth is a realm
of heaven, / and mortals are like the gods.' These verses have been
read as an adynaton, that is, as the expression of a logical impossibility. If they were put into effect, they would bring about the over-
throw of the existing order and the end of the absolutist state. That
is why they must be practised in secret, in the sanctuary of the lodge
(or in Sarastro's utopian space on the operatic stage). The freemasons pursue their ideals as the avant-garde of a coming world, trust-
ing in their gradual self-accomplishment. With respect to the coming

world of bourgeois democracy, Koselleck therefore interprets this process as the 'pathogenesis of the bourgeois world'. From within the horizon of the eighteenth century, we are witnessing the genesis of a double structure in the sense of *religio* or *philosophia duplex*. The communicative space of society splits in two, and Enlightenment 'emigrates into the private underground'.[69] The formation of secret societies flows from the enlightened citizen's 'exodus' (Manfred Agethen[70]) from social and political relations which, to his critically sharpened sensibility, appear to be (currently still) irreconcilable with his notions of reason and justice. The social function of secrecy, providing shelter from censorship and persecution, also plays a role here. Nothing connects people so strongly as their complicit knowledge of exclusive secrets.[71] The lodges formed an 'enclave culture' (Mary Douglas[72]) within society as a whole. The higher the walls separating them from the outside world, the stronger was the sense of solidarity within, as invoked and celebrated in the fraternal 'chain songs'. By setting themselves apart from the outside and creating inequality (between the 'profane' and 'brothers'), they generated equality on the inside.

The distinction between politics and morality, outside and inside, has social effects in the distinction between public space (politics) and non-public space (morality), and it has psychological effects in the emergence of a new attitude of reserve towards politics and the state. At any rate, that is the diagnosis of the Enlightenment offered by Reinhart Koselleck in his 'pathogenesis of the bourgeois world'. This inner reserve towards the space of politics is manifested in what he calls the 'hypocrisy' of the Enlightenment.[73]

A similar critique of the secret societies is offered by Carl Schmitt. In his *Leviathan* (1938), he accuses 'the quiet ones in the country' of ruining the absolutist state with their distinction between inside and outside and the 'inner reserve' which resulted from it:

> The absolute state can demand anything, but only in externals. *Cuius regio, eius religio* had been realized, but the *religio* had slipped away, in the interim, into a completely different and unexpected new realm: the private sphere of the free-thinking, free-feeling and in his convictions absolutely free individual. Those who pioneered the development of this inner reserve were very different from each other and even stood opposed to each other: secret leagues and clandestine orders, Rosicrucians, Freemasons, Illuminati, mystics and pietists, sectarians of all kinds, and above all here again the restless spirit of the Jew, who knew how best to exploit the situation until the relationship between public and private, attitude and conviction was turned on its head.[74]

In Schmitt's eyes, the freemasons and the 'restless spirit of the Jew' (there follows a lengthy polemic against Mendelssohn and his *Jerusalem*) used the instrument of lodge secrecy to withdraw from the totalizing grasp of the absolutist state while directing their forces, at the same time, towards the creation of a transnational society. Together with the Jews, they therefore number among the natural enemies of Schmitt and his total state.

4

Religio Duplex and Freemasonry

The eighteenth century was the century of Enlightenment. But it was also the Golden Age of secret societies, whose obsession with secrecy stood at odds with everything the Enlightenment held dear.

Hugh B. Nisbet[1]

Secret Society Novels

The actualization of ancient – in particular, Egyptian – mysteries for the self-understanding and rituals of secret societies went hand in hand with their individualization. Interest was now shown in the individual who trod a path from the fictions and illusions of 'popular religion', via the different stages of disillusionment and initiation into ever greater secrets, all the way to enlightenment (or 'epopty'). Emphasis was placed on the psychological effects of initiation, which 'not only touched the eye and ear but seized all the senses, causing listeners and spectators to break into cold frightful sweats, holy shudders and shivers of delight. All these suddenly alternating, contrasting emotions gave rise to a sense of reverential awe.'[2] Schiller writes of the Egyptian mystagogues: 'They introduced new ideas to the soul with a certain sensible solemnity, and, through all kinds of preparations befitting this end, placed the mind of their apprentice in a preliminary state of passionate sensitivity that made it receptive to the new truth.'[3] The 'holy shudders' and other affects accompanying the initiate's induction belong to the register of the sublime. We will become acquainted with several of the key passages further below.

Among the Illuminati, each member of the lower degrees was required to submit a monthly report on his moral progress (and that of his confrères) to his superiors. This new interest in individual experience had a long pre-history in the exercises of self-scrutiny and self-examination which, presumably starting out with Augustine's *Confessions*, received enormous impetus in the Reformation, in the Jesuit Order, in Pietism and in Puritanism. In the eighteenth century, pedagogy, cultivation of the self (*Bildung*), biographical development and human formation moved to the forefront of literary production, giving rise to the *Bildungsroman*. The genre got underway with *Télémaque* (1699) by François de Salignac de la Mothe-Fénelon. The novel *The Travels of Cyrus* (1727)[4] by Chevalier Andrew Michael Ramsay, who soon after was to play a leading role in the masonic Grand Lodge that formed in Paris, adhered to this model.[5] Matthias Claudius translated Ramsay's novel into German in 1780.[6] Both novels can also be understood as 'mirrors for princes', meaning that they aimed to bring about the ennoblement of society by educating and moulding the princes to whom they were addressed. Fénelon was tutor to the grandson of Louis XIV, while Ramsay taught the young Comte de Sassenage and briefly also the British pretender to the throne, Charles Stuart.

The first secret society novel or *Geheimbundroman*, *Séthos*, which appeared anonymously in 1731, took its cue from these models. Its author was the Abbé Jean Terrasson,[7] a highly distinguished Greek scholar known (among other things) for editing and commenting on the *Historical Library* of Diodorus Siculus. Terrasson transposed the educational career of his hero to ancient Egypt and hence to that dual world, split between outside and inside, public sphere and secrecy, where the pathway to knowledge took the form of initiation. Terrasson's account of the testing and induction of Prince Sethos occupies all of Books Three and Four in Claudius's translation, taking up some 170 pages. Through a deed of heroic valour, the young Prince Sethos has proved himself worthy of initiation into the mysteries of Isis. He succeeded in capturing a giant snake that had laid waste to the land and terrorized its inhabitants.[8] His initiation begins at Khufu's pyramid, which he and Amedès, his leader and hierophant, enter from the north. Once inside, they must climb down a deep shaft which brings them to an extensive system of underground canals, caverns and passageways. Sethos must then walk through a fiery furnace, swim through surging waters and, last but not least, execute an audacious aerial vault that catapults him into the temple of Isis.[9] Two drinks are offered him there: the draught of oblivion, which makes him forget all the false doctrines and ideas that had previously clouded his judgement, and the draught of remembrance, which allows him to retain everything he is about to be taught. This period of instruction lasts several months. At the end of this phase he is ready to face his final test: he is appointed as judge to decide the case of two quarrelling brothers. Having passed the test with flying colours, he is now free to roam the extensive subterranean world beneath the pyramids. A solemn procession rounds out the proceedings.

As its subsequent reception history would demonstrate, Terrasson's invention of the Egyptian initiation ritual was a masterpiece of literary imagination. Until deep into the nineteenth century – until Gérard de Nerval, who in *Le Voyage en Orient* (1851) has this ritual explained to him by a Prussian officer while visiting Khufu's pyramid – Terrasson's depiction remained the definitive representation of the Egyptian mysteries.[10] Like Ramsay before him in his *Travels of Cyrus*, Terrasson adorns his *Séthos* with a plethora of learned footnotes alluding to ancient sources, thereby lending the appearance of a scholarly monograph to his text, which he passes off as the translation of a Greek manuscript. His contemporaries, particularly the freemasons, largely fell for this fiction and took his account of the Egyptian induction at face value, believing it to be an accurate historical reconstruction supported by the source materials. Consequently, Terrasson's readers thought they knew far more about the Egyptian mysteries than even the boldest interpretation of the meagre ancient sources could have delivered at the time. Terrasson's flight of fancy was inspired by his historical and antiquarian interests, but he showed scant regard for the theological and philosophical issues. He thus declined to broach the religious ideas at stake in the Egyptian mysteries, which Cudworth had so impressively elaborated into an Egyptian arcane theology. He was evidently unfamiliar with Cudworth's work, available only in English at the time, yet unlike Ramsay, he also seemed genuinely uninterested in this aspect of the ancient Egyptian world.[11] His sole, brief reference to the content of *religio duplex* can be found on pp. 179–80 of Thomas Lediard's English translation. In an hour-long morning 'conference', 'the general principles of the Egyptian religion' are explained to Sethos. The teacher:

> inculcated the notion of only one God [footnote: Lactantius B[ook] 1[12]], who by his knowledge conceiv'd the world, before he formed it by his will. But to comply with the frailty of mankind, they were allow'd to adore the different attributes of his essence, and the different effects of his goodness, under the symbols of the stars, as the sun and the planets; of renown'd personages, as Osiris, Jupiter, Mercury; and even of terrestrial bodies, as animals and plants. [. . .] The Egyptians

by virtue of this confus'd idea of unity in the divine being, and of multiplicity in his symbols, are the first authors of what has been the most sublime in philosophical opinions, and the most gross in popular superstitions.

The opposition between 'popular superstitions' and 'philosophical opinions', hence the structure of *religio duplex*, is thus emphasized clearly enough, but the content of this idea remains extremely sketchy.

This gap was filled by an unnamed reviewer whose discussion of the novel (in the 1777/78 German translation by Matthias Claudius) appeared in the 1782 *Freymäurer-Bibliothek (Masonic Library)*.[13] The reviewer highlights three aspects of the novel: as a 'political novel' à la Fenelon (by which its function to serve as a 'mirror for princes' is obviously intended), as a 'commentary on [Egyptian] mores and customs, antiquities, laws, even geography and history' and 'as a contribution to the history of freemasonry in the oldest times'. The first aspect relates to the fictional and educational character of the work, the second to its antiquarian-historical instructiveness and the third to its importance for the history of freemasonry. In the spirit of contemporary Viennese research into mysteries, the novel is here taken as an historical document and as proof of freemasonry's venerable pedigree. This specific focus of interest explains why the reviewer dwells only upon the initiation ritual, which he revisits in considerable detail. The question of what was actually revealed to the prince after he had been successfully tested then prompts the reviewer to offer his own reflections on the matter. These place Terrasson's description of the Egyptian mysteries in the light of *religio duplex*. How is it possible that the ancient Egyptians, this wisest of all peoples, could have adopted so seemingly abstruse a religion as the animal cult? Two answers suggest themselves. The first is that there may well be a great deal of wisdom in this choice: the broad populace, after all, relies on symbols of an unrepresentable god; in this regard, animals – creatures symbolizing the creator – make better candidates for worship than statues or even living human beings (the Dalai Lama is cited as an example here). Second, however, the sages of Egypt introduced the mysteries in order that those select mortals deemed capable of apprehending the truth might be taught, 'to speak with Jacob Böhme – for I do not wish to be understood by all – God is Nothing and Everything!' In Böhme, rooted in the tradition of negative theology, one can in fact find such sentences as these: 'He [God] is Nothingness and Everything and He is one will.'[14] The formula 'Nothing and Everything' goes beyond Cudworth's and Lessing's *hen kai pan*, installing a mystical negative theology in place of a Spinozist pantheism. The most up-to-date ideas about what exactly was revealed to initiates in the great mysteries are thus projected by the reviewer into the space left as good as empty by Terrasson.

Ramsay's and Terrasson's novels started a trend. Three years later came Charles de Fieux de Mouhy's novel, *Lamékis, ou les Voyages extraordinaires d'un Egyptien dans la terre intérieure*,[15] whose loosely interconnected episodes, set in subterranean Egypt, anticipate many elements of the later gothic novel.

The significance of the secret society novel, which spread across Europe at the same time as the masonic lodges, took a long time to be fully appreciated. The eighteenth-century *Bildungsroman* or novel of personal development, as exemplified in Jean-Jacques Rousseau's *Émile ou de l'education* (1762) and Christoph Martin Wieland's *Geschichte des Agathon* (*History of Agathon*, 1766/67), has rightly been brought into connection with the aforementioned Protestant, Puritan and Pietistic traditions of an individualistic inwardness of religious spiritual formation,[16] but the initiatory aspect and importance of secret societies were neglected. Linda Simonis has now drawn our attention to the immensely important literary role played by secret societies and their rites of initiation within the framework of the alliance between Enlightenment and secrecy that was so characteristic of the eighteenth century.[17] As Rosemarie Nicolai-Haas has shown, the secret society novel arrived in Germany in the late 1780s with Matthias Claudius's translations of Terrasson's *Séthos* and Ramsay's *Travels of Cyrus*, quickly stimulating a native tradition of *Bildungsromane*. These included Adolph von Knigge's *Die Verirrungen des Philosophen oder Geschichte Ludwigs von Seelberg*[18] (*The Blunders of the Philosopher or The History of Ludwig von Seelberg*, 1787), Christoph Martin Wieland's *Peregrinus Proteus* (1789–91),[19] Wilhelm Friedrich Meyern's *Dya-Na-Sore oder Die Wanderer*[20] (*Dya-Na-Sore or The Wanderers*, 1787–91), Karl Philipp Moritz's two novels *Andreas Hartknopf* (1786) and *Andreas Hartknopf's Predigerjahre* (*Andreas Hartknopf's Years of Preaching*, 1790), which Linda Simonis has interpreted as initiatory secret society novels,[21] Jean Paul's *Die unsichtbare Loge* (*The Invisible Lodge*, 1793), and above all Goethe's *Wilhelm Meisters Lehrjahre* (*Wilhelm Meister's Years of Apprenticeship*, 1795) and the two-volume novel *Das Heimweh* (*Homesickness*, 1795) by Johann Heinrich Jung-Stilling, which represents the attempt to connect the Pietistic and initiatory aspects: here the masonic and freethinking mysteries paradigm is reinterpreted in a Christian-Pietistic sense and the kingdom of God conceived as a secret society into which the hero is inducted in several stages of initiation.[22] In parallel with *The Magic Flute* and leaning

heavily on Claudius/Terrasson, his induction in the substructure of
the pyramids is imagined as a passage through fire and water. The
link between Enlightenment and secrecy emerges with particular
clarity in the context of this Egyptian induction, where the initiate is
catechized in the principles of Kantian philosophy:

> In order not to tax my readers with philosophical speculations, I will
> only remark in a few words here that I became thoroughly convinced,
> through these and other demonstrations, that what we call space, size,
> extension and shape have no existence apart from us in the things
> themselves, but that we have an innate idea in our souls which we call
> space, and that we therefore transpose size, extension and shape into
> the things outside us. While the entire world consists of infinitely many
> things that are not identical to us, their position in relation to each
> other, their extension, size and shape are all formed in our eyes through
> their qualities, which are unknown to us. If our eyes had a different
> structure then the shapes, locations and sizes of all things would also
> be completely different. [. . .] All our concepts relating to space may
> therefore only be applied in the physical world, not to the spiritual
> world. [. . .] Our sensible reason is grounded wholly and solely on time
> and space, therefore it cannot possibly make any judgments and con-
> clusions that do not relate to extensive and intensive size, to the mutual
> influence of things existing apart from each other and following on
> from each other, and to a thing's characteristic mutability in time. That
> is why sensible reason, the PSYCHIKOS ANTHROPOS, simply cannot
> be used to judge and demonstrate in the ethical realm of God; here it
> must believe.[23]

Initiation, mysteries and secret societies play a role in other *Bildungsromane* from around the turn of the nineteenth century as well,
such as Novalis's *Heinrich von Ofterdingen* (1802) and the mystery
novels of Rostorf (Karl Gottlob Albrecht von Hardenberg),
Pilgrimmschaft nach Eleusis (*Pilgrimage to Eleusis*)[24] and Isidorus
Orientalis (Otto Heinrich Graf von Loeben), *Guido*.[25] The plot of
The Magic Flute stands in this tradition of secret society novels and
Bildungsromane as well.[26] In these works, the relationship between
exoteric and esoteric religion is dealt with from the viewpoint of an
individual whose path of development takes him from the former to
the latter.

Secrecy and the underground are positively connoted in all these
novels, in keeping with the self-image of an elite that had itself been
driven underground by the authorities. In the literature of the late
eighteenth century, however, a quite different evaluation of secrecy
also makes itself felt. A new semantic paradigm, bound up with the
republican and democratic ideals of the increasingly influential middle

class, expresses itself in the rejection of secrecy as well as in the structure of dual religion itself. I will explore these changes in the next chapter. A more specific phenomenon further contributed to these changes, a fear of conspiracy which took hold in the 1780s and represents the shadow side, so to speak, of the contemporary alliance between Enlightenment and secrecy. It led to tensions between individual secret societies as well as between these societies and the secular and ecclesiastical authorities. Just as the Catholic Church and the political establishment of the *ancien régime* believed themselves to be undermined by the lodges, so the lodges feared infiltration by agents of Church and state. Secrecy offered shelter not only to free-thinking wisdom but to crime, fraud, conspiracy and espionage as well. In 1781 Goethe wrote to Lavater:

> I have traces, not to say news, of a great mass of lies that steal about in the dark, which you seem to know nothing about. Believe me, our moral and political world is riddled with catacombs, cellars and sewers, as is often the case in a great city. Nobody seems to think or reflect about their interconnections and the conditions under which their denizens live; but those who know something of this will find it much more understandable if, here or there, now or then, the earth crumbles away, smoke rises out of a crack, and strange voices are heard. Believe me, what lies below the ground goes about its business just as naturally as what lies above the ground, and he who does not exorcize demons by daylight, under the open sky, will be loath to summon them in a basement at midnight.[27]

As an expression of this widespread fear of clandestine plots and conspiracies, Pope Clement XIV[28] dissolved the Jesuit Order in 1773 at the urging of the European princes. This only fuelled a new fear of 'crypto-Jesuits', whom many freemasons suspected of intriguing against their lodges.[29] After the discovery of the Bavarian-Austrian land-swapping scandal in 1784[30] and the diamond necklace affair in Paris in 1785/1786, satirically reworked by Goethe in his comedy *Der Groß-Cophtha* (*The Great Cophtha*), this general fear of conspiracy took on a new lease of life: Friedrich Schiller captured it with unmatched precision in his unfinished novel, *Der Geisterseher* (*The Clairvoyant*, 1786–8). In this text, Schiller turns on its head the basic principle of the initiatory *Bildungsroman* by having his hero, the prince, succumb to a process of moral and spiritual destruction through his dealings with a secret society. His drama *Don Carlos*, written around the same time, paints in the figure of Marquis Posa a portrait of an Illuminatus who, for all his ambivalence, nonetheless displays unmistakably positive characteristics.[31]

Another text taking a critical stance on secrecy was Wieland's *Reise des Priesters Abulfauaris ins innere Afrika* (*Journey of the Priest Abulfauaris to Inner Africa*, 1770), which shows just how tenuous the border between priestly fraud and legitimate fiction could be.[32] The first part of the narrative offers a caustic satire on colonialism. It tells how the Egyptian priests of Isis 'civilized' an African tribe, teaching their new subjects to wear clothing (and so opening up a lucrative market for the Egyptian flax and linen industry) and exploiting the local gold deposits. In the process, they not only exported Egyptian fashion to the 'negroes' but all the civilizational vices of an over-refined and hypertrophic sexuality as well, plunging the tribe into misery. To prevent the situation getting out of hand, Abulfauaris introduces his 'negroes' to the mysteries of Isis, but he takes advantage of the darkness, and the confusion of a beautiful initiate, to have his way with her while wearing an Anubis mask.[33] Among all his sins, he ruefully acknowledges at the end of his 'confessions', this was the blackest. These confessions form the second part of the narrative and show what the practice of the Egyptian *religio duplex* might have looked like from the inside, from the viewpoint of an initiate who knows the truth about the fictitious deities while nonetheless confirming the populace in its idolatrous ways.

> You admit to yourself that all these things owe their supposed divinity to the unthinking superstition of the rabble: and you, who should have joined forces with your brothers to teach them better ideas, you support them in their superstition? – O Abulfauaris, son of Menofis, I fear you are a deceiver! (34–5)

Abulfauaris assuages his stricken conscience with two considerations. On the one hand, 'the religion of the Egyptians, however repellent and bizarre it may seem in the eyes of a foreigner, has become so closely intertwined with the state that they have come to depend on each other for their peace and continued existence' (36). On the other hand, the deceit was perpetrated with the best of intentions: 'If it is fraudulent to conceal truths from the rabble whose radiance they cannot endure: then this is a salutary, necessary fraud; and with that the matter ceases to merit this name' (37). Yet these arguments fail to afford Abulfauaris lasting satisfaction. Above all, 'the distinction between the uncouth souls of the rabble and the sensitive and cultivated souls we claim for ourselves' strikes him as dubious. Why should not everyone be taught the truth? That fateful distinction does not lie in the nature of the matter or the nature of humankind; it arose historically. Hermes, 'the great founder of our order, bequeathed us a very simple religion; such a religion as was needed by a people that had just been assembled by him and had received from him the initial formation to a proper state; and as good a religion as they were able to endure' (42). His 'secret doctrine' was intended 'to bind more tightly his newly founded republic, and to remedy the insufficiency of his laws by inculcating the belief in a glorious reward for virtue and a severe punishment for sin after death' (43) – in other words, it boiled down to a political theology. So much for the Egyptian religion in its original state. 'The admission of the heroes of our people into the pantheon laid the groundwork for its expansion, and the hieroglyphs subsequently gave an opportunity for the number of holy things to increase almost to infinity' (43). The 'expansion' of religion, and the consequent emergence of 'middle orders' between the initiated and the uneducated people, thus led to the structure of *religio duplex*, which this late text by Wieland already presents as a symptom of decadence.

Finally, Herder's damning verdict on the secret societies, delivered in a letter to the Göttingen philologist Christian Gottlob Heyne dated 1 September 1786, should not go unmentioned in this context:

> I have a deadly hatred of all secret societies and, after all my experiences with them both inside and out, I wish them to the d[evil]; for what crawls under their cover is the creeping spirit of despotism, deceit and intrigue.[34]

Herder had entered the lodge 'To the Sword' in Riga in 1766, and on 1 July 1783, under the name of Damasus Pontifex, he had joined the Illuminati lodge 'Amalia' in Weimar. He remained a member until his death.

Secrecy under the Banner of Nature and Revelation

The interest in mysteries cannot be fully explained by the dualism of morality and politics which Reinhart Koselleck, as we have seen, declared to be the hallmark of the age. Moral concerns were certainly at stake in the lesser mysteries, as interpreted by Warburton. Here the neophyte had drummed into him the doctrine of the 'future state' with all its terrors and promises, without which – Warburton argued against Bayle – moral laws could never be firmly anchored in people's hearts and minds. The real borderline, however, ran between the lesser and greater mysteries, and this had nothing to do with politics and morality. Beyond this borderline lay disillusionment (in its negative aspect) and 'vision' (in its positive aspect). How are we to understand the distinction that was made here? What was the vision beheld by the initiate, or rather, how did the eighteenth century envisage it? That which revealed itself in the vision was described, in the texts of the time, using the concepts 'nature' and 'truth'. Clement of Alexandria writes of the 'innermost shrine of truth': 'The truly sacred word, deposited in the innermost shrine of truth, was by the Egyptians indicated by what were called among them adyta' – from *adyton*, an off-limits, strictly interdicted space. Plutarch and Proclus report on the image of Neith-Athena in Sais, 'whom they also call Isis'.

In Plutarch we are dealing with the famous passage in the ninth chapter of *On Isis and Osiris*, a key text for the construction of the Egyptian religion as a *religio duplex* and one that was cited time and again. In this chapter, Plutarch discusses the significance of secrecy and initiation in Egyptian religion and gives three examples of how the Egyptians expressed this principle: first, by setting up sphinxes in front of their temples, which showed that 'their religious teaching contained wisdom hidden in enigmas'; second, through the veiled image at Sais; and, third, through the divine name Amun, which according to Manetho means 'the hidden one' (*to kekrymmenon* – which, incidentally, is almost correct).[35] According to Plutarch, the veiled image at Sais is a seated statue of Athena-Isis with the inscription, 'I am all that has been, is, and shall be; no mortal ever lifted my garment (*peplos*)'.[36] The same inscription is delivered by Proclus in his *Timaeus* commentary, albeit with three crucial alterations. 'No mortal' appears here as 'no one', thereby including gods as well as human beings. Instead of *peplos* (a woollen garment worn on the upper body) he writes *chitōn* (a finely woven undergarment), lending a sexual connotation to the act of 'lifting' (*apokalyptō*). This connotation is strengthened by a detail missing from Plutarch's version: 'the fruit of my body is the sun'. For all that it may sound similar, the sentence thus has quite a different meaning in Proclus; it refers not to an epistemological aporia – the inviolable seclusion of truth – but rather to the parthogenesis of the sun from the body of a maternal primal goddess. We can be certain, then, that Proclus did not copy the sentence from Plutarch but derived it independently from another source.

In the eighteenth century, 'Isis' was generally taken to be synonymous with 'nature' – not in the sense of the visible *natura naturata* but the invisible *natura naturans*. She is 'Mother Nature', as Kant makes clear in the famous footnote to the third Critique where he cites the inscription to the 'veiled image at Sais': 'Perhaps nothing more sublime has ever been said, or any thought more sublimely expressed, than in the inscription over the temple of Isis (Mother Nature): "I am all that is, that was, and that will be, and my veil no mortal has removed." '[37] That is nature, as apolitical as it is amoral, knowing neither friend nor foe, neither good nor evil: the all-encompassing, all-one. What distinction could draw a border here and oppose a counterpart to that which embraces everything?

The dividing line that is drawn here runs between reason and faith or nature and revelation. That is how Theodor ·Ludwig Lau had already defined dual religion: *Rationis & Revelationis* – 'Religion is double: as religion of reason and as religion of revelation.'[38] The border between revelation and reason or faith and reason separates the God of the Fathers from the philosophers' god. The opposite of 'nature' is called 'revelation' (*revelatio*, the lifting of the veil). 'Nature' is hiddenness incarnate, the veil assumed by the all-one godhead in order that it may manifest itself. Nature is the 'structurally' secret, that which *cannot* be unveiled, and at the same time, given the prevailing circumstances, it is also the 'strategically' secret, that which *should not* be unveiled in the interests of the 'people' and the state. We need to supplement the dialectic of politics and morality with the dialectic of revelation and nature if we are to understand the idea of *religio duplex*, and hence the significance of the Egyptian mysteries for the eighteenth century. The split extends further, however, for only in the realm of 'nature' is that decisive borderline drawn which we encountered earlier in connection with Cudworth: that between deism and atheism. Nature is either the visible, phenomenal world, *natura naturata*, or the invisible, self-concealing *natura naturans*, Kant's 'Mother Nature', the deity of the 'veiled image at Sais'.

Friedrich Schiller's ballad, 'Das verschleierte Bild zu Sais' ('The Veiled Image at Sais'), was written in 1795, at a time when, after years of intensive study of Kantian philosophy, he had begun working on his letters on aesthetic education and his studies on the 'sublime'. The Egyptian mysteries became important for him in the context of these studies. Here what was communicated to the initiate was the experience of the sublime. 'The sublime object', Schiller wrote in his essay 'On the Sublime', 'is of a dual sort. We refer it either to our power of apprehension and are defeated in the attempt to form an image of its concept; or we refer it to our vital force and view it as a power against which our own dwindles to nothing.'[39] Initiation into the greater mysteries stages an experience of the sublime by first instilling in the initiate a real fear of death (as drastically described in the Plutarch fragment handed down by Stobaeus and dramatized in the trials by water and fire of *The Magic Flute*), so threatening his 'vital force', and then challenging his 'power of apprehension' by letting him glimpse the truth.

Schiller sticks to Plutarch's version in his ballad but makes one important change: the deity of his veiled image is neither Athena nor Isis but truth itself. The ballad tells the story of a failed initiation, showing what was at stake in this confrontation with the sublime. A youth 'burning with a thirst for knowledge' had travelled to Sais to be initiated into the mysteries, but he lacked the patience to slog his way through the various stages of induction. One night his over-whelming curiosity got the better of him and he removed the veil with his own hand.

What did the youth see? In his *Critique of the Power of Judgment*, Kant asserts that the presentation of the sublime 'can never be any-thing other than a merely negative presentation, which nevertheless expands the soul'.[40] He cites the biblical ban on graven images as an example of this principle of negative presentation: 'Perhaps there is no more sublime passage in the Jewish Book of the Law than the commandment, *Thou shalt not make to thyself any graven image, nor any likeness either of that which is in heaven, or on the earth, or yet under the earth, etc.*'[41]

The sublime cannot and should not be represented. Schiller respects this principle by not revealing to us what the youth actually saw. Instead, he only spells out the consequences of this unprepared epopty:

Ever from his heart
Was fled the sweet serenity of life,
And a deep anguish dug for him an early grave.

In the light of Warburton's interpretation of the greater mysteries, whose final stage the youth so recklessly anticipated, the experience of this encounter must be understood as the loss of all life-serving fictions and illusions. The thought of the all-one, all-encompassing, impersonal god is the greatest challenge which our human powers of apprehension and representation can possibly face; it places both mind and soul in acute mortal danger. Only those who have passed a series of harsh trials which instil in the initiate a real fear of death and transform him in his innermost self – the trials by fire and water, for example – can hope to meet this challenge. In his thirst for knowl-edge, the youth made the fatal mistake of skipping the long path to initiation and surrendering himself unprepared to the sight of truth. The vision he rushed to behold should have come at the end of a period of preparation lasting years or even decades, and even then it is vouchsafed only to the select few.

Schiller's seminal contribution to the theme of Egyptian mysteries, however, is his essay 'Die Sendung Moses' ('The Legation of Moses', 1789/90). Written several years before the ballad, the essay may be considered the classic account of ancient Egypt as the primary model for a *religio duplex*. Here this view of Egypt found its most prominent and influential expression.[42] In his essay, Schiller adopted Warburton's political interpretation of the Egyptian *religio duplex*, painting an impressive portrait of an Egyptian arcane religion dedicated to serving an anonymous, impersonal and all-encompassing deity. For Schiller, this idea of god represents the epitome of the sublime. 'Nothing is more sublime', he writes, 'than the simple grandeur with which they [the Egyptian initiates] spoke of the creator of the world. In order to distinguish him in a more striking way, they gave him no name at all.'[43]

To substantiate his thesis about the Egyptian god's anonymity, Schiller refers to the treatise *Asclepius* in the Corpus Hermeticum, where it is stated that god 'is nameless, since He is one and all, so that one must either call everything by His name or call Him by the name of everything'.[44] The self-etymology provided by Yahveh, *ehjeh asher ehjeh*, 'I am what I am' (Exod. 3:14), is also interpreted by Schiller as the withholding of a name. According to Schiller, Moses had appropriated this idea from the Egyptian mysteries, into which – as a prince brought up at Pharaoh's court and groomed to rule his people – he had been initiated up to the final stage of epopty. The all-one, anonymous god who revealed himself to Moses in the burning bush is the same deity who, in the 'veiled image at Sais', conceals herself more than she reveals herself as 'everything that was, is and shall be'. Again, the most sublime aspect of this deity is a figure of negation: the veil that guards her from mortal sight. Schiller reads the veil as an allegory of the 'theoretically-sublime', that is, of the unrepresentable, ineffable and inconceivable. Thus he writes in his treatise *On the Sublime* (1793):

> Everything that is veiled, everything mysterious, contributes to the terrible and is therefore capable of sublimity. Of this kind is the inscription that could be read at Sais in Egypt above the temple of Isis: 'I am everything that is, that has been, and that will be. No mortal has lifted my veil.' Precisely this uncertainty and mysteriousness gives man's conceptions of the future after death something of the dreadful.[45]

With the concept of the sublime, Schiller emphasizes the dreadfulness and inscrutability of the idea of god proclaimed in the mysteries, features of a negative theology which Cudworth, too, had brought into connection with the all-one. In the moment of epopty, the initiate is exposed to the sight of the unveiled truth, and hence to the abyss of negative theology and to nothingness. This was the experience that proved too much for the youth at Sais.

Schiller's Moses, by contrast, has seen the truth without flinching. He is free of all the illusions of popular religion. All the rituals, images and doctrines in which religions articulate the divine into a pantheon melt away before the truth of the all-one deity. With this god, Moses sets out to free his people from their Egyptian bondage. Two obstacles stand in the way of this noble plan: first, he cannot initiate an entire people into these mysteries, since that would take decades and would, moreover, lead only the fittest and most intellectually able candidates to knowledge; second, the all-one deity of the mysteries lacks the qualities required of a national god. The latter must bear a name and have certain characteristics. He must judge and save, reward and punish, and he must favour his people over all others. In place of the supreme, nameless being, Schiller's Moses therefore proposes the 'national god' Yahveh, another life-serving and politically expedient fiction, in order to salvage at least part of the truth, the idea of god's unity. With that, Moses betrays the mysteries in two ways: he betrays them to the people, who had been kept in the dark about them by the Egyptians; but he also betrays and falsifies (albeit with the best of intentions) the sublime idea he takes from them. We thus encounter in Schiller as well the motif of a politically motivated pious fraud. In Schiller's account, the fraud pays off: Moses succeeds in emancipating his people and founding a free community beholden only to the law. Then, 140 years later, Arnold Schoenberg and Sigmund Freud showed Moses running aground on precisely this dilemma, failing in his attempt to translate the sublime into comprehensible, colloquial language. In Schoenberg's operatic retelling, Moses sinks despairingly to the ground: 'O word, o word that I lack.' In Freud he is even bludgeoned to death by the Israelites.

Schiller based his essay on a treatise on the *Hebrew Mysteries* by his friend and fellow Illuminatus Carl Leonhard Reinhold.[46] Reinhold interprets the mysteries as the 'oldest religious freemasonry', whereby 'freemasonry' is synonymous with esotericism. But what does this mean in conjunction with the adjective 'religious'? This concept can only be understood in the light of its opposite. This is called 'scientific' freemasonry. The inventor of this distinction and terminology was the philosopher Anton Kreil. Kreil and Reinhold were both members of the Viennese lodge 'True Concord', and their writings on the Egyptian and Hebrew mysteries must be seen in the context of this lodge's ambitious project to research all the ancient mysteries. This project was undertaken with the aim of finding models for their lodge rituals and general orientation for their situation in an enlightened-absolutist society. So what was meant by 'religious freemasonry'? Reinhold illustrates this by means of the Israelite 'school of prophecy'. Just as the Egyptian initiates were the forerunners of 'scientific freemasonry', so the Israelite institutions of Sanhedrin and especially the 'school of prophecy' were the forerunners of 'religious freemasonry'.[47] The concept is thus intended polemically. It designates the twilight phase of mystery culture. So long as only the highest initiates have an inkling of the truth, so long as the complex hierarchical and hieroglyphical architectures of dual religion remain focused on the vanishing point of the all-one deity, this system is unobjectionable. Things take a turn for the worse when the key goes missing, when the inner sanctum of the mysteries is filled by a void, and when this void, and nothing more, is what must be kept secret at all costs. Then the mysteries become an elaborate charade of secret nods and handshakes, and religion degenerates into blind faith. With these warnings, Reinhold returns at the end of his book to freemasonry. As representatives of an 'authentic and true school of prophecy in freemasonry', he names the 'Strict Observance', the 'Holy Order of the Golden and Rose Cross' and the 'clerisy' of the Orientalist and theologian Johann August Starck. They form the contemporary front of religious freemasonry, their occultist rigmarole lying poles apart from the programme advanced by the Illuminati: the transformation of blind faith into an organ of reason, and ultimately the reformation of society into an autonomous collective of responsible citizens who have outgrown the need for state governance, police, surveillance and censorship.

In the light of this polemic, the diagnosis of Hebrew religion as 'religious freemasonry' thus appears as a damning indictment.[48] In Israel, the Egyptian religion of reason regressed into an instrument of blind faith. To be sure, that is not stated in so many words, only intimated to those who know what the expression 'religious freemasonry' means. Schiller, for one, understood it very well. The Viennese lodge in which this distinction was developed had pledged itself to 'scientific freemasonry' and glimpsed its model, perhaps even its origin, in the priestly orders of ancient Egypt, which, as Anton Kreil and Ignaz von Born reported, pursued their scientific, philosophical and theological investigations in underground libraries, laboratories, research institutes and places of worship. Just as Egypt was considered the birthplace of scientific freemasonry, so Israel was seen as the origin of religious freemasonry.

Ignaz von Born and the Vienna Mysteries Project

The 'True Concord' lodge in Vienna stood at the centre of freemasonic research into the mysteries. It boasted over 200 members and, as a bastion of the Enlightenment in Austria, it exercised a function comparable to that of an Academy of Sciences.[49] In the five to six short years of its existence, its members composed no fewer than fourteen studies – frequently of monographic proportions – on the Egyptian, Cabiric, Phoenician, Samothracian, Eleusinian, Dionysian, Pythagorean, Mithraic and Neoplatonic mysteries. Almost all these studies appeared in the pages of their house periodical, the *Journal für Freymaurer (Journal for Freemasons)*:

> Ignaz von Born, *Ueber die Mysterien der Aegyptier (On the Mysteries of the Egyptians)*: 1 (1784), 15–132.
>
> Karl Joseph Michaeler, *Ueber Analogie zwischen dem Christenthume der erstern Zeiten und der Freymaurerey (On Analogies between Christianity in the Earliest Times and Freemasonry)*: 2 (1784), 5–63.
>
> [Joseph Anton von Bianchi], *Ueber die Magie der alten Perser und die mithrischen Geheimnisse (On the Magic of the Ancient Persians and the Mithric Mysteries)*: 3 (1784), 5–96.
>
> Ignaz von Born, *Ueber die Mysterien der Indier (On the Mysteries of the Indians)*: 4 (1784), 5–54.
>
> Anton Kreil, *Geschichte des pythagoräischen Bundes (History of the Pythagorean League)*: 5 (1785), 3–28.
>
> Karl Haidinger, *Ueber die Magie (On Magic)*: 5 (1785), 29–56.
>
> Anton Kreil, *Geschichte der Neuplatoniker (History of the Neoplatonists)*: 6 (1785), 5–51.
>
> Carl Leonhard Reinhold, *Ueber die kabirischen Mysterien (On the Cabiric Mysteries)*: 7 (1785), 5–48.
>
> [Anton Kreil], *Ueber die wissenschaftliche Maurerey (On Scientific Masonry)*: 7 (1785), 49–78.
>
> Carl Leonhard Reinhold, *Ueber die Mysterien der alten Hebräer (On the Mysteries of the Ancient Hebrews)*: 9 (1786), 5–79.
>
> Augustin Veit von Schittlersberg, *Ueber den Einfluß der Mysterien der Alten auf den Flor der Nationen (On the Influence of the Mysteries of the Ancients on the Bloom of Nations)*: 9 (1786), 80–116.
>
> Anton Kreil, *Ueber die eleusinischen Mysterien (On the Eleusinian Mysteries)*: 10 (1786), 5–42.

Carl Leonhard Reinhold, *Ueber die größern Mysterien der Hebräer* (*On the Greater Mysteries of the Hebrews*): 11 (1786), 5–98.

Michael Durdon, *Ueber die Mysterien der Etrusker, insonderheit ueber die Geheimnisse des Bachus* (*On the Mysteries of the Etruscans, particularly on the Mysteries of Bacchus*): 12 (1787), 5–164.

Michaeler's detailed study of the Phoenician mysteries belongs in this series as Nr 15. Michaeler had it published as a free-standing monograph rather than letting it appear in the *Journal for Freemasons*,[50] just as Reinhold later published his lectures in book form with Göschen.

This research project was the brainchild of Ignaz von Born[51] (1742–91), the Master of the Lodge. Born opened the series of studies with a treatise 'On the Mysteries of the Egyptians', which at 117 pages assumed the dimensions of a monograph. His image of the scientific and practical activities of the kings and cultural heroes of Egypt largely draws on Book I of Diodorus's *Bibliotheca Historica*: *Hermes* taught the arts and sciences (I.43.6); *Menes* arranged the mysteries (I.45: there is no word of 'mysteries' in Diodorus, who states that Menes 'instructed the people to worship the gods and make sacrifices'; above all, he brought an end to the simple life and introduced a luxurious way of life); *Sesostris* brought order into public administration (Diodorus talks about this king, whom he calls Sesoosis, in chapters 53–8);[52] *Urocheos* dammed the Nile to the east of Memphis (I.50: Diodorus incorrectly writes 'Uchoreus' for Ochureus).[53] The list concludes with two fundamental statements which Born, undeterred by a lack of corroborating evidence in the ancient sources, places in the mouths of his priestly historians: '*Osiris* was a mortal. We call the sun [. . .] by his name,' and 'The knowledge of Nature is the ultimate purpose of our application. We worship this progenitor, nourisher and preserver of all creation in the image of *Isis*. Only he who knows the whole extent of her power and force will be able to uncover her veil without punishment.'[54] A little later, Born comes back to the veiled image at Sais: 'The inscription on the column of Isis in the temple at Sais expresses how they [the priests] gauged the full extent of this science: "I, Nature, am all that was, is and shall be; no one has ever completely unveiled me."' A great many natural-scientific writings of the seventeenth and eighteenth centuries feature a picture of the unveiled Isis as a frontispiece.[55] Born, too, imagines the project of a scientifically and alchemistically oriented freemasonry as an unveiling of Isis, albeit one undertaken in a spirit of reverence rather than of disenchantment.

Osiris and Isis – Diodorus also identifies the Egyptian gods as deified mortals[56] – established the basis for civilization among the Egyptians;[57] Thoth or Hermes I invented a symbolic script that Hermes II then developed into hieroglyphic writing, erecting two pillars on which he 'had engraved the full extent of the Egyptian sciences';[58] finally, Hermes III, by-named 'Trismegistus', gathered together the 'scattered remnants' after a catastrophic flood had devastated his country, and he restored the arts and sciences to their former glory and dominion. Learning and science thus take centre stage in Born's retelling of Egyptian history.

Sesostris, this 'Egyptian Solomon' (34), split his kingdom into thirty-six provinces[59] and organized the justice, welfare and education systems together with the divine cults. 'Religion was always included, since this has always been the most powerful bridle for steering the people wheresoever the regent wills' (37): that is a principle of radical Enlightenment, which unmasks every religion (including Christianity, although Born possibly would not go that far) as political theology.[60]

The other passages from Diodorus to which Born refers in this section concern the famous mausoleum of Ozymandias (i.e., the Ramesseum),[61] the city of Memphis supposedly built by 'Uchoreus', obelisks, colossal statues, and – of course – the pyramids. It is typical of his intellectualistic bias that Born interprets the pyramids as repositories of learning, erected in order to preserve the cultural memory of Egypt:

> The example of the earliest Egyptians, who in a similar way engraved their history and secrets into the columns of Thoth, or, as others claim, upon the walls of underground caves; the testimony of Pliny, who declares the hieroglyphs on the obelisks to be philosophical observations (Hist. Nat. lib. 36 cap. 9); the durability of the materials they selected for the task; the solidity they gave these masses of stone; the majestic simplicity of these buildings, through which they sought nothing other than to afford them permanence and fame; the figure of a pyramid, i.e. a body that has a widespread base and ends in a tip – all these conditions make it more than likely that they were erected with the sole intention of being inscribed with the full extent of their political, civic and ecclesiastical learning, such that they were destined to become the Bible of the Egyptians, as it were. (43–4)

The Egyptians were thus not only the first people to build capacious storehouses for their arts and sciences, designed specifically to withstand the vicissitudes of the ages; they also passed on this learning to visitors from abroad, who took it with them to the four corners of the earth: first Orpheus, Musaeus, Melampus, Daedalus and Homer, then Pythagoras, Plato, Eudoxus, Democritus, Aenopis (= Oenopides), Telecles and Theodorus, as well as (in the legislative sphere) Moses,[62] Solon and Lycurgus.[63] It is characteristic of the Illuminati's pessimistic view of history that they posited a common origin of human knowledge which, having once sunk into oblivion, was now to be reconstructed from the traces it had left scattered all over the earth.

The second section dwells on the 'composition, duties and expertise of the Egyptian priesthood'. Born first sketches the essential features of the Egyptian religion, which 'for want of any revelation' recognized the divine in the effects of natural forces, above all the sun. The original cult consisted in offerings of fruit in thanksgiving for the harvest,[64] then bread was added and finally, with the raising of livestock, animal sacrifice also became common, a line of development that unmistakably traces a path of decline. Still, the Egyptians never went so far as to perform human sacrifice. Those chosen to officiate this cult constituted a caste segregated from the rest of society, but 'happily, before they could degenerate into a company detrimental and injurious to the well-being of Egypt', they were split up and instructed by Thoth in a manner 'that made them worthy to become the keepers of their country's laws, its higher learning and its most sublime secrets, and to take part in the felicitous administration of Egypt, whose welfare was the singular goal of this remarkable priesthood' (48). In a word: before the Egyptian priests had a chance to 'degenerate' into clergymen, monks and Jesuits, they were trained by Thoth to become servants of society, that is, freemasons.

The conditions for entering these priestly orders were strict, and they strangely paralleled the conventions of freemasonry. The candidate had to be a 'free man'; artisans, farmers and shepherds were barred from serving the gods, as was 'the female sex'.[65] What Diodorus says about the priests is music to Born's ears:

> The priests are the first to deliberate upon the most important matters and are always at the king's side, sometimes as his assistants, sometimes to propose measures and give instructions, and they also, by their knowledge of astrology and of divination, forecast future events, and read to the king, out of the record of acts preserved in their sacred books, those which can be of assistance. [. . .] They also pay no taxes of any kind, and in repute and power are second after the king. (I.73.4–5)

That describes fairly accurately the role the freemasons aspired to play in the Josephinian state. To be sure, it is no less utopian a depiction of conditions in ancient Egypt as they appeared to Diodorus (or rather his source, Hecataeus of Abdera) than it is of conditions in late eighteenth-century Vienna. The synods established by Ptolemy corresponded to the typical strategy, pursued by colonial overlords all over the world, of giving their regime a consensual veneer by winning over the indigenous elites, but the priests were far from being 'always at the king's side'. What Hecataeus offers here is a mirror held up to his king, Ptolemy I, reflecting back an image of how he ought to rule, not how he actually ruled. In exactly the same way, Born had Joseph II in mind when he reached back to Diodorus's presentation of Egypt as an enlightened monarchy, presided over by a king who received guidance from a philosophically educated elite; earlier still, Bossuet had painted a similar picture for the benefit of Louis XV.[66] Born viewed ancient Egypt through Josephinian spectacles: seen from this point of view and in this light, Diodorus's report on Egypt must have seemed to him by far the most credible and illuminating. For Diodorus's source on Egyptian matters, Hecataeus of Abdera, had himself viewed Egypt through glasses which can best be characterized as 'Josephinian'. He travelled to the country in the aftermath of Alexander the Great's conquest with the aim of settling down there, studying its culture and history, writing up his research, and so giving the Diadochi king Ptolemy I a tool for ruling his new kingdom in harmony with its traditions and institutions. Like the Viennese freemasons, he evidently considered the optimal form of government to be an enlightened monarchy, one committed to good laws and the general welfare of the country. Traditional Greek political theory distinguished between the arbitrary rule of Oriental despotism and the lawfully constituted forms of government found in the Greek *polis*, whether these were democratic or oligarchic. Like Plato and Isocrates before him, Hecataeus saw in Egypt the ideal conjunction of law and monarchy.[67] Diodorus (Hecataeus) paints the portrait of a monarch whose thoroughly ritualized daily routine is prescribed right down to the minutiae by laws and watched over by priests. 'All their acts were regulated by prescriptions set forth in laws, not only their administrative acts, but also those that had to do with the way in which they spent their time from day to day, and with the food which they ate' (I.70.1). This was done 'in order that the king . . . might follow no low practices; for no ruler advances far along the road of evil until he has those about him who will minister to his passions' (I.70.2).

When it came to the Egyptian priestly 'orders', Born based his account on Porphyry (i.e., Chaeremon), Herodotus, Plutarch, Clement of Alexandria, Apuleius and Iamblichus, as well as Diodorus. Here, then, his range of sources was much broader. Priests were circumcised and subject to strict entrance examinations, purity laws, dietary regulations and standards of dress. Besides officiating at divine worship, their main task was to devote themselves to scientific study, particularly in theology, philosophy, the natural sciences, medicine, mathematics, geometry, geography, astronomy and philology. The priesthood was separated into different ranks (prophets, stolists, hierogrammatists, horologists and pastophors), each charged with mastering a different section of the Hermetic corpus. Here Born refers back to Clement's famous depiction of an Egyptian priestly procession, in which representatives of each rank step forward with their insignia of office and announce which volumes of the Hermetic texts they specialize in. The Egyptian priesthood stands as model for Born's concept of a 'scientific' freemasonry. His authority on theological matters is Iamblichus, from whose work *On the Egyptian Mysteries* he cites a passage summarizing the Egyptian idea of God:

> Prior to all things was God, He alone, older than the sun, immoveable, and abiding in the solitude of his own unity. [. . .] No conception we make of him is worthy of Him. He is self-begotten and truly good. Is there anything greater and older than Him? The fountain of all good things, the root of all entities and all intellect. He is [. . .] His own creator. The beginning of all things and God of Gods, the One and primordial being, from whom entity and essence are derived.[68]

For Born, this Neoplatonic credo epitomizes the ancient Egyptian arcane theology with which he so unabashedly identifies. To the Egyptian priesthood, the many deities worshipped by the people are only visible symbols or hypostases of the invisible, inconceivable One: 'What the people saw as particular, distinct gods was for the priest a representation of the different qualities of the unique God he came to know in his mysteries' (59). Along with the sublime idea of God, 'the recollection of death was deeply impressed upon the initiates, and the immortality of the soul explained in the mysteries, whence it was transplanted into the mysteries of all peoples' (60). While polytheism may thus have been the religion of choice for people on the streets, the priests in their temples paid homage to an esoteric monotheism instead.

The third section draws parallels to freemasonry. The most important consists in the rite of initiation, for which Born cites the only surviving ancient report on an initiation into the mysteries of Isis, the famous passage from Book XI of Apuleius's *The Golden Ass* (94–101).[69] Here he finds information about the teachings and tests

which lay in store for the candidate during his novitiate. These related
to his seriousness, resolve, self-control, strength, patience and not
least his solvency, as well as giving him a first indication of the
'sublime concepts of God and Nature' (as was also customary in
freemasonry). The actual initiation began with a day of purification
and ten days of fasting. Finally, the novice was clothed in linen and
led into the temple. The nocturnal proceedings that followed were
protected by a vow of silence; Apuleius hints at them in images:

Accessi confinium mortis	I came to the boundary of death,
et calcato Proserpinae limine	and after treading Proserpine's threshold
per omnia vectus elementa remeavi,	I returned having traversed all the elements.
nocte media vidi solem candido coruscantem lumine,	At midnight I saw the sun shining with brilliant light;
deos inferos et deos superos accessi coram	I approached the gods below and the gods above face to face
et adoravi de proxumo.	and worshipped them in their actual presence.

In the morning the newly consecrated priest was presented to the
cheering crowd *ad instar solis*, 'like the sun god', and his initiation
'celebrated like a re-birth'. Born sees similarities with the masonic
rites in the period assigned for preparation, in the determination of
the day of initiation by the high priest, in the convocation of priests
for the initiation that evening, and in the initiation itself: in both
cases, the initiate is led into the temple by the priest, 'he is threatened
in dark chambers by the fear of death and traverses all the elements
until he arrives back at his former position', and he sees 'bright light
at midnight' (99).

The dazzling image of the Egyptian priesthood which Born derives
from the Greek sources is offered to his brothers as the model for a
'scientific' freemasonry, founded on the reverential study of nature
rather than on revelation. The Egyptian priests were the standard-
bearers of an enlightenment which they had to keep secret only
because the time was not yet ripe for the truth to be made known to
all. Secrecy was a strategy necessitated by the still imperfect state of
social and political relations, not a condition intrinsic to the matter
itself: that is the 'historical significance' of the Egyptian mysteries.
'We too reveal to the initiate, as soon as he has seen the light, that
we are not destined to remain a secret and concealed society, but that

we gathered behind closed doors, when tyranny and vice carried all before them, in order to oppose them all the more resolutely' (89).

Subterranean Egypt

Up until the late eighteenth century, the image of ancient Egyptian culture as a *religio duplex* rested almost exclusively on the grammatological theory which ascribed to the ancient Egyptians a dual culture of writing, split between a secret pictographic script used in the mysteries and a supposedly alphabetic script for general use. In 1774, however, a work appeared in French that lent this image a new topological basis and plausibility. In the sixth section of his *Philosophical Dissertations on the Egyptians and Chinese*, a foray into comparative ethnography,[70] Cornelius de Pauw produced a surprising link between Egyptian architecture and the mysteries. He saw the antagonism between popular and arcane religion in Egypt not only in the use of two systems of writing but also, far more visibly, in the difference between above-ground and below-ground construction. De Pauw was one of the first to draw on modern travellers' reports as well as classical authors for his description of ancient Egyptian culture, and he thereby acquired a far more vivid picture of Egypt as a *religio duplex*, even if it rested on as serious a misunderstanding as the interpretation that posited a double culture of writing. The subterranean installations which we interpret today as tombs were interpreted by de Pauw and his contemporaries as cult spaces and repositories of learning for the arcane religion. I quote from Captain J. Thomson's English translation of the *Recherches philosophiques sur les Egyptiens et Chinois*, which came out in 1795, twenty-one years after both the French original and its translation into German:

When we reflect on the prodigious excavations, made continually by the Egyptians in their mountains, and the singular predilection of the priests for those caverns, where they passed the greater part of their lives, it is no longer doubtful, that, in former times, they had lived like Troglodytes. [. . .] If any thing can be compared to what these extraordinary people erected on the surface of the earth, it must be their subterranean labours. Some ancient authors had good information, that different apartments were constructed an hundred and fifty feet below the pyramids, communicating with each other by passages, to which Ammianus Marcellinus has given the Greek name of *syringes*. The only one of these now known is that leading through the most northern of all the pyramids; and it becomes every year more imperfect, from the rolling in of sand and ruins. Yet Prosper Alpin assures us, that, about the year one thousand five hundred and eight-five, a man, having descended there with a compass, arrived at the place where the way divides into two ramifications, one take a southern, and the other an eastern direction. This could no longer be traced by Maillet, Greves, Thevenot, Vansleb and Father Sicard, who came many years later [. . .].

Herodotus knew beyond a doubt that, after descending below ground, a person could pass into the apartments of the pyramid of the labyrinth. As this is exactly the case in that of Memphis, the interior disposition of which is perfectly well known to the present day, we have every reason to believe, that the same mode of construction was common to the other monuments of that kind. [. . .] Strabo has indicated a *Serapeum*, or chapel of Serapis, amidst the moving sands to the west of Memphis, which appears to have been the real spot where the mouths of the different galleries, leading below the pyramids of *Gizeh*, were united.

Among the crypts and grottos of Heptanomis and Thebais, those of *Alyi* and *Hipponon* are large enough to contain a thousand horses: we know those of *Speos Artemidos*, of *Hieracon, Selinon, Antaeopolis*, and *Silsili*; as well as the syringes, or subterraneous passages mentioned by Pausanias, in the vicinity of the vocal statue [note: Lib. i in Attic. cap. 42.] But although travellers meet with others every day, they have not yet discovered the one hundredth part of such excavations. (2: 36–8)

De Pauw then comes to speak of the 'caves' of Biban el Moluk (= the Valley of the Kings), which he interprets as 'the tombs of the earliest dynasties or the first royal families'. He explicitly contradicts those who consider the pyramids to be the oldest royal tombsites. Egypt nonetheless has 'caverns', he continues, 'which were never used as sepulchres'. Examples include:

that of Diana, or the *Speos Artemidos*, still seen at *Beni-Hasan* [. . .]. Many others of the same kind were cut in the rocks of Ethiopia; where, we learn from Bermudez, the priests initiated, or offered sacrifices, and even retired to study.[71] We have been told of a certain Pancrates, who did not leave those dreary abodes during a period of twenty-four years;[72] and it is generally supposed, that Orpheus, Eumolpus, and Pythagoras, were admitted there likewise.

On considering this mode of studying under ground, it no longer appears astonishing, that the priests contracted the habit of throwing a mysterious veil over all their real or imaginary knowledge. [. . .] It is truly interesting to observe, that the custom of retiring into cells, practised by the priests, gave rise to the mysteries of antiquity. Without this, none perhaps would ever have been invented; and wheresoever those of Egypt were received, the mode of celebrating them in caverns was likewise adopted [. . .].

The mysteries seem originally to have been a secret instruction, given only to the priests, who, prior to their consecration, experienced a panic terror. They were afterwards conducted by dark windings to a place very full of light; and this suggested the idea of copying the phenomena of thunder and lightning [. . .]. All the priests without exception were initiated, as Diodorus says, in what were called the mysteries of the god Pan; and not one of them escaped a panic terror in the obscurity of the subterranean passages. (2: 40–2)

It is unlikely that the Egyptian royal tombs (which Champollion, drawing on the passage from Ammianus Marcellinus, still called 'syringes') and the other tombsites covered with writing have ever been subjected to a more fanciful interpretation. It should also be noted that these 'syringes', which de Pauw locates 'an hundred and fifty feet below the pyramids', actually lie over 600 kilometres south of the Pyramids of Giza in the Valley of the Kings near Thebes. For de Pauw, they function not only as repositories of learning but as assembly halls and places of study as well. To support this claim he adduces, among other ancient passages, Lucian's reference to a priest named Pancrates, who is said to have spent twenty-three years of his life underground:

'Well now, one of my fellow passengers on the way up was a scribe from Memphis, an extraordinarily able man, versed in all the lore of the Egyptians. He was said to have passed twenty-three years of his life underground in the tombs, studying occult sciences under the instruction of Isis herself.'

'You must mean the divine Pancrates, my teacher,' exclaimed Arignotus; 'tall, clean-shaven, snub-nosed, protruding lips, rather thin in the legs; dresses entirely in linen, has a thoughtful expression, and speaks Greek with a slight accent?'[73]

In his *Recherches sur les initiations anciennes et modernes* (Paris 1779), Claude Robin then makes an explicit connection between the subterranean architecture described in travellers' reports and Terrasson's imaginative reconstruction of initiations under the pyramids. I cite a lengthier excerpt:[74]

In their caves, the aspirant found wells of a terrifying depth, into which he descended by means of footholds cut into the rock. He then had to traverse long and winding passageways, where he encountered ghosts under a thousand hideous forms, monsters to be fought, streams to be crossed, infernos to be braved: everything that could disturb the senses and frighten the imagination was placed in his path, and death seemed to present itself to him under a thousand different aspects; plaintive and mournful cries could be heard in the distance; he was dazzled by sudden flashes of light, then plunged unawares into pitch darkness; the noisy play of machines raised him up, let him fall, painted for him gales, thunderclaps and raging torrents. At the least sign of terror and weakness he was escorted into other subterranean chambers, where he was condemned to pass the remainder of his days. The priests believed that timid and cowardly men were incapable of guarding the secret of their mysteries inviolate; they detained them there in order that they could not disclose what they had seen. After these preliminary preparations, which were called the trials by water, fire and air, the initiate was led to a place beautified by all that art could add to nature: a soft and tender light made the objects more interesting, the air was perfumed by a pleasant assortment of flowers, and the melodious sound of a thousand instruments proclaimed to the initiate the joy of seeing him emerge as the vanquisher of evil spirits and the elements. This place was the symbol of the satisfaction and happiness that a man feels upon surmounting the obstacles and battles he had to endure before advancing to truth and virtue.[75]

The most original contribution on the Egyptian mysteries to appear in the Viennese *Journal for Freemasonry* owed much to these descriptions. The anonymously published essay was the work of Anton Kreil.[76] In it, he represents the Egyptian arcane religion as the primitive form of 'scientific freemasonry'. All Egypt, so one could read in de Pauw, was undermined by subterranean halls, chambers and passageways covered from wall to wall with priestly hieroglyphs. This network of bunkers could have had only one purpose: to serve the secret religion of the initiates as a cultic stage, research institute and storage facility for arcane knowledge. In his treatise on 'scientific freemasonry', Kreil proposes that the initiates had so successfully planned this secret religion and science to last for eternity that it was still alive today, in the form of the 'scientific freemasonry' practised by 'True Concord' and other lodges affiliated with Illuminism. The Egyptians developed three institutions to bring this about: the art of building underground, hieroglyphic writing (as a codification of the truth illegible to the uninitiated), and a secret Order charged with safeguarding and handing down the truth, the 'mysteries of Isis'.

According to this interpretation, the underground complexes built by the Egyptians arose not only from political considerations regarding the fictions of popular religion and Platonic concerns about the incomprehension of the masses, but from fear of oblivion as well. Kreil cites as evidence a passage in Ammianus Marcellinus, also mentioned by de Pauw, in which it is stated that the Egyptian priests began their extensive excavation projects because 'they had fore-knowledge that a deluge was coming, and feared that the memory of the ceremonies might be destroyed':

> There are also subterranean fissures and winding passages called syringes, which, it is said, those acquainted with the ancient rites, since they had foreknowledge that a deluge was coming, and feared that the memory of the ceremonies might be destroyed, dug in the earth in many places with great labour; and on the walls of these caverns they carved many kinds of birds and beasts, and those countless forms of animals which they called hieroglyphic writing.[77]

This does in fact appear to have been the motive behind the decorative principle of the late Egyptian temples, if not of the Egyptian tombsites: their walls, pillars and passages, covered from top to bottom with inscriptions and pictures, can be understood as a means of notating and conserving religious learning feared to be under threat from Hellenism, if not from flooding.[78] In the late antique tradition, the flood evidently appears as a cipher for the memory loss entailed by the decay of Egyptian culture and the attendant decline in knowledge of the hieroglyphs. For example, Dio Chrysostom writes of this amnesia:

> I learned about it in Onuphi, in Egypt, from a priest who spoke very good Greek. He said that their entire ancient history was either written in the temples or on stelae and that, after the stelae were destroyed, only a few still remembered it. Much that had been written down had been lost owing to the ignorance and carelessness of later generations.[79]

The 'stelae' undoubtedly refer to the famous stelae on which Hermes is said to have recorded his learning.[80] This motif goes back to a story about Manetho that had been preserved by Eusebius and passed down to Syncellos:

> In the time of Ptolemy Philadelphus he [Manetho] was styled high-priest of the pagan temples of Egypt, and wrote from stelae[81] in the Siriadic land [Egypt],[82] traced, he says, in sacred language and holy characters by Thoth, the first Hermes. After the Flood they were trans-lated into hieroglyphic characters by Agathodaemon, son of the second Hermes, and arranged in books in the temple-shrines of Egypt.[83]

Iamblichus speaks of these books when mentioning his sources at the very beginning of his 'Letter to Abammo' (= *On the Egyptian*

Mysteries). These stelae are also mentioned in a particularly imaginative description, dating from the 1740s, of an Egyptian underground complex devoted to the pursuit of wisdom:

> Surrounded with these pillars of lamps are each of these venerable columns, which I am now to speak of, inscribed with the hieroglyphical letters with the primeval mysteries of the Egyptian learning. [. . .] From these pillars, and the sacred books, they maintain, that all the philosophy and learning of the world has been derived.[84]

Why did the Egyptian priests keep their wisdom hidden? 'Noble and virtuous men are never wise for themselves alone,' Kreil asserts, 'but stake [. . .] all their happiness on employing their learning for the greater good of humankind. If, then, wise men at the height of their powers choose to keep secrets, this can only be because their learning includes knowledge that would be harmful to the people, or liable to be misused by them, or that would enlighten the people on matters concerning which they were better left in the dark' (68). In their eagerness to pass on this knowledge nonetheless, the Egyptians looked beyond the confines of their own society to encompass all humankind in their gaze, 'for they built not for their own age and their own nation, but for the millennia and the human race' (69).

Theoretically, their learning could thus still be extant. If so, then 'it is extant in a secret society, preserved in mysteries of some kind'. How could such a secret society continue to recruit new members over the centuries? The key selection criteria would surely be 'uprightness, intellectual acumen and above all steadfastness, presence of mind and discretion'. Through 'the constantly renewed, constantly evoked image of death, their life's goal,' the novices would have to be

> gradually transposed into that calmer, more serene state of mind in which one tends to regard the worth of things more cold-bloodedly, to become more attentive [. . .] to one's calling, and [. . .] to know and cherish a higher contentedness. This thought of death would have to be kept night and day at the forefront of aspirants' minds, so as to deprive [. . .] the baser drives which so often set man at odds with himself of their bedazzling, deceiving, one-sided and turbulent force; to lift them out of their own selves and spread them over their entire race; to raise them to that more sublime plane where they would do good not by disposition, nor merely out of sympathy, but as a matter of principle. [. . .] Finally they would have to [. . .] adapt the hieroglyphs to the spirit of each age and nation, so that [. . .] they would

always mislead the rabble and help increase the obscurity of the arcane meaning. (70–1)

'Those [. . .] are the measures which would need to be taken if secrets unintelligible to the uninitiated were to be bequeathed to the next generation; and that is also the real plan by which the mysteries of the ancients were instituted. [. . .] It is the plan of masonry as well' with its three degrees: in the apprenticeship, emphasis is placed on 'steadfastness, equanimity, presence of mind and discretion' (which, as 'the wise teaching of these boys', Tamino wishes to have 'forever engraved upon [his] heart'). 'In the second degree, we are urged to pursue the sciences and exercise the mind. In the master degree [. . .], the image of death, this physical removal into the coffin, the eternal resting place awaiting all, this preliminary trial of lying in that cramped container' is said to have 'a wonderful effect on the minds of all those capable of nurturing wisdom.' One reads these words differently knowing, as we shall see (p. 108), that it was Leopold Mozart in whose heart those very feelings were stirred in the presence of his son, who had just gone through the same experiences during his induction into the rank of master mason.[85]

In effect, the eighteenth century's fantasies about subterranean Egypt turn Plato's parable of the cave on its head. In Plato, people dwell in a cave illuminated by the artificial light of their conventional, symbolically mediated representations. Only a few philosophers succeed in finding the exit and ascend to the daylight of truth. When they return to the cave to enlighten the remaining troglodytes, they meet with fierce resistance. If this model is turned upside down, what results is the picture of a society that lives in the daylight of its ideas and prejudices – which are not only symbolically mediated but also institutionally validated in the form of state and Church, school, court, police and army – while banishing its philosophers underground, where they are free to pursue the truth under the shelter of secrecy. This image of a split-level society, a society divided between superstructure and substructure, publicity and secrecy, accords with what the polyhistor Reimmann termed *philosophia duplex*,[86] and it encapsulates how people pictured ancient Egyptian culture at the time. It also corresponds to the image the freemasons made of themselves as an elite that had taken cover in an underworld of secret ritual. We are dealing here with a structure of mutually reinforcing projections. On the one hand, this period constructs an image of ancient Egyptian culture that reflects its own circumstances; on the other hand, however, it views this construction as a model that can provide it with orientation for its self-understanding, its problems and their possible solutions.

The Magic Flute: Opera Duplex

The ideas of *religio duplex* and the Egyptian mysteries find their clearest expression in Mozart and Schikaneder's opera *The Magic Flute*.[87] It could even be called an *opera duplex*, with an exoteric exterior and an esoteric interior: on the outside, a popular fairy-tale opera, magic opera and machine opera in the tradition of the Viennese *Volkstheater*; on the inside, a masonic mystery play. In this respect, *The Magic Flute* occupies an absolutely unique position in the European operatic literature.[88] In its pronounced dualism, it was both unprecedented and without sequel. That makes it one of the great enigmas in the history of art.

Mozart was a committed and active freemason, and his 'Beneficence' lodge worked closely with 'True Concord'.[89] It was thus only a matter of time before he came into contact with that lodge's great theme, the Egyptian mysteries. It can even be shown that he was familiar with Anton Kreil's work on the 'scientific freemasonry' practised by the ancient Egyptians in their underground research institutes. As the protocols of 'True Concord' indicate, Kreil presented his theory at two meetings at which Mozart was also present, held on 16 and 22 April 1785; for it was at these meetings that his father Leopold was elevated to the rank of Fellowcraft and then Master mason.[90]

It is easy to surmise that the picture Kreil painted of the Egyptian world as a *religio duplex*, split between the sublime truth cultivated below ground and the colourful, popular polytheism celebrated above, might have inspired Mozart to write an *opera duplex* that would bring the ideals of the masonic Enlightenment to the stage in the guise of a fairy-tale and magic opera. Such an idea could only have been realized in the tradition of baroque world theatre that still lived on in the Viennese *Volkstheater*, not in the Italian-influenced court theatre. Schikaneder was the ideal partner for this project. This construction presupposes, of course, that Mozart made a significant contribution to the libretto (which is not how Wolfgang Hildesheimer imagines it, although Friedrich Dieckmann's fictional 'Mozart narrative' takes a different view of things[91]). Since both composer and librettist worked in the same place and in the closest personal contact, there are no letters between them to shed light on this question.

With its contrast between superstition and wisdom, *The Magic Flute* owes much to the model of *religio duplex*, while at the same time treating this model not as an ideal, but as a provisional state to

be overcome in the fullness of time. This faithfully reflects the programme of the Iluminati, who tolerated the alliance between Enlightenment and secrecy as a merely temporary pact necessitated by the
inhospitable climate of the times. In *The Magic Flute*, 'soon' and
'then' are the keywords which register this consciousness of living in
a time of transition, a time already brightened by the dawning of a
better future. Freedom of thought, the primacy of reason, concord,
equality, and fraternity on the basis of good laws: these and other
Enlightenment ideals may not yet have been realized and may still
need to be attained, but they appear on the horizon as short-term
goals. This 'soon' characterizes the time of the opera; it refers in the
foreground to the imminent fulfilment of Tamino's and Papageno's
longing for love, and in the background to the impending reign of
light and reason ('Soon superstition shall vanish'). This hope determines the opera's thematic content on two levels: on the level of the
individual lifetime in the sense of 'soon' (the hope that Tamino might
'soon' pass the tests), and on the level of historical time in the sense
of 'then' ('then earth will be a realm of heaven').[92] In *The Magic Flute*,
the time of transition extends from the fairly recent rule of Pamina's
father, who has handed down in trust the instrument and emblem of
his rule, the 'sevenfold circle of the sun', to the priestly Order, to the
approaching coronation of Pamina and Tamino; in the conception of
history developed by the masons, and especially the Illuminati, it
extends all the way back to a primeval age pre-dating even the ancient
Egyptians. According to the Illuminati, the loss of paradisiacal
freedom went hand in hand with the establishment of states, and it
can only be regained through their abolition. *The Magic Flute* does
not go quite so far. Sovereign authority is not to be abolished but
tempered with virtue and justice:

> When virtue and justice
> Strew with fame the path of the great,
> Then earth is a realm of heaven,
> And mortals are like gods.

Tamino and Pamina's path of initiation, like the formative journey
embarked on by the hero of the education novel, depicts in miniature
the historical process of universal Enlightenment.

The libretto of *The Magic Flute* has been much maligned, above
all due to the supposed illogicality of its plot structure. The charge
of illogicality, at least, can be refuted in the light of the mysteries
theory elaborated by the Viennese lodge on the basis of Warburton
and Terrasson's research, as I will show in what follows. This requires

Table 1

Initial situation	First stage	Second stage	Third stage
The illusions of popular religion	Purification (disillusionment: liberation from illusions)	Lesser mysteries: trials, teaching	Greater mysteries: near-death experience, epopty (vision of truth)

that a slight adjustment be made to Warburton's schema, such that the neophyte's disillusionment now moves further to the front, to the beginning of his path of induction, as shown in table 1.

The neophyte must first break free of the illusions and fictions of popular religion in which he has previously lived. That is a painful process, since it leads him from light into darkness, from the above-ground world into the underworld. The light of popular religion proves to have been a false light, but it initially makes way not for the true light but for darkness. The youth, hitherto so sure of his way, loses his bearings and becomes a 'seeker'. That is the masonic concept for the neophyte who requests admission into the lodge and volunteers to undergo the process of initiation. As a seeker, Tamino walks the path from darkness to the true light, a path that divides into two phases: the lesser and greater mysteries. All are admitted to the lesser mysteries, where they are tested and offered instruction; that is why even Papageno makes it this far. Entrance to the greater mysteries, by contrast, is reserved only for the strongest and noblest natures, those who are called to rule, and even then only after a prolonged period of preparation. Here they are subjected to nothing less than a confrontation with death. The decisive, oft-cited passage occurs in a fragment ascribed to Plutarch. Only those who have passed through these mortal terrors are qualified to contemplate the truth.[93]

Let us now examine the opera in the light of this information. *The Magic Flute* is an opera in two acts, each of which is divided in turn into two roughly equal halves: a sequence of numbers with spoken dialogue and a through-composed finale. We thus have four sections, and Mozart has emphasized this structure by ending each section in the same key signature in which it began. If we attempt to project the phases of induction onto these four sections, we arrive at the structure shown in table 2.

The opening scenes in the realm of the Queen of the Night, including the scene with Monostatos and Pamina in the 'Egyptian room',

Table 2

ACT ONE		ACT TWO	
Part One	Part Two	Part Three	Part Four
Overture and No. 1 to No. 7 Duet	Finale	No. 9 March to No. 20 Aria	Finale
Illusion: Tamino enters the realm of the Queen of the Night and adopts her view of things ('rescue the abducted princess')	*Disillusion:* Tamino begins to suspect the real state of affairs and turns into a 'seeker'	*Lesser mysteries (with Papageno):* First test: resisting the Three Ladies Second test: silence towards the beloved	*Greater mysteries (without Papageno):* Near-death experiences (Pamina's suicide attempt, passage through fire and water, 'night and death', enlightenment)
E flat major	C major	F major	E flat major

have their counterpart in popular religion. They thus serve to cast a spell of illusion over Tamino and the spectators. The second section brings Tamino's disillusionment in the speaker's scene. He enters this scene full of self-certainty: 'To me, rescuing Pamina is a duty.' And he leaves it in an utterly benighted state of disorientation: 'Oh endless night, when will you pass?' He has cast aside his illusions but still wanders in the dark. In short, he has become a seeker.

The first part of Act Two is devoted to the lesser mysteries, to which Papageno is also admitted. They consist of three stages: the postulants are offered instruction; they are transported through darkness, thunder and lightning into a state of fear and terror; and they must learn to exercise self-control by maintaining silence towards the women who are trying to seduce them into speaking.

The next section, the second Finale, delivers the greater mysteries. Here it is a question of death and enlightenment. Only those destined to rule, we recall, are authorized to take this final step; that is why Papageno has no place here. Death is continually being invoked in this section: it begins with Pamina's suicide attempt; then we find Tamino before the gates of terror, 'which threaten danger and death for me'; 'if he can conquer the fear of death', the armoured men sing, 'he will soar from the earth up to heaven'. Surprisingly, Pamina, 'a woman unafraid of darkness and death', turns up here as well, and the two lovers 'by the power of music [. . .] walk cheerfully through the dark night of death'. Papageno, tormented by pangs of love, likewise arrives at the threshold of death and also wants to take his own life; through this experience he proves himself worthy of salvation, if not enlightenment, and gets his Papagena. Tamino and Pamina, however, are rewarded with enlightenment at the end: 'the theatre transforms into a sun', the stage directions read.

Mozart not only remained an active member of the lodge until the end of his life – his last completed composition, KV 623, was written to consecrate a new 'temple' – but apparently even toyed with the idea of establishing his own lodge. In 1800, Constanze sent the music publishers Breitkopf and Härtel 'an essay, in large part written in my husband's hand, about an order or society he wanted to set up, called Grotta'; unfortunately, the essay has gone missing. Constanze's two letters to the publishing house relating to this matter date from 27 November 1799 and 21 July 1800. The name 'La Grotta' evidently refers to a *fabrique* or garden folly that featured heavily in contemporary landscape design. It was particularly popular in parks owned by freemasons, and one would probably not be mistaken to see it as an imitation of the legendary subterranean installations built by the Egyptians. Such grottoes, which usually included a waterfall and sometimes also a cluster of quasi-Egyptian statues, could be found in many masonic gardens around Salzburg and Vienna. Descriptions of these grottoes sometimes read like stage directions for *The Magic Flute*. The name contemplated by Mozart for his future lodge was thus anything but casually chosen. It combined impressions of these masonic gardens with the idea of a 'subterranean Egypt', as described above all by Anton Kreil in his lodge lectures on ancient Egyptian 'scientific freemasonry': 'In short, everything was pocked and interlaced with grottoes, caves and underground passages. One finds that, wherever the Egyptian mysteries were adopted, they tended also to be celebrated in grottoes or underground caves.'[94]

Although the specific goals that informed Mozart's plan can no longer be ascertained with any certainty, one thing seems clear: in one crucial respect, this lodge would have emancipated itself from the laws of freemasonry by standing open to both sexes. Schikaneder's libretto has often been criticized as particularly tasteless on account of the misogynist utterances of Sarastro and his sphere: 'A woman does little, chatters a lot'; 'for without him [the husband] all women tend to stray outside their own sphere of activity'; 'Beware of womanly wiles: this is the brotherhood's first duty!' But this reproach fails to take into account that the hierarchy and ideas of the Sarastro world are themselves belied by the subsequent course of events. When Pamina takes Tamino by the hand – 'I myself shall lead you; love guides me' – to venture with him the passage through fire and water, she refutes Sarastro's 'a man must guide your steps', such that, by the end, even the priests are forced to concede that 'a woman unafraid of darkness and death is worthy and will be consecrated'. Through their joint consecration, the provisional reign of the Order is overcome, and with it the rigid antagonism that speaks even through the critique of religion found in the writings of the 'True Concord' circle. *The Magic Flute* thus practises enlightenment not only insofar as it participates in the masonic Enlightenment of the Viennese scene, but even and especially insofar as it goes beyond it.

5

In the Era of Globalization
Religio Duplex as Dual Membership

> If the world continues to exist for countless numbers of years, the universal religion will be a purified Spinozism. Reason, left to itself, leads to nothing else, and it is impossible that it should.
>
> G. Chr. Lichtenberg[1]

Globalization, Cosmopolitanism and Cultural Memory

Waves of globalization and universalist initiatives

Some years ago, Walter Mignolo suggested that a distinction be made between 'global designs' and 'cosmopolitan projects'.[2] Whereas global designs envisage an economic, political or cultural unification of the world 'from above', cosmopolitan projects understand themselves as a counter-movement which strives to create conditions for the peaceful coexistence, or 'conviviality', of different cultures and nations. Together, they make up what Mignolo calls 'coloniality', the signature of a globalized modernity. 'Coloniality' designates a world that is both constituted and riven by the 'colonial difference' between colonizing and colonized societies. Guided by this concept, Mignolo shifts the origins of modernity as an age of globalization, which historians usually place in the late eighteenth century, back to the Renaissance.

The history of 'global designs' can be traced much further back in time, however, and the history of 'cosmopolitan projects' likewise has roots in antiquity. Whether the world which 'global designs' make it their mission to unify coincides with what we know and conceive today as the 'global(ized)' or 'planetary' world is not important; what matters instead is what was understood by the 'world' as the sum of all known countries and peoples. The experience of globalization, in the sense of a unification of the world, gets under way once people have the impression of living in a single world with all other known nations, tribes and kingdoms, however broadly or narrowly circumscribed the horizon of that world may be. This unification of the world typically results when the network of trade contacts extends to the four corners of the world as it is known at the time. That was probably first the case in the late Bronze Age (1500–1100 BCE), when the 'ancient world' constituted itself as a field of interlinked, interacting states.[3] This form of globalization – presumably the first – can be characterized as 'internationalism'. It rests on the construction of a common framework, a platform of shared norms and principles, on the basis of which individual nations can draw up treaties, wage wars, establish trade relations, exchange emissaries and gifts and, in short, enter into all possible kinds of relationships with each other. The common framework was both cultural (through the introduction of Babylonian as a lingua franca) and religious (through the cultural technique of religious translatability). Treaties had to be sealed by solemn oaths and the gods who were invoked in these oaths had to be recognized by both parties. It was therefore imperative that relations of equivalence could be established between the gods by whom oaths were sworn. This cultural technique was already pioneered by the Mesopotamians in the third millennium BCE, when the bilingualism of this culture made it necessary to correlate Sumerian and Akkadian deities. In the late Bronze Age it spread throughout the entire known world and made possible its unification.[4] The 'ancient world' emerged around 1500 BCE with the entry of Egypt and the Aegean into the network described by Volkert Haas as the 'Near Eastern cultural *koine*'.[5]

This network collapsed with the transition to the Ice Age (1100–800), only to be built up anew from the eighth century BCE under quite different circumstances. Now the quest for unification no longer reflected the search for international contacts but was pursued in the interest of imperial hegemony. This model of globalization merits the name 'imperialism'.[6] It was complemented by the ancient form of colonialism through emigration and trading colonies; it was in this form that the Phoenicians and Greeks, for example, vied with each other for supremacy in the Mediterranean in the first half of the first millennium BCE. The Assyrians had already beaten them to it with the network of trading colonies they established in the Near East from the early second millennium. They were also the first who, in consequentially and aggressively pushing the goal of an imperialistic unification of the world, extended their borders far beyond their traditional territory, building up an ethnically diverse, multifaith, polyglot state. In this project they were followed by the Babylonians and surpassed by the Persians, who themselves had to make way for the even vaster empire of Alexander and its various successor states. The last, practically global mega-empire in this series, dwarfing all its predecessors, was the Roman Empire.

Each of these steps towards globalization was accompanied by the emergence of universal ideas and cosmopolitan concepts. The first stirrings of universalistic thought coincided with the rise of the great empires in the East (Assyrians, Babylonians, Persians) and helped give shape to the period referred to by Karl Jaspers as the 'axial age'.[7] By that he meant an epoch of intellectual breakthroughs, occurring at roughly the same time in China (Confucius, Laozi, Mencius), India (Buddha), Persia (Zoroaster), Israel (Isaiah) and Greece (the pre-Socratics, Plato, Aristotle), which collectively brought forth the (intellectual) world we still live in today: here, too, a genealogy of modernity.[8] The philosophies (Greece, China) and world religions (Zoroastrianism, Judaism, Buddhism) to which this epoch gave rise can be understood as 'cosmopolitan projects' in Mignolo's sense of the term. The Hellenistic-Roman epoch, the 'ecumenic age' (Eric Voegelin[9]), witnessed the birth of a cosmopolitan consciousness, particularly associated with Stoicism, that affirmed the notion of 'man' as a global citizen and the idea that all gods and religions are ultimately one and the same. The Book of Daniel in the Bible, written towards the beginning of this epoch in the second century BCE, introduced the idea that empires succeed each other in time as well as supplanting each other in space, a concept that decisively influenced Western thought right through to modernity.[10]

After the fall of the Roman Empire, the Arabs took up the imperial project of globalization, conceived for the first time as the unification of the world under one religion. They amassed a comparably large empire by embarking on an unprecedented campaign of conquest. For all its violence and impatience towards 'infidels', the Arab globalization of the world between the seventh and twelfth centuries at least developed a model of tolerance in its concept of the three 'book religions' – the basis for the ring parable in Lessing's *Nathan der Weise* (*Nathan the Wise*), as we will see in the next section. From the fifteenth century onwards, Europe then launched a counter-movement that brought it, in the course of military conquests and colonizing expeditions, voyages of discovery and trade missions, to the furthest reaches of a new, now truly global world. New cosmopolitan projects corresponded to this wave of globalization, as Walter Mignolo has emphasized in relation to Spain and the New World.

The European Enlightenment reacted to the modern unification of the world with new cosmopolitan and universalistic concepts which were now no longer grounded in theology, like the *orbis Christianus* of the Renaissance, but in philosophy.[11] The Christian tradition was relativized as late antique and Arabic alternatives came into view. That is especially true of the concept of a 'natural theology' (*theologia naturalis*), for which models could be found above all in Stoic cosmotheism, but also in the Arab world. One such model was the novel *Haiy Ibn Yaqzan* (*Alive, Son of Awake*) by the Andalusian doctor Abu Bakr Ibn Tufail (1110–85).[12] Taking as its point of departure the question of what kind of religion and theology would be conceived by a man who grew up on a desert island, bereft of any tradition, guidance or revelation and wholly dependent on his observations of nature, the novel can be read as a *Bildungsroman avant la lettre*. It was translated into several European languages in the seventeenth and eighteenth centuries and enjoyed considerable success. Lessing no doubt was familiar with it.

All gods are one: religious cosmopolitanism

The secret societies of the late eighteenth century, above all the Illuminati, pledged themselves to developing universalistic ideas and cosmopolitan projects in a quite special way. 'The mason', we read in a manifesto of the Viennese 'True Concord' lodge, 'serves all humanity, serves it in all zones, under all forms of government, in public or in secret; how then can one country, one fraction of the earth's surface, make exclusive claims on his heart?'[13] The mason is a cosmopolitan. I will come back to this link between masonry and cosmopolitanism a little later. For now, what interests me is how the late eighteenth century reprised the universalistic-cosmopolitan conceptions of earlier epochs. In the cosmopolitanism of the Illuminati, in particular, we find repeated the same basic attitude to life prevalent in late antiquity, which had already arrived at similar ideas when confronted with similar experiences of a globalizing convergence of peoples in the Roman Empire. This attitude finds typical expression in a masonic cantata by Mozart, set to a text by Franz Heinrich Ziegenhagen (KV 619):

You who revere the
Creator of the boundless universe,
Call him Jehovah or God,
Call him Fu, or Brahma.
Hark! Hear the words
From the trumpet of the Almighty!
Its eternal sound rings out
Through planets, moons and suns.
Mankind, listen to it too!
Love me in my works, love order, regularity and harmony!
Love yourselves and your brothers!
Let physical strength and beauty be your adornment, clarity of
    understanding your nobility![14]
Extend to one another the eternal hand of brotherly friendship
    which a delusion, not truth, has deprived you of for so long!
Smash the bonds of this illusion, rip to shreds the veil of this
    prejudice,
Divest yourselves of the garment which cloaked mankind in
    sectarianism!
Turn into sickles the iron that hitherto shed the blood of men!
Blow up rocks with the black powder which often discharged bullets
    into a brother's heart!
Do not imagine that true unhappiness exists on my earth! [. . .][15]

'Call him Fu [Buddha], or Brahma' – the name hardly matters. All particular religions ultimately gesture towards the same all-one concealed god, and all in their own way embellish this *deus absconditus* with the names, rites and images which the people demand, and which the wise men who rule over them relativize with an eye to the concealed truth, without thereby devaluing such trappings and declaring them to be indifferent; for they know that the truth is aimed at, if never actually captured, in these names, rites and images. Goethe encapsulated this attitude to life in the formula: 'Names are sound and smoke', while Schiller expressed it in a couplet:

You ask which religion I profess?
None! And why? From religion.

Schiller uses the word 'religion' in a twofold sense here which we will re-encounter in more recent authors in the next chapter. Religion is the particular, historical religion someone professes as the member of a religious community, and it is also knowledge of a concealed, universal truth ultimately aimed at by all religions, coupled with respect for the paths taken by other religions.

Hellenistic cosmopolitan motifs resurface in the eighteenth century with this awareness of a concealed truth common to all religions and the idea that all names given to their gods by the nations and religions of the world ultimately refer to the same universal deity. Cultural memory furnishes the conceptual categories and historical examples with which the epoch articulates its new attitude to life. A favourite citation of the eighteenth century, for example, is an epigram which the late Roman poet Ausonius had engraved on a statue of Liber Pater at his country estate, Lucaniacus. It bears the inscription: 'An Outlandish Medley to a Marble Statue of Liber Pater in My Country House, Having the Attributes of All Gods' – the personification of multireligious hybridity, so to speak.[16] I give the text according to the edition and translation by Hugh G. Evelyn White:

> The sons of Ogyges call me Bacchus,
> Egyptians think me Osiris,
> Mysians name me Phanaces,
> Indians regard me as Dionysus,
> Roman rites make me Liber,
> The Arab race thinks me Adoneus,
> Lucaniacus the Universal God.[17]

Another of the most frequently cited texts of enlightened cosmopolitanism was a passage from the *Metamorphoses* of Apuleius; it is referred to by Toland in his *Clidophorus*, for example. It lists the predications ascribed to Isis as a supreme goddess encompassing all other (female) deities. Having been transformed into an ass and survived countless scrapes and misadventures, Lucius awakens on the shore of the Mediterranean near Thebes as the full moon rises over the sea. He witnesses a theophany that prompts him to address the moon in the following terms:

> O Queen of Heaven – whether thou art Ceres, the primal and bountiful mother of crops [. . .], or whether thou art heavenly Venus who [. . .] art worshipped in the shrine of Paphos, or the sister of Pheobus who [. . .] art now adored in the temples of Ephesus, or whether as Proserpine . . . thou art propitiated with differing rites – whoever thou art, [. . .] by whatever name or ceremony or face thou art rightly called, help me now in the depth of my trouble.[18]

The goddess answers him in a dream and begins her self-presentation with a catalogue of names:

> Lo, I am with you, Lucius, moved by your prayers, I who am the mother of the universe, the mistress of all the elements, the first off-spring of time, the highest of deities, the queen of the dead, foremost of heavenly beings, the single form that fuses all gods and goddesses; I who order by my will the starry heights of heaven, the health giving breezes of the sea, and the awful silences of those in the underworld: my single godhead is adored by the whole world in varied forms, in differing rites and with many diverse names. Thus the Phrygians [. . .] call me Pessinuntia [. . .]; the Athenians [. . .] call me Cecropeian Minerva; the Cyprians [. . .] call me Paphian Venus, the Cretans Dictynna, the Sicilians Ortygian Proserpine; to the Eleusinians I am Ceres, to others Juno, to others Bellona and Hecate and Rhamnusia. But the Ethiopians, together with the Egyptians who excel by having the original doctrine, honour me with my distinctive rites and give me my true name of Queen Isis.

The goddess presents herself as a supreme deity who unites all the gods and goddesses in her appearance (*facies*: the moon) and is worshipped by different nations under different names and rituals. That is the Hellenistic, globalized form of the ancient Egyptian cultic topography. But alongside these many ethnic names she also has a 'true name', albeit one used only by the nations boasting the oldest and most authentic tradition: the Egyptians and the Ethiopians.[19] That does not make the other names 'false', nor does it degrade the rites practised by other nations into idolatry and superstition. These countless cults do not err in not knowing the right name; rather, each communicates with the deity in its own way. Among all these cults, Philae enjoys the status of a centre, but it does not hold a monopoly on religious truth.

This globalized form of predication is especially characteristic for the Hellenistic Isis. One of four hymns which Isidorus of Narmuthis had engraved on pillars in the temple of Thermuthis at Medinet Mad (first century BCE)[20] reads:

> All mortals who live on the boundless earth,
> Thracians, Greeks and Barbarians,
> Express your fair name, a name greatly honoured among all.
> [But] each speaks in his own language, in his own land.
> The Syrians call you: Astarte, Artemis, Nanaia,
> The Lycian tribes call you Leto, the lady.

The Thracians also name you as Mother of the gods,
And the Greeks [call you] Hera of the Great Throne, Aphrodite,
Hestia the goodly, Rhea and Demeter.
But the Egyptians call you Thiouis[21] [because they know] that you,
being one, are all other goddesses invoked by the races of men.[22]

Late antiquity's fundamental belief in the universality of religious
truth and the relativity of religious institutions and names, which
resonates so strongly in the eighteenth century, manifests itself in this
tradition of calling the supreme deity by whatever name it happens
to be given in different nations. In his text *On Isis and Osiris*, widely
read in the eighteenth century, Plutarch could write at the beginning
of the second century that, 'in the same way as the sun, the moon,
the sky, the earth and the sea, which are common to everybody, bear
different names among different people,' so too 'the sole reason
(*logos*) which has laid out all things, the sole providence which
governs all [. . .] have different honours, titles and holy symbols
among the different peoples'.[23]

Like the author of the poem set to music by Mozart, Celsus could
argue in his text against the Christians that 'it makes no difference
whether you call God the Most High, or Zeus, or Adonai, or Sabaoth,
or Amun like the Egyptians, or Pappaeus like the Scythians'.[24] At
the very birth hour of the first 'world religions', Judaism and Christianity, which insisted on professing the *one*, irreplaceable name,
there rose up against them a world religion in the literal sense of the
term, albeit one that could never exist as a religion as such, only as
the cosmopolitan wisdom of the concealed convergence of all religions. This basic attitude towards life and the world recurred in the
epoch of the Islamic global empire, from the eleventh to the thirteenth
centuries, and again in the epoch of European Enlightenment following on from the worldwide conquests of the sixteenth and seventeenth
centuries.

The parable of the ring: tolerance as a cosmopolitan project

Perhaps the most prominent example of such a resuscitation of cultural memory is the parable of the ring in Lessing's *Nathan the Wise*
(published in 1779 and first performed in 1783, two years after
Lessing's death). The idea that a universal yet concealed truth stands
behind the various religious traditions here receives more forceful and
representative expression than in any other eighteenth-century text.[25]
The parable of the ring relativizes the truth claims made by the three

monotheistic faiths. All three lay claim to an absolute truth which, although vital for the salvation of all humankind, could only have been bestowed on one of them by divine revelation. The parable relativizes this claim without denouncing it as mendacious or fraudulent, and it thereby performs a balancing act between two positions which, in the eighteenth century more than any other, had been placed in a high state of intellectual and spiritual tension. On one side stood the orthodox positions claiming sole validity for their own version of the truth: the hierarchy of the Catholic Church, but also the rabbinate, which banished Moses Mendelssohn, and the institutions of Lutheran and Reformed orthodoxy. On the other side, the atheism of the radical Enlightenment expressed itself with a hitherto unheard-of radicalism in the 'priestly fraud' thesis, voiced in treatises like the infamous *De tribus impostiborus* (*On the Three Imposters*), in the writings of Thierry d'Holbach, and in countless unpublished manuscripts of a clandestine controversial theology.[26] It was a stroke of genius on Lessing's part to offer this spiritually divided century a solution in the simple form of the parable.

All the more surprising, then, that this parable, however much it may seem custom-made for the spiritual situation of the time around 1780, was in fact an *objet trouvé*, a find from a quite different era. According to Lessing's own testimony, he took it from Boccaccio's *Decameron*, written in the plague year of 1348.[27] That takes us back more than 400 years, but Boccaccio, too, would have chanced upon the story somewhere else rather than thinking it up for himself. The most likely historical context for the genesis of the ring parable is that of the medieval religious dialogues, conducted between representatives of the three religions (Judaism, Christianity and Islam) in the Islamic world, in Baghdad and Andalusia. While these constituted a literary genre in their own right, they certainly also took place in the form of actual disputations. Islam was experiencing something of an enlightenment at the time, which had an influence on Judaism (Maimonides) and Christianity (Thomas Aquinas) as well.[28] Even if Islam naturally upheld the superior truth of the Koran, the conception of the three holy books and the three book religions, the 'people of the book' (*ahl al kitāb*), still implied an idea of tolerance that was far in advance of anything the West had to offer at the time. The ring parable could only have arisen from this fertile ground.[29] With that we have arrived in the very time and in the very world where Lessing sets his *Nathan*, and our admiration for his feat of cultural 'recycling' grows ever greater. Lessing transcribed the parable almost word for word. Only the motif of the real ring's power 'to render of God and man beloved' is missing in Boccaccio, and with it the figure of the 'modest judge' who advises the three brothers to display this power by performing good deeds.

The basic idea behind the parable – that the truth is concealed and that there is nonetheless an authoritative revelation – goes even further back in time. According to Diodorus, Isis made some twenty-five replicas of the mummified body of her husband Osiris and gave one to each province of Egypt. She assured each province that it had received the god's real body, and hence the true tomb of Osiris, but this knowledge was to be kept strictly secret.[30] We can thus isolate three temporal layers in the parable of the ring: the ancient enlightenment that gave rise to the Isis legend; the twelfth-century Islamic-Jewish enlightenment that gave rise to the ring parable; and the European Enlightenment in which Lessing re-actualized that parable.

The question of truth is bracketed out in the ring parable. That there is such a thing as the truth is never called into doubt. The true ring exists but it cannot be determined; the truth is concealed and can only ever be aimed at, never directly possessed. We must, as Goethe says, 'divine it from its manifestations'. For Lessing, these manifestations consist in deeds. What causes the truth to be made manifest is not the best theology but the best praxis – that best suited to making the agent 'beloved of God and[31] man'. What matters is thus not what one knows about God but how one lives one's life, quite in keeping with Mendelssohn's understanding of the Mosaic laws (to be explored in the next section), but also with the masonic ideal of beneficence. Secrecy has withdrawn from the sphere of esoteric doctrine into the absolute unfathomability of authenticity or truth.

Lessing's drama, and the parable staged at its heart, can only fully be understood when we take into account the highly polemical context in which the play intervenes. With his dramatization of the anecdote about Saladin and the rich Jew Melchizedek, Lessing marks out his position in a theological controversy that preoccupied both him and a large part of the critical public sphere in Germany (which Lessing's writings had done much to create) during the last seven years of his life.

From 1770, Lessing was employed as librarian in Wolfenbüttel, where he edited a series 'On History and Literature: From the Treasures of the Ducal Library in Wolfenbüttel'. Importantly, this series was exempt from censorship. From 1774 to 1778, he published in it six excerpts from a manuscript which, far from numbering among the treasures of the Wolfenbüttel collection, had been given him by the heirs of its author, the Hamburg Orientalist Hermann Samuel Reimarus.[32] Its purported discovery in the library was intended to bypass the censor's office, which would otherwise never have cleared this work for publication. Reimarus was a radical deist who recognized only the natural religion of reason and rejected all revelation. In the fragments edited by Lessing, he denied both the Old and New Testaments any 'divinity', interpreting them instead as purely human, historical products. Lessing's actual aim with this publication was to provoke the so-called 'neologists', a school of Protestant theologians who sought a compromise with deism and set out to reduce Christianity to a moral doctrine compatible with reason. Lessing wanted to show them what radical deism entailed, where it leads and how impossible such a compromise would be. He also felt obliged to defend religion against the anonymous author's attacks by adding his own 'editor's counterpropositions' to the fragments.[33]

   These counterpropositions, however, represented the real provocation. They brought not only the neologists into the fray but the orthodox clergy as well, above all the Hamburg chief pastor Johan Melchior Goeze, a disputatious theologian and battle-hardened polemicist who saw it as his spiritual duty to oppose all false doctrines vehemently and without delay.[34] Lessing had argued in his 'counterpropositions' that a distinction needed to be made between the letter and the spirit, that is, between the Bible and religion: 'In short, the letter is not the spirit, and the Bible is not religion. Consequently, objections to the letter and to the Bible are not by the same token objections to the spirit and to religion.'[35] The Bible, both Old Testament and New, was an historical document and a human artefact. This much he was prepared to concede to Reimarus. Religion, however, was a different matter altogether. *It* comes from God, and the Bible contains only so much of it as could be grasped by the people for whom it was written. At the same time, the Bible includes a great deal that goes beyond true religion. These additions were fabricated for the sake of improved public understanding. The Bible *contains* religion without being identical to it. Religion existed before the Bible, the Gospels were written long after Christ's death, and it was later still that the Church Fathers propounded their dogmas concerning the Trinity and the exact nature of Christ, matters passed over in silence in the New Testament. Enlightened Bible criticism therefore does not apply to religion itself, only to its textual fixation. Lessing is perfectly happy to concede to his unnamed antagonist that the Bible qua human, historical document is riddled with contradictions and irrational reports. For all that, the truth of religion is left intact.

   To the orthodox Lutheran Goeze, who insisted on the principle of *sola scriptura*, Lessing's defence of religion must have seemed far more scandalous than the attacks mounted against it by the anonymous author. The Bible is the word of God, His absolute, absolutely definitive revelation, the sole foundation of religion. Whoever calls scripture into question has left the fold of the Protestant Church. Goeze repeatedly challenges Lessing, in the peremptory tone of a grand inquisitor, to declare what he actually believes in, accusing him of being just as much a deist, just as attached to natural religion, as his ostensible adversary. Lessing, in other words, is an enemy of revelation.

Goeze composed several polemics against Lessing, and Lessing responded in kind with no fewer than eleven essays. In these essays, collected under the title *Anti-Goeze* I–XI, Lessing demonstrates his superiority over his opponent in two ways: not only does he emerge – needless to say – as the incomparably more brilliant, multifaceted and imaginative essayist; he also shows himself the more knowledgeable and able theologian, better versed in history and less constrained by dogma. Lessing's father was a theologian of the same orthodox observance as Goeze. There was thus something of a belated father–son conflict to his quarrel with the Hamburg chief pastor. During his time in Wittenberg (1752–4), Lessing had been much concerned with theological questions of interreligious tolerance, and he had devoted his final years in Breslau (1763–5) to studying the early history of Christianity, the genesis of the canon and the Church Fathers. Asked by Goeze what he actually believed in, if not in scripture and its absolute truth, his answer was the *regula fidei*: Christ's core message, which had not been set down in writing once and for all but could be expressed in various ways. Based on the oral transmission of the disciples, it could help us better understand the writings of the early Church as well as provide us with a criterion for their canonicity.[36] Although Lessing's arguments were couched in historical and cultural terms, they were informed by his abiding theological interest in revoking the Church's absolute claim to truth and reformulating the concept of revelation.

As the ever more heated controversy with Goeze threatened to descend into a mud-slinging contest, Duke Karl not only cancelled Lessing's censorship privileges but banned him from penning any more theological-critical polemics. Lessing was thus forced to turn to other genres. One such instance was his philosophical text on the *Erziehung des Menschengeschlechts* (*Education of the Human Race*), the first part of which he had already appended to his 'Counterpropositions'.[37] Distancing himself from Reimarus, the radical opponent of revelation, Lessing makes clear there in what sense he is prepared to accept the idea of a revealed truth: not as a one-off historical event

but as a continuously unfolding, trans-historical process; a phyloge-
netic education, so to speak, which transcends human reason only to
the extent that it spurs it on. Here, too, an attempt is made to scale
down the concept of revelation advanced by positive religion until it
no longer clashes with the principles of the natural religion of reason.
Nathan the Wise needs to be seen in this context. It takes up the
controversy with Goeze at another level and represents the twelfth
'Anti-Goeze', so to speak. In a letter to his brother, dated 7 November
1778, Lessing writes that he chose this subject matter because it
would enable him 'to fall into the enemy's flanks from another side'.[38]
The play's direct relevance to the Goeze controversy is further underscored in a letter from 6 September 1778 to his friend Elise Reimarus,
the anonymous writer's daughter. Informing her of the ducal prohibition on indulging in any more theological polemics, he adds: 'I must
see whether I will at least be allowed to preach undisturbed from my
old pulpit, the theatre.'[39] The Nathan drama was written with polemics rather than edification in mind, as the following remarks likewise
attest: 'It will be enough if, [. . .] among a thousand readers, only
one learns to doubt the evidence and universality of his religion.'
'Nathan's attitude towards *every* positive religion has always been
my own.'

'Positive' religion stands opposed to 'natural' religion. The former
finds support in a canon of revealed texts and their orthodox interpretation. The latter means, in Lessing's words, 'recogniz[ing] one
God [and] try[ing] to form the worthiest ideas of him. [. . .] Every
human being, in proportion to his powers, is disposed and committed
to this natural religion.'[40] Yet Lessing by no means wants to reject
positive, revealed religion in favour of its natural counterpart. 'The
indispensability of a positive religion, whereby natural religion is
modified in each state according to that state's natural and fortuitous
condition, I call its inner truth; and this inner truth is as great in one
as in the other. All positive and revealed religions are consequently
equally true and equally false.'[41] This is precisely the message of the
ring parable. They are equally true and equally false because they are
all equidistant from the concealed truth envisaged by natural religion.
There are nonetheless differences between them: 'The *best* revealed
or positive religion is that which contains the fewest conventional
additions to natural religion, and imposes the fewest limitations on
the good effects of natural religion.'[42] Lessing's conception of *religio
duplex* allowed him, in Hugh Nisbet's words, 'to discover a certain
truth in revelation and natural religion alike, in both orthodox Christianity and Reimarus's critique of Christianity'.[43] This 'both/and' is
the principle of *religio duplex.*

Moses Mendelssohn and the Idea of a 'Religion of Mankind'

With the idea of a supra- or interreligion, a natural religion available to everyone regardless of their native positive religions, the principle of double religion – that is, the antithesis between popular religion and mysteries or superstition and wisdom – is universalized into an anthropological constant. That was already the case in Hellenism and late antiquity, when the Isis religion and philosophical movements like Stoic cosmotheism each regarded themselves as just such an inter-religion. The opposition between public and arcane religion becomes that between particular (or positive) and universal (or natural) religion. This transformed understanding of *religio duplex* was most clearly expressed by Moses Mendelssohn. In his account, 'popular religion' is represented by individual world religions like Christianity, Judaism and Islam, while the 'mysteries' become the foundation for a universal, natural and cosmopolitan theology shared by the entire human race. In his treatise *Jerusalem oder über religiöse Macht und Judentum (Jerusalem, or, On Religious Power and Judaism,* 1783),[44] he critically engaged with the idea of revelation, and the existence of sacred revealed scripture, which the competing world religions (and they alone) used to bolster their claim to ownership of exclusive salvific truths.

It should first be pointed out that neither the Egyptian mysteries nor dual religion, as we have understood it to this point, are discussed in Mendelssohn's text. Including his voice here entails a change of theme, or at least a drastic expansion and displacement of the thematic framework. That is precisely my intention, however. With the help of his treatise, I want to raise the theme of dual religion to a higher plane and place it in a setting that could make it interesting beyond the eighteenth century.

Mendelssohn's *Jerusalem* begins by investigating the relationship between the state and religion. The state's role is to promulgate laws and ensure that they are obeyed, thereby creating a space where all law-abiding citizens may live in peace and security. Religion's role is to develop principles, to justify moral convictions, and to inculcate values, attitudes and norms deriving from those convictions. The state is responsible for how people associate with each other, that is, for order and security. The rights and duties that result for humans as citizens must be regulated by *laws* and backed up by force, if necessary. Religion is responsible for how people associate with God. The rights and duties that result for humans from their relationship

with God are expressed in *commandments*. These can never be
backed up by force but can only be made comprehensible on rational
grounds. Once again, we recognize here Koselleck's distinction
between politics and morality. What is crucial is that Mendelssohn
reserves the application of force for the state: 'The state is armed with
physical force and makes use of it, if need be; the force of religion is
love and benevolence' (22). State and religion, however, do not exist
in isolation from each other; rather, it is the task of religion 'to con-
vince the people in the most emphatic manner of the truth of noble
sentiments and persuasions; to show them that duties to man are also
duties to God' (19). These duties to God and man include obedience
towards the state. This is the point at which state and religion come
together. On the basis of this separation of powers between state and
Church, Mendelssohn arrives at the radical conclusion that, in the
religious sphere, there can be no property, no rights, no laws and no
government or ecclesiastical authority of any kind. 'The weapons it
uses are grounds and convictions; its power is the divine force of
truth' (66). 'The right of proscribing and banishing,' the excom-
municate Mendelssohn continues, 'which the state, at times, may
think fit to exercise, is directly contrary to the spirit of religion' (66).
Mendelssohn demands that every form of ecclesiastical law be abolished since the use or threat of force required to implement this law
is incompatible with religion. As Mendelssohn explains, 'all ecclesiastical restraint is unlawful, all external authority in theological
matters, usurpation' (72).

Starting out from these reflections, Mendelssohn turns in the
second part of his investigation to address the problem of revelation,
and with it the distinction between nature and revelation that divided
the eighteenth-century world no less than the distinction between
politics and morality. Moses Mendelssohn shared with his contemporaries their predilection for thinking in antitheses. We have already
seen him making a distinction between politics and religion or state
and Church, ascribing law and force to the one side, truth and con-
viction to the other. He now introduces this distinction into the
religious sphere by differentiating between two forms of religion,
which – and this is what makes his conception so novel and so interesting in our context – are meant to complement rather than exclude
each other: revealed religion and natural religion. For this dualism to
be conceived in terms of complementarity rather than mutual exclusiveness, the concept of revelation with its uncircumventable, absolute claim to truth must first be taken down a notch or two. It cannot
refer to any absolute, universal truths that would license one religion
to exercise compulsion and force in their name.

In his preface to Manasseh Ben Israel's *Rettung der Juden (Vindication of the Jews*, 1782), Mendelssohn had already written:

> I know of no rights over persons and things that are connected to doctrinal opinions and rest upon them, rights that men acquire when they agree with certain statements and lose when they cannot consent to them or will not do so. Least of all do I know of any rights and powers over opinions granted by religion, and wielded by the Church. The true, divine religion does not arrogate any power with regard to opinions and judgments; does not give us any title on worldly goods, no right to consumption, possession and property; does not acknowledge any other power than the power to win with the help of reasons, to convince, and to make happy by way of conviction. The true, divine religion needs to use neither arms nor fingers; it is pure spirit and heart.[45]

For Mendelssohn, the 'true, divine religion' is religion as it should be, a regulative idea. Above all, it is a matter of nature, not revelation, hence a matter of reason, not faith. Any religion that considers itself obliged to impose its divinely revealed doctrinal opinions by means of force has already severed its connection to true religion. In Mendelssohn's eyes, the Jewish religion is not a religion of revelation at all:

> I believe that Judaism knows nothing of a revealed religion, in the sense in which it is taken by Christians. The Israelites have a divine legislation: laws, judgments, statutes, rules of life, information of the will of God, and lessons how to conduct themselves in order to attain both temporal and spiritual happiness: those laws, commandments, &c., were revealed to them through Moses, in a miraculous and supernatural manner; but no dogmas, no saving truths, no general self-evident positions. Those the Lord always reveals to us, the same as to the rest of mankind, *by nature and by events*; but never in *words* or *written characters* (89).

Judaism knows something of revelation, to be sure, but its validity is limited to the Jewish people rather than applying to humankind as a whole. Mendelssohn makes three distinctions here: first, between dogmas and 'rules of life'; second, between 'natural' and written revelation; and, third, between natural and supernatural revelation. Dogmas pertain to 'eternal truths'. From a Jewish point of view, they are naturally revealed to *all humankind* and can be read, at least in rough outline, by virtue of the reason with which we have been endowed by the creator. They are therefore a matter of reason, not of faith. According to the Jews, they can and should never be codified in writing: 'They were entrusted to living, intellectual instruction, which keeps pace with all the changes of times and circumstances' (110). To make this point clear, Mendelssohn distinguishes between two kinds of truth: 'eternal truths' and 'historical truths'. He further divides 'eternal truths' into 'necessary' truths – for example, the truths of mathematics and logic, which 'are true so and not otherwise, because they are thinkable so and not otherwise' (90) – and 'casual' truths, which are true because they happen to have been realized so and not otherwise (physical truths, for example). Truths of the former category come to light through proof, those of the latter through observation. Historical truths, by contrast, refer to 'things which did occur at one time and perhaps will never occur again' – for example, the exodus from Egypt – and 'propositions which, through a confluence of causes and effects, have become true in one point of space and time, and which, therefore, can be conceived as true in respect to that point of space and time only' – for example, the handing down of the commandments on Sinai (91). Historical truths can only be attested; they cannot be proven. 'In historical matters, the narrator's reputation and his credibility constitute the only evidence. We cannot be persuaded of any historical truth, unless by testimony. Were it not for authority, the truth of history would vanish along with the events themselves' (95). That is why historical truths need to be authenticated through words, writing and authority (for example, that of Moses). In other words, the revelation accorded the Jews is an historical truth, not an eternal truth.

Only 'historical' truths can and may be written down, not 'eternal' truths, and one such historical truth is the law revealed to Moses:

> I should think that, in respect to historical truths only, it was consistent with the dignity of Supreme Wisdom to instruct mankind in a human manner; that is, by means of words and writings [. . .]. But the eternal truths, so far as they are of use for the welfare and happiness of man, on the contrary, God teaches in a manner more to suit the Godhead; not by words or written characters, which may be intelligible here and there, to this or that man; but by creation itself, and its internal relations, which are legible and intelligible everywhere, and to all men. Nor does he certify them by signs and miracles, which effect only historical belief; but he stirs the mind created by him, and affords it an opportunity to observe those relations of things, to observe its own self, and to become persuaded of the truths of which it is destined to acquire knowledge here on earth. (95–6)

It is thus not only necessary to distinguish between nature and revelation, but also within revelation between natural and historical revelation. Natural revelation is ahistorical; it is equally accessible at all times to all human beings. Mendelssohn therefore explicitly contradicts his friend Lessing:

> I, for my own part, have no conception of an 'education of the human race', such as my late friend Lessing himself let some historiographer of mankind put into his head. They picture to themselves this collective thing, the 'human race', as a single individual, and think, Providence has put it here on earth, as it were, in a school, to be trained from an infant to an adult. In the main, the human race (if the metaphor will hold good) is, in almost every age, infant, adult, and greybeard at once, only in different places and regions. [. . .] Man goes on; but mankind is constantly swinging to and fro, within fixed boundaries; but, considered as a whole, retains, at all periods of time, about the same degree of morality, the same quantity of religion and irreligion, of virtue and vice, of happiness and misery [. . .] (99, 101)

Mendelssohn certainly did not subscribe to the nascent belief in progress shared by many of his contemporaries, at least insofar as humankind in general is concerned.

After this long excursus on the concepts of truth and history, Mendelssohn comes back to his main argument, which I would like to cite in the new and trenchant form in which it is repeated:

> Judaism boasts of no *exclusive* revelation of immutable truths indispensable to salvation; of no revealed religion in the sense in which that term is usually taken. Revealed *religion* is one thing, revealed *legislation* is another. The voice which was heard on *Sinai*, on that memorable day, did not say, 'I am the Lord, thy God, the eternal, self-existing Being, omnipotent and omniscient, who rewards men, in a future life, according to their works.' All this is the *universal religion of mankind*, and not Judaism. And it was not the universal religion of mankind, without which they can neither be virtuous nor saved, that was to be revealed there. [. . .] [The divine voice called out instead:] '*I am the Lord thy God, who led thee out of the land of Egypt; who delivered thee from bondage, &c.*' An historical fact, on which the legislation of that *particular people* was to be founded, since laws were to be revealed there; commandments, judgments, but no immutable theological truths. [. . .] All these are historical truths, from their nature, resting on historical evidence, which *must* be attested by authority, and *may* be corroborated by miracles. (102–4)

Revelation, then, is restricted to laws that have a particular – Jewish – validity. Yet it is also clear that this divine book [. . .] is well known to include withal an inscrutable treasure of rational truths and theological dogmas [. . .]. All the laws refer to or are founded on immutable self-evident truths, or put one in mind of, and cause one to ponder on them: hence our Rabbis justly observe, that the laws and dogmas stand in the same relation to each other as the body does to the soul. (105)

Or, as Paul says, as the letter does to the spirit (105). Here Mendelssohn is also alluding to the double meaning of the sign, the division of scripture into *sensus literalis* and *sensus mysticus*, in describing which he strikes an almost mystical tone:

The more you search therein, the more you are amazed at the depth of knowledge hid in it. [. . .T]he nearer you approach, the chaster, the more innocent, affectionate, and wishful the look with which you are gazing at her, the more she will unfold to you of her divine beauty, over which she throws a thin gauze, that it may not be profaned by vulgar and unholy eyes. (105–6)

In the *Zohar* it is written: 'The Holy One, blessed be He, enters all the hidden things that He has made into the holy Torah, and everything is found in the Torah. And the Torah reveals that hidden thing and then it is immediately clothed in another garment where it is hidden and not revealed.'[46] The Torah – the veiled image at Sinai. Neither dogmatic fidelity to the text nor blind faith, however, is capable of accessing the quite inexhaustible wealth of 'rational truths' to be discovered in the Torah. Rational truths are not believed in but recognized through reason; likewise, laws are not believed in but obeyed in confidence and trust. The Christian concept of faith is no less foreign to the Jewish religion than the Christian concept of revelation.

There is not, among all the precepts and tenets of the Mosaic law, a single one which says, 'Thou shalt believe this', or 'Thou shalt not believe it'; but they all say, 'Thou shalt do', or 'Thou shalt forbear' [. . .]. Nay, the word in the original language, which they are wont to translate 'to believe' [*emunah*, J.A.], in most cases, properly means 'to trust in', 'to rely on', 'to have full confidence in what is promised or caused to be expected'. (106)

This argumentation contains a striking paradox: through these laws, human action, which is irreducibly temporal and historically conditioned, is prescribed for all time (subject to divine repeal); yet insight into what might be considered atemporal, historically

invariable truths – the existence and essence of God, the meaning of
life, the immortality of the soul, and so on – can never be fixed once
and for all, only improvised in the form of oral commentary as
history unfolds. Higher, absolute truths are revealed, but they are
revealed to all people and never through the written or spoken word;
Moses was only given laws. We are dealing here with deeds rather
than beliefs, with orthopraxy rather than orthodoxy. Judaism rests
on the law, not on theology. The Jews are free to think whatever they
like about God, but they are beholden to obey the law.

Accordingly, there are no theological dogmas in the Bible.

> They were entrusted to living, intellectual instruction, which may keep
> pace with all the changes of times and circumstances, and be altered
> according to a pupil's exigencies, and suited to his abilities and powers
> of comprehension. [. . .] In the beginning, it was expressly forbidden
> to write more on the law than God had caused Moses to signify to the
> nation. 'What has been delivered to thee orally,' say the Rabbis, 'thou
> art not permitted to put down in writing.' (110–11)

It might be objected that Judaism is awash with textual commentary.
Mendelssohn claims that this was due to historical circumstances, the
expulsion of the Jews in the diaspora. 'They called that licence, the
destruction of the law; and said with the Psalmist: "There is a time
when we must make a law void for the sake of the Lord"' (111).
Through their dialogic set-up, however, the Talmud and Midrash
deliberately avoid any kind of theological-dogmatic fixation and
attempt to preserve the spirit of orality.[47]

In my books *Moses the Egyptian* (1997) and *The Price of Monotheism* (2003), I characterized the distinction between true and false
in the realm of religion as an achievement of monotheism, and I went
on to identify it as one of the sources of religious violence. Although,
historically speaking, Akhenaten may have been the first to make this
distinction and to impose it on his subjects by abolishing the old
religion and introducing a new one, I chose to associate it with the
biblical figure of Moses because it first made history in that form. It
is very significant in this context that the most influential conceptions
for relativizing and overcoming the Mosaic distinction arose from
within Judaism, the very religion that looks to Moses as its founding
father. Mendelssohn's distinction between Judaism and Christianity,
along with that between a 'universal religion of mankind' and individual religions, is a milestone on this path. In my eyes, moreover, it
speaks in Judaism's favour that it leaves the 'eternal truths' in a
state of discursive flux rather than seeking to set them in stone. The

'universal religion of mankind' can never be reduced to a system of binding precepts. Perhaps the linguistic distinction between surface structure and deep structure can furnish a model for the relationship between the 'universal religion of mankind' and the individual religions, which can and will only ever exist in the plural. The 'deep religion' revolves around eternal truths which can never be prescribed, only aimed at in discursive approximation; it forms the common reference point for the individual 'surface religions', which provide vital orientation and certainty within their respective spheres of influence. The problem with Christianity, in Mendelssohn's view, is that it tends to understand itself as the universal religion of mankind, as the expressive form assumed by 'deep religion' in the surface structure.[48] In this spirit, theologians like Karl Barth[49] and Dietrich Bonhoeffer[50] rejected the term 'religion' for Christianity, since religion only exists in irreducible plurality. With their cultic concretization and collectivization of the individual's intensely personal, spiritual relationship with God, religions are necessarily a form of idolatry. The then cardinal Joseph Ratzinger asserted: 'Christian faith is not based on poetry and politics, these two great sources of religion; it is based on knowledge. It is the worship of that being which is the foundation of everything that exists, the "true" God.'[51] All this entails an identification of Christianity with Mendelssohn's universal religion of mankind. In this regard, Christians will have to follow the example of Mendelssohn's Jews by stepping back and recognizing their religion as one among many, each of which worships 'the "true" God' in its own way[52] – or rather, which has long done so; for all these considerations are already contained in Lessing's ring parable, placed in the mouth of a Jew but addressed primarily to the author's fellow Christians, particularly the Hamburg chief pastor Johan Melchior Goeze. Such considerations belong on the higher plane of a wisdom untouched by theological dogmatism or scientific metaphysics, a wisdom found in all religions and directed at the point where they converge beyond all distinctions, including the Mosaic distinction.

Patriot and Cosmopolitan: Lessing's 'Ernst and Falk', with a Glance at Herder and Wieland

Like the drama *Nathan the Wise* and *The Education of the Human Race*, Lessing's 'dialogues for Freemasons' *Ernst and Falk*, published in 1778, were offshoots of the controversy with Goeze over orthodoxy and freedom.[53] These dialogues explicate the problem of tolerance by means of the dialectic of identity and difference. What unites us is also what divides us from everyone else. The first of the five conversations deals with the essence of freemasonry, a subject on which Ernst receives only vague and evasive answers to his queries from Falk. Lessing's reluctance to provide definitional clarity bespeaks the same wariness towards dogmatic stabilization which, in a different register, animates Mendelssohn's characterization of Judaism as a religion that entrusts general precepts on eternal truths to living dialogue but not to writing. Lessing, too, is content to leave in a state of 'discursive flux' the question of what the true, eternal and utopian freemasonry might be. In the following, lightly abridged passage from the second dialogue, however, he expresses its goals and purpose with the utmost clarity:

Falk.   [. . .] Then let us assume that the best constitution has been invented, and that everyone in the world lives under this constitution. Would everyone in the world therefore only constitute a single state?

Ernst. Well, hardly. Such an enormous state would be impossible to administer. It would have to divide itself up into several little states, all of them would be administered according to the same laws.

Falk.   In other words, people would continue to be Germans and French, Dutch and Spanish, Russians and Swedes, or whatever else they might be called. [. . .] For isn't it the case that each of these little states would have its own interest? And every member of these states would share his own state's interest? [. . .] These diverse interests would often come into collision, just as they do now; and two citizens of two different states would no more be able to meet each other in an unbiased frame of mind than a German is now when he meets a Frenchman or a Frenchman when he meets and Englishman. [. . .] Civil society [. . .] cannot unite people without dividing them; and it cannot divide them without placing gulfs between them, without constructing dividing walls through their midst.

    [. . .] It's not enough for civil society to divide people up into different nations and religions. – Such a division into a few large parts, each of which formed a whole in itself, would still be preferable to no whole at all. – No; civil society also continues to make divisions within each of these parts, so to speak ad infinitum.

Ernst. How so?

Falk.   Or do you believe that a state is conceivable without class differences? [. . .] There will therefore be higher-ranking and lower-ranking members. – Even if all the property of the state is initially distributed equally among them, this equal distribution cannot last for more than two generations. One man will know how to make better use of his property than another. One will nevertheless have to distribute his less well-managed property among more descendants than the other. There will therefore be richer and poorer members.

Ernst.   That goes without saying.

Falk.   Now just consider how much evil there is in the world which is not occasioned by this difference between classes.

Ernst.   [. . .] All right, people can only be united through division! And only through incessant division can they remain united! That's just the way things are. And they can't possibly be otherwise. [. . .]

Falk.   [. . .] If people cannot be united into states other than through such divisions, do such divisions therefore become good?

Ernst.   Hardly so.

Falk.   Do they therefore become sacred, these divisions?

Ernst.   What do you mean by sacred?

Falk.   So that it might be forbidden to lay hands on them?

Ernst.   With what intention?

Falk.   With the intention of not letting them become any more firmly entrenched than is strictly necessary. With the intention of rendering their consequences as harmless as possible.

Ernst.   How could that be forbidden?

Falk.   But it cannot be required either; not by civil laws! – For civil laws never extend beyond the boundaries of the state which made them. And this would in fact transcend the boundaries of each and every state. – Consequently, it can only be an *opus supererogatum* [i.e., a work performed beyond the call of duty]; and one can only wish that the wisest and best members of every state might voluntarily undertake this *opus supererogatum.*
           [. . .] It is most desirable that there should be men in every state who have got beyond national prejudices and know exactly where patriotism ceases to be a virtue.
           [. . .] It is most desirable that there should be men in every state who are not susceptible to the prejudice of their native religion and do not believe that everything must necessarily be good and true which they accept as good and true.

> [. . .] It is most desirable that there should be men in every state who are not overawed by social rank or repelled by social inferiority; men in whose company the exalted willingly cease to stand on their dignity and those of inferior rank boldly assert themselves.

Ernst. Most desirable!

Falk. And what if these wishes were fulfilled?

Ernst. Fulfilled? – Such a man can no doubt be found here and there and from time to time.

Falk. Not just here and there; and not just from time to time.

Ernst. At certain times and in certain countries, there may be even more than one of them.

Falk. What if such men were to be found everywhere now? And if they must continue to exist at all times?

Ernst. Would to God it were so!

Falk. And if these men did not live in ineffectual isolation, and not always in an invisible church?

Ernst. A fine dream!

Falk. Let me be brief. – And what if these men were the Freemasons [. . .] who had made it *part* of their business to reduce as far as possible the divisions which so much alienate people from one another?[54]

The problem which the freemasons are called on to solve – and not just those who call themselves by that name, but also the everlasting, non-institutionalized freemasonry 'grounded in human nature and in civil society'[55] – concerns the divisions among men necessarily entailed by their union; for civil society 'cannot unite people without dividing them; and it cannot divide them without placing gulfs between them, without constructing dividing walls through their midst'. The psychologist Erik H. Erikson characterized this dynamic as 'pseudospeciation'.[56] Lessing identifies three factors contributing to such pseudospeciation: one political, dividing people into citizens of different states; one religious, dividing them into followers of different religions; and one social, dividing them into members of different estates or classes.[57] The eighteenth century had left behind it the terrors of religious pseudospeciation, in the form of the confessional warfare of the sixteenth and seventeenth centuries, but it was yet to experience those of political and social pseudospeciation (in the guise of nationalism and class conflict, respectively), and even today the call to consign it to history by creating a cosmopolitan culture has lost none of its urgency.

It might nonetheless be asked whether a secret society is the right means to achieve this goal. It was a question also asked by Johann Gottfried Herder, who came to the opposite conclusion in one of his *Briefe zur Beförderung der Humanität* (*Letters for the Advancement of Humanity*), entitled 'Conversation on a Visible-Invisible Society'.[58] He follows Lessing's second dialogue almost word for word up to the point where Falk identifies the freemasons, as a community made visible, with the 'invisible church' of men who work against the forces dividing people into nations, religions and classes. In Herder's version, Lessing's Falk has become 'He', Ernst 'I'. This 'I' now confronts the freemasons with a quite different society:

> What if, apart from your society, there was another, freer society [. . .], one not closed, but open to the entire world; one that doesn't express itself through rituals and symbols, but in clear words and deeds; one that doesn't exist in one or two nations only, but among enlightened people throughout the world [. . .]? Particularly if I had long lived in this society, which has existed and will exist at all times, and had found in it my Fatherland, my most intimate friend?

When 'I' identifies this society as 'the society of all thinking people in all parts of the world', 'He' responds: 'It may be big enough, but it is, alas, a scattered, invisible church.' This is exactly what Lessing's Falk had denied the freemasons were: 'And if these men did not live in ineffectual isolation, and not always in an invisible church?' The 'visible society' that Herder's 'I' opposes to the freemasons is the republic of letters: 'It has convened, it is visible. Faust or Gutenberg was – how shall I put it? – its Grand Master, or rather its first serving brother. Everything I encounter there raises me above all divisions within civil society, preparing and training me for commerce, not with *such* and *such* human beings, but with human beings *as such*.' Herder decisively repudiates the idea and form of secret societies: 'No true light can remain hidden, even if one wanted to hide it; and the purest light is not to be found in the crypt. [. . .] All such symbols may once have been good and necessary; as I see it, however, they are no longer so. In our times we have to use the opposite method: *pure, bright, revealed truth*.'[59] The alliance between Enlightenment and secrecy still upheld by Lessing is replaced, in Herder's account, by their irreconcilable antagonism: Enlightenment spells an end to secrecy. In a similar vein, he writes in his dialogue 'Glaucon and Nicias':

Instead of the false light cast by all arcane learning, which leads you astray like Aeneas in the underworld, how glad I am to see the clear light of the midday sun, the universal, public, unmistakeable truth! Everyone appears before it with his opinion: good or bad, tenable or misleading, it is considered, tested, confirmed or rejected [. . .] If, then, a secret society loves the truth, it should step into the light with its arcane learning, its Gnostic gospels, and let the old monastic parchment be lit up by the sun's rays.[60]

The 'great business' driving both Lessing and Herder is the same, however: the 'great, noble edifice of humanity'. 'But don't you believe', 'He' says in response to this plea, 'that even the word *humanity* might become tainted?'

That fate was indeed not spared it. The eighteenth-century scholars' dreams for the betterment of the human race have long since been unmasked as a Eurocentric and imperialistic projection. The printing presses have not made the world a better and more enlightened place; nor can we expect this of the Internet, which has brought us a good deal closer to Herder's ideal of a global community of citizens communicating incessantly with each other, forthrightly advertising their own views and criticizing those of others irrespective of national, religious and class borders. That does nothing to alter the fact that Lessing and Herder's 'great business' is not only still on the table but has become more pressing than ever.

The 'great business' – overcoming pseudospeciation or the 'clash of cultures' through cosmopolitan thoughts and deeds – serves the cause of peace. That emerges particularly clearly from another of Herder's *Letters for the Advancement of Humanity*. In the 119th letter from the Tenth Collection, he lists seven 'dispositions of peace' inculcated by his 'great peace woman', *pax sempiterna*: 1. Horrors of war; 2. Reduced respect for heroic glory; 3. Horror of false statecraft; 4. Purified patriotism; 5. Feelings of justice towards other nations; 6. No presumptions in trade; and 7. Activity. The fifth disposition is of particular interest in our context: 'there must gradually awaken a *common feeling* so that every nation feels itself into the position of every other one'. What is called for is a universal, cosmopolitan empathy.

Every nation must gradually come to feel it as unpleasant when another nation gets disparaged and abused. [. . .] Under whatever pretext someone steps over the border in order to cut off the hair of his neighbour as a slave, in order to force his own gods upon him, and in order in return to steal from him his national sacred objects in religion, art, manner of representation, and mode of life – he will find in the heart of *every nation* an enemy [. . .]. If this feeling grows, then there will arise imperceptibly an *alliance of all civilized* [gebildeten] *nations* against every individual presumptuous power.[61]

What Herder could not have imagined at the time, and has since emerged as the main problem, is a power's 'presumption' in acting not against others but against its own populace; but in this context, Herder is concerned less with safeguarding human rights than with preserving peace.

Dispositions four ('purified patriotism') and five belong together and jointly articulate Herder's idea of dual membership. A purified patriotic disposition stipulates 'horror and contempt for every empty invasion of your people into foreign lands, for useless interference in foreign quarrels, for every empty aping and participation that disturbs our business, our duty, our peace and welfare.'[62]

Christoph Martin Wieland seems to have adopted a similarly negative stance towards the link between cosmopolitanism and secret societies. Hugh B. Nisbet has drawn attention to the connections between Lessing's *Ernst and Falk* and Wieland's 'cosmopolite'.[63] These can be understood in terms of mutual influence. Just as *Ernst and Falk* evidently draws on the account of the 'Cosmopolitan Order' given in Wieland's *Geschichte der Abderiten* (*History of the Abderites*), so Wieland's essay 'Das Geheimniß des Kosmopolitenordens' ('The Secret of the Cosmopolitan Order') seems to represent a reply to Lessing's masonic dialogues. In the *Abderites*, Lessing might have read in 1774:

> There is a kind of mortal already mentioned here and there by the ancients under the name of *cosmopolites*, who – without arrangement, without a badge, without maintaining a lodge, and without being bound by oaths – constitute a kind of brotherhood that hangs together more closely than any other order in the world. Two cosmopolites come, the one from the east, the other from the west, see one another for the first time, and are friends, not by virtue of a secret sympathy that is, perhaps, to be found only in novels; and not because sworn duties bind them to it, but *because they are cosmopolites*.[64]

The great advantage of the cosmopolites consists in the fact that there are no false brothers in their ranks; for one does not *become* a cosmopolite, one already *is* one:

> Their society has no need of excluding the *unclean* from their number as the Egyptian priests did in former times by means of secret ceremonies and forbidding customs. These exclude themselves; and one can

no more *appear to be* a cosmopolite if one is not than one can pass oneself off without any talent as a good singer or violinist. [. . .] It is not possible to imitate the way the cosmopolites think, their principles, their convictions, [. . .] because, for all who do not belong to their order, they are a true mystery. Not a mystery that depends upon the reticence of their members or upon their precautions against being overheard; but rather a mystery over which nature itself has draped its veil. For the cosmopolites could without hesitation have it made known with trumpets sounding throughout the entire world and might safely count on no one's understanding anything about it except themselves. The circumstances of the matter being as they are, nothing is more natural than the cordial understanding and mutual trust that establish themselves between two cosmopolites at once in the first hour of their acquaintance. [. . .] For it belongs [. . .] to the *nature of the matter* that everything that can be said about it is an enigma to which only the members of this order have the key. The only thing that we can still add is that their number has at all times been *very small* and that they, the *invisibility* of their society notwithstanding, have maintained from time immemorial an influence in the things of this world whose effects are the more certain and more lasting because they make no noise and are mostly attained by means whose *apparent* direction confuses the eyes of the multitude.[65]

It seems obvious to me that Nisbet's supposition is correct and Lessing was spurred on to his conception of the true and immemorial freemasonry by this description of the cosmopolites. A clear sign of this is the motif of invisibility taken up and at the same time modified in Lessing's 'invisible church'. For the society now constituted by his eminently 'desirable' men is no longer that: it has become visible. The invisibility of the Cosmopolitan Order is precisely the point underscored by Wieland in his essay 'The Secret of the Cosmopolitan Order', published in the *Teutschen Merkur* (*German Mercury*) in 1788.[66] The cosmopolites, he contends there, form an 'invisible society' whose 'secret' consists in its not being an 'Order' at all, or even a society. Wieland's cosmopolites operate programmatically, as it were, under a cloak of invisibility: a man does not become a cosmopolite by being initiated into some Order; he either is one or he isn't, and if he is then he simply belongs (442). The cosmopolites differ from all other secret societies in that 'they neither have a secret *to conceal* nor do they make one of their principles and convictions' (445).

Cosmopolites bear their name, *citizens of the world*, in the most authentic and eminent sense. For they regard *all nations* on earth as so many branches of a *single family*, and the *universe* as a *state* in which they, together with countless other rational beings, are the *citizens*, in order – *under general laws of nature* – to further the perfection of the *whole* by each in his own way looking out for his own prosperity. (446)

Wieland does not want to have this true, utopian, invisible freemasonry, which Lessing sees at work in all epochs of human history, assume visible form in an organized secret society.

Yet Lessing, to come back to him one last time, is well ahead of this critique (if indeed it is one). The programme he ascribes to his true freemasons is far removed from the goals of institutionalized freemasonry; indeed, it is assigned to the human race as a whole. To be sure, neither Lessing nor Wieland is out to *replace* the traditional divisions of the human race into different nations, states and religions. They merely want to *extend* the possibilities for human association and identification to another level. The goal is to relativize entrenched partitions along lines of nationality, religion and class by cultivating a sense of belonging to an overarching category, which Lessing, Mendelssohn and Herder unite in calling 'humanity'. This goal is as topical as ever. It is essentially no different, for example, to what the Nobel Prize-winning economist Amartya Sen is trying to do today to avoid the 'clash of cultures'.[67] Sen deconstructs an all too monolithic understanding of identity by pointing to the irreducible plurality of attachments and allegiances shared by us all. He criticizes the compartmentalization of human beings into 'cultures' and 'religions', and he rejects the 'Western' monopolization of universalistic concepts and perspectives. Discovering the worldwide commonality or generalizability of ideas like human dignity, human rights, tolerance, democracy, freedom of opinion, freedom of religion and freedom of choice is surely more important than reclaiming or denouncing such ideas as 'Western'.[68] We must learn, above all, to deal with these commonalities dialogically and dialectically, treating them as the basis on which differences can be articulated and negotiated in the first place. The great achievement of Lessing and Mendelssohn is to have conceived globalization and universalism not only under the banner of unification, but under that of difference as well. Nothing lies further from Mendelssohn's intentions than to equate his goal of a Jewish Enlightenment with an abandonment of his native religion through its complete assimilation to Christian and secular European civilizational ideals. He advocated the principle of dual membership, as expressed in the nineteenth century in Samson Raphael Hirsch's *torah îm derekh 'erets* ('Torah with the way of the land'), a formula that asserts the compatibility of an

Orthodox-Halakhic way of life with a European, worldly education. This bears comparison, perhaps, with what Walter Mignolo calls 'critical cosmopolitanism'.[69] Today it can no longer suffice to see in the stranger only my brother and to enfold him into my own world with the open arms of philanthropy. That was a position still open to the sixteenth century, when 'my own world' was defined as the *orbis Christianus*, and to the eighteenth, when it was detheologized and redefined as humanity. Even Jaspers' axial age theory, for all his declared intention to overcome the Eurocentric perspective, ultimately amounts to an 'inclusion of the other'.[70] What matters more is to recognize the other – with his different religion, culture and skin colour – *as other*, on the basis of commonalities that will need to be determined in each case. For all their pride in man's emergence from his self-incurred tutelage, many people in the eighteenth century had no qualms about imposing this tutelage on millions of others by enslaving and colonizing them. Now those who once were condemned to silence have rediscovered their voice, and when they raise it, it behoves us to hear what they have to say about our differences and commonalities.

There is no more room for mysteries in this conception of a two-tiered religion. The concept of Mendelssohn's 'religion of mankind' and Lessing's cosmopolitanism can never be institutionalized, and it will always be left to individuals to orient themselves in relation to it. They must learn to cope with living and thinking on both levels at once. Yet while the religion of mankind is not the province of mystery and esotericism, it does not spell an end to secrecy as such, only to strategic secrecy. In the freemasonic construction, secrecy fulfilled four basic functions: first, it welded together the self-appointed guardians of this secret; second, it marked them off from other groups and the world outside; third, it created within the group the wish for ever greater secrets to be divulged with each promotion; and, fourth – and this is the most problematic aspect – it caused those in the know (the elite) to wield power over those they kept in ignorance (the 'people'). 'Enlightenment of the individual to keep the others in the dark generates power, and establishes slavery,' wrote Adam Weishaupt. 'Enlightenment to enlighten others generates freedom.'[71] This form of secrecy is banished under conditions of freedom; there is nothing the least bit secret about cosmopolitanism and human rights. It makes way, however, for a structural secrecy that goes to the very heart of the matter: the secrecy of truth, whose concealed existence relativizes all positive truths without vitiating them in the process. That is the real secret of human existence.

Homo Duplex

Lessing, Mendelssohn, Herder and others may be considered the Protestant reformers of *religio duplex*. The form they gave this idea ensured its continuing relevance in the centuries to come. This reform implied at once a turning outward, towards cosmopolitanism, and a turning inward. The opposition between popular and arcane religion was relocated within the individual, this time in the sense of a 'both/ and' – a dual membership – rather than an 'either/or'. Knowing about the universal religion of mankind did not mean having to renounce one's particular, native religion. This dual membership was cultivated in the secret societies oriented towards the Enlightenment. Time and again it was emphasized that the lodges were not out to transform society but to 'ennoble' the individual. Masons would continue to carry out their civic or 'profane' duties and activities as before, even if the goal was naturally for such ennoblement to be reflected in their daily work and thereby to exert an indirect influence on society at large. The double life they practised in their lodges was meant to produce the kind of person for whom thinking and feeling on two levels or in two horizons, that of humanity and that of particular allegiances, would be second nature.

The opposition between popular and arcane religion had traditionally been defined as an antagonism between sensuality and spirituality. Where the people needed rites, festivals, and visual and tangible representations of the sacred, the wise worshipped the divine 'in the mind and in the truth'. In the light of the new individualism, however, man came into view in both his sensuous and spiritual aspects, and towards the end of the eighteenth century their reconciliation, not their antagonism, became the order of the day. With respect to society, we have already cited the demand voiced by Hölderlin, Schelling and Hegel in their 'System Programme': 'Mythology must become philosophical and the people rational, while philosophy must become mythological, in order to make the philosophers sensuous.' In his *Letters on Aesthetic Education*, likewise a product of the 1790s, Schiller places the demand that the spiritual become sensuous and the sensuous spiritual at the door of the individual. Their opposition, conceived within the framework of the *religio duplex* model as an antagonism between popular religion and mysteries, now takes up residence within man as two contrasting drives:

> The first of these, which I will call the *sensuous* drive, proceeds from the physical existence of man, or his sensuous nature. Its business is

to set him within the limits of time [. . .]. This state, which is nothing but time occupied by content, is called sensation, and it is through this alone that physical existence makes itself known. [. . .] The second of the two drives, which we may call the *formal drive*, proceeds from the absolute existence of man, or from his rational nature, and is intent on giving him the freedom to bring harmony into the diversity of his manifestations, and to affirm his person among all his changes of condition. [. . .] It annuls time and annuls change. It wants the real to be necessary and eternal, and the eternal and the necessary to be real. In other words, it insists on truth and on the right.[72]

What Schiller is calling for here is a new type of individual, 'homo duplex', who will bring the sensuous and formal drives into harmony in his own person; and hence, by extension, a culture and society in which feelings are no longer suppressed by principles and principles no longer overwhelmed by feelings. The individual he has in mind 'is not to strive for form at the cost of reality, nor for reality at the cost of form; rather is he to seek absolute being by means of a determinate being, and a determinate being by means of infinite being'.[73] Translated into the problematic of *religio duplex*, this means that we should neither repudiate a personal God or traditional religion in favour of the philosophers' god or a universal religion of mankind, nor should we take the opposite route, which today goes by the name of fundamentalism. We should instead seek to combine both, a goal 'that man can only approximate over time without ever attaining it'.[74] Schiller describes the form taken by this combination as a 'reciprocal relationship', identifying art as the principle of such interaction. We have not yet spoken of art in discussing the idea of *religio duplex*, but it makes sense to think again of *The Magic Flute* in this context, which is not only an *opera duplex* – popular theatre and mystery play in one – but also and especially a work of art that places both elements in a 'reciprocal relationship' of the greatest aesthetic luminosity.

The secret society novel, as a subgenre of the eighteenth-century novel of education or *Bildungsroman* showing the effect of Enlightenment on personal development, already attested to an individualization of the *religio duplex* concept. The hero of this novel may be characterized as *homo duplex* insofar as he cultivates a dual religion and a dual membership in society. This idea also has a long history in religious, philosophical and sociological anthropology, although there it has a rather different meaning. As traditionally employed, the distinction between two aspects, forms, natures, layers or mental states in humankind ultimately derives from that between nature and society. In a way, that is already true even of the two concepts of the

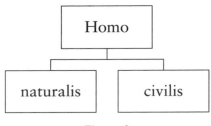

Figure 3

'soul' in ancient Egypt. These differentiate strictly between an individual 'corporeal soul', *Ba*, which animates the body in life and departs from it after death, and a 'social soul', *Ka*, which stitches the individual into a genealogical chain of forebears and descendants and integrates him into the community.[75] The concept of the 'inner man' in Paul and Augustine also implies a distinction between inside and outside: between the individual self, absorbed in its relationship with God, and the social self, fixated on its role in society.[76] Richard Weihe, who has devoted a thorough, historically far-reaching investigation to the distinction between face and mask or self and role, traces the concept of *homo duplex* back to Boccaccio.[77] Boccaccio and, a century later, Nicolaus of Cusa define *homo duplex* as *homo naturalis* and *homo civilis*.[78] Man is at once a natural being prone to animal drives and a social being determined by societal norms, values and feelings (see figure 3).

Nicolaus of Cusa invests the *naturalis* pole with concepts like 'sense-endowed, mortal' and *civilis* with 'reason-endowed, immortal'.[79] Richard Weihe compares this with several modern dualisms like Carl Jung's distinction between 'individual, true nature' (*naturalis*) and 'personality, mask, collective' (*civilis*),[80] Helmuth Plessner's 'authentic self' and 'social role',[81] and Émile Durkheim's 'bodily, instinctive, individual and amoral mental states' (*naturalis*) and 'social, collective, moral mental states' (*civilis*).[82] Returning to the late eighteenth century, this overview can also accommodate Schiller's idea of *homo duplex* with its dualistic theory of drives: 'material drive, drive for self-preservation' (*naturalis*) and 'formal drive, cognitive drive' (*civilis*).[83]

With its distinction between 'mere' and 'such-and-such' humans, Lessing's *homo duplex* model appears at first to inscribe itself into this tradition:

When a German at present meets a Frenchman, or a Frenchman an Englishman (or vice versa), it is no longer a meeting between a *mere* human being and another *mere* human being who are attracted to one another by virtue of their common nature, but a meeting between *such* a human being and *such* a human being who are conscious of their differing tendencies. This makes them cold, reserved, and distrustful towards one another, even before they have had the least mutual inter-action or shared experience as individuals.[84]

That sounds as if natural or 'mere' man (*homo naturalis*) had been covered up, through his socialization in a state, by 'such-and-such' a man (*homo civilis*), and all that had to be done now was reverse the process by laying bare the natural substrate of every human being. Lessing considers the political difference by which someone becomes a 'German', for example, to be a 'prejudice' that must be done away with. Yet the goal worked towards by Lessing's freemasons is that man should become a citizen of the world, not that he should revert to the state of nature; hence the thrice-emphasized 'in the world' when Lessing is describing the masons' sphere of activity.[85] Their 'secret' consists in their deeds rather than in some occult doctrine. Whoever would act in the world must cast aside his prejudices, but this means progressing from *homo civilis* to the higher level of *kosmopolitēs*, not regressing to *homo naturalis*. Two things are clear: this progression is reserved only for 'the wisest and best members of every state',[86] and it does not imply that the borders and differences which transform a 'mere' human being into 'such-and-such' a human being will be abolished. States, religions and classes are here to stay – human beings will not metamorphose into citizens of the world, nor will nations make way for a global society – but, here and there, the 'wisest and best' will always see through the prejudicial, illusory, or – to speak with Benedict Anderson and Cornelius Castoriadis – 'imaginary' nature of these differences, and thereby learn to expand their sphere of influence to the world at large. Accordingly, freema-sonry is a 'countermovement against the unavoidable evils' (Koselleck) of political, religious and social pseudospeciation, not a movement to be rid of them entirely.[87] Lessing's mason is a *homo duplex* in the sense that he is socialized on two levels, as a citizen of his nation and of the world.

With that, we encounter a new characterization of *homo duplex*, corresponding to the turn taken by the *religio duplex* idea in Mendelssohn and Lessing. Our point of departure is the insight, shared by anthropologists and sociologists like Plessner, Gehlen and Durkheim, that sociality is also part of human nature, the *homo naturalis*. We could speak here of a drive to bond.[88] The crucial line of differentiation therefore does not run between individual 'nature' and social 'culture', but between an instinct-driven proximate social-

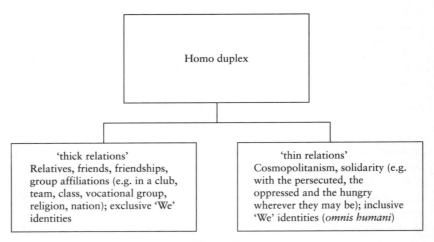

Figure 4

ization and an acquired remote socialization. We can draw on Michael Walzer and Avishai Margalit's distinction between 'thick' and 'thin' relations to help make sense of this (figure 4).[89] In this figure, Lessing's freemasons represent the right column, although they think of themselves solely as a modern, institutionalized and organized form of a type of human being that has existed since time immemorial in the most diverse cultures, an elite found at all times and in all places. For Lessing and Mendelssohn, admission to this elite is not determined by birth, class or race. It requires a mentality that must be inculcated through education, training and testing.

Once we consider that what the scholars of the seventeenth and eighteenth centuries imagined as the elite religion of the wise and the initiate basically involved worshipping at the shrine of an all-one, impersonal Supreme Being, it becomes clear how *religio duplex* and *homo duplex* belong together in late eighteenth-century thought. In the subterranean Egyptian nurseries of wisdom, in the mysteries of the Greeks and Orientals and in the lodges of the freemasons, Rosicrucians and Illuminati, a new human being or new cosmopolitan consciousness was to be nurtured, one that would prove capable of thinking and feeling beyond the horizon of its quasi-natural 'thick relations'. This is what was understood at the time by 'philanthropy' or 'beneficence' as the noblest goal of freemasonry, and it could only be achieved, so it was believed, by following the path of mysteries towards a fundamental and far-reaching transformation, or 'ennoblement', of human nature.

Prospectus
Religio Duplex Today?

In the twentieth century we come across the idea of dual religion where we least expect to find it, perhaps: in the Indian lawyer, philosopher and activist Mahatma Gandhi. The India specialist and constitutional law expert Dieter Conrad, who passed away in 2001, drew attention to this in his posthumously published book, *Gandhi and the Concept of the Political*. Alluding to Lessing's dialogues for freemasons, he calls this principle of dual religion 'Gandhi's masonic secret'.[1] Gandhi distinguished between particular religions – Hinduism, Buddhism, Islam, Judaism, Christianity and the like – and a true religion or religion of truth aimed at by them all. With reference to particular religions, Gandhi insisted on the separation of Church and state, striving for an independent state in which all religions, especially Hinduism and Islam, could peacefully coexist. Whenever he stresses the inseparability of religion and politics, however, he has in mind the general religion of truth, 'the universal and all-pervading spirit of Truth'. Indeed, no area of life remains untouched by the claims of religious – and for Gandhi that means moral – responsibility. Gandhi did not believe 'that there can or will be on earth one religion'. For him, particular religions exist only in the plural. He did believe, however, that it was possible 'to find a common factor and to induce mutual tolerance'.[2] He gave the name 'Religion' (with a capital R) to this common denominator of all religions: 'there are many religions, but Religion is only one'.[3] This concept of a capitalized Religion has its counterpart in Mendelssohn's 'religion of mankind'. Unlike particular religions, Religion is never institutionalized and is always an individual affair. In a different context, Gandhi explains his concept of Religion in this higher sense (although here he leaves the word in lower case):

> Let me explain what I mean by religion. It is not the Hindu religion, which I certainly prize above all other religions, but the religion which transcends Hinduism, which changes one's very nature, which binds one indissolubly to the truth within and which ever purifies. It is the permanent element in human nature which counts no cost too great in order to find full expression and which leaves the soul utterly restless until it has found itself, known its Maker and appreciated the true correspondence between the Maker and itself.[4]

The religion of mankind, to draw on Mendelssohn's concept here, touches the individual in his innermost essence or 'heart', about which Augustine said that it is restless until it rests in God. According to Conrad's reading of Gandhi's statement, cultivating this inner religion or religiosity 'means continually relativizing the various expressions it brings forth in the form of particular religions. Above all, it means abolishing their irrational antagonisms'[5] – and also, we might add, the Mosaic distinction, which precisely in India had such tragic repercussions in the appalling massacres and political enmity that poisoned the relationship between Muslims and Hindus. With this conflict unfolding before his eyes, Gandhi worked for a relativiza-, tion of particular religions and their divergent creeds in view of an overarching religion of (hidden) truth. The same pacifistic conception of mutual recognition informed the ways in which scholars of the Renaissance developed the idea of *prisca theologia* or *philosophia perennis* and discovered the Hermetic tradition, and those of the late eighteenth century, building on these traditions, worked for interfaith understanding. For Gandhi, this individualized religion of a universal truth anchored in human nature was synonymous with 'God' – as he states on many occasions, 'Truth is God'[6] – but also with morality: 'the essence of religion is morality'.[7] Beholden only to the inner law (*svadharma*), the individual religion or religiosity therefore has less to do with mysticism than with the 'humanitarian, moral common sense'[8] preached by the Enlightenment. All historical religions are called before its judgement seat to justify themselves and, if necessary, relinquish their claims to truth: 'nothing that flies in the face of reason, universal truth and morality can be recognized as a sacred scriptural tradition or revelation'.[9]

In the same sense, our current age of globalization demands that we learn to think on two levels. It is not so much a question of tolerating the other as of recognizing difference. The London rabbi and philosopher Jonathan Sacks encapsulated this demand with admirable clarity in his book *The Dignity of Difference* (2002).[10] Like Mendelssohn, Sacks distinguishes between universal truths and religious truths. 'Judaism,' he writes, 'is a particularistic monotheism. It believes in one God, but not in one religion, one culture, one truth. The God of Abraham is the God of all mankind, but the faith of Abraham is not the faith of all mankind.'[11] 'God is universal, religions are particular. Religion is the translation of God into a particular language and thus into the life of a group, a nation, a community of faith.'[12] God exists only in the singular, religions only in the plural. Religions establish identity, and identity implies difference.[13] 'God is the God of all humanity, but between Babel and the end of days no single faith is the faith of all humanity':[14] that sums up Mendelssohn's distinction between the religion of mankind and particular religions. Jonathan Sacks occupies a standpoint defined as 'cosmopolitan' by sociologist Ulrich Beck:

> Universalism means that religious differences are levelled so that what they have in common consists in the lowest common moral denominator. Cosmopolitanism, by contrast, emphasizes the dignity and the burden of difference, the indissoluble interconnection and opposition of universalism and particularism.[15]

To be sure, this form of cosmopolitanism is impossible without universalism, the construction of a higher level of general ideas, principles, values and norms. Universalism, as I understand it, is not the opposite of cosmopolitanism but its condition of possibility. The levelling of religious differences, on the other hand, should be understood as an effect of globalization.

Although religious truths are never universal, they are not for that reason simply relative, according to Jonathan Sacks.[16] Within their ambit, in the horizon of a given religion, they are *absolute*. In this context, Sacks draws on Michael Walzer's distinction between 'thick' and 'thin' relations. The relation that a religion establishes between God and his worshippers – and Sacks traces the word *religio* back to *religare* ('to bind back'), not *religere* ('to take into careful account')[17] – is a 'thick' one; it has to do with love. Whereas science may set out in search of universal truths, religion, like love, aims at the particular and the individual. That is 'what distinguishes the God of the philosophers from the God of the Hebrew Bible'.[18] Sacks makes clear that the former leaves him just as cold as Pascal; yet if God, as he writes, is universal in opposition to the particular religions, then this universal God is not 'the God of the Hebrew Bible', and the biblical

God can only be a particular God. The god of the philosophers is a hidden god, one who transcends all conceptions that human beings may have of him. It is the God of Schoenberg's Moses, to whom Aaron justly complains: 'Can you love what you dare not even conceive?' This is also the God Jonathan Sacks has in mind when he calls him 'universal'. It is the God he *thinks* but not the God he *loves*. As rabbi and philosopher, Sacks inhabits a dual religion, rejoicing in his God from within the framework of his religion, with all the thick relationships and convictions it affords him, while knowing full well that there are other religions with equally thick relationships and convictions.

What is peculiar about Sacks' version of *religio duplex* and the principle of dual membership is that he anchors them in the Bible itself. For him, the opposition is not one between the extra-biblical and consequently universal god of the philosophers and the biblical God, but between the God of Noah and the God of Abraham, or more precisely, between the covenant God made with Noah and mankind and the covenant he made with Abraham and his 'seed', the nation he would go on to father. 'On the one hand,' Sacks writes, 'we are members of the universal human family and thus of the (Noahide) covenant with all mankind. [. . .] On the other hand, we are also members of a particular family with its specific history and memory.'[19] That is the definition of dual religion. Admittedly, Sacks does not use this concept, and he would presumably also be unwilling to accept it. For him, one membership is a question of 'thin', abstract, philosophical terminology, the other a matter of 'thick' feelings and commitments: a ' "thick" or context-bound morality'.[20] He refers in this context to Michael Walzer, who ties the opposition between universal humanity and particular societies to the concept of memory:

> Societies are necessarily particular because they have members and memories, members with memories not only of their own but also of their common life. Humanity, by contrast, has members but no memory, and so it has no history and no culture, no customary practices, no familiar life-ways, no festivals, no shared understanding of social goods. It is human to have such things, but there is no singular way of having them. At the same time, the members of all the different societies, because they are human, can acknowledge each other's different ways, respond to each other's cries for help, learn from each other, and march (sometimes) in each other's parades.[21]

What Walzer identifies here are precisely the two levels of *religio duplex* in modern, secular form. It is by no means obvious, however, why the 'other' level, the level of humanity, should present itself as so colourless or 'thin'. In this regard, much seems to have changed in the fifteen years since Walzer's book appeared, and those changes are still afoot. It is simply not true that there is no memory and no history on this level; nor that there can be no 'shared understanding' of goods, goals and values. We are witnessing a growing awareness of the wrongs done to those on the losing end of globalization, a growing willingness to donate to the victims of catastrophe, a growing solidarity with the suffering and oppressed throughout the world, and above all, a growing number of NGOs and other possibilities of becoming active as a global citizen through donations, petitions and protests. The Internet, in particular, has fundamentally altered our perceptions of distance and proximity, 'thickness' and 'thinness'. There are ever more platforms and forums for worldwide communication and interaction (Facebook, Myspace, Twitter, and so on), an ever growing number of worldwide days of remembrance, and ever more intensive efforts to anchor particular historical experiences on a transnational and even global level, thereby creating something like a memory of the human race. The redoubled commitment to a globalization of human rights and other universal values likewise points to the cultivation of a kind of universal culture or civilization, a global polity whose values and norms will need to be respected by the particular religions, too. Human sacrifice, for example, is unthinkable today, not for particular religious reasons but in view of universal norms, and it is only a matter of time until, say, the religiously sanctioned refusal of human rights (especially women's rights) or the mutilations still perpetrated in the name of many religions and traditions will be globally outlawed and abolished. As humanity becomes more closely knitted together in an age of globalization, membership on this level will and must become 'thicker' over the coming decades, building a sense of solidarity, concern and mutual recognition. Societies 'have' no memory, but they can make one. Why should humanity as a whole not make one? It is already well on the way to doing so. In the introduction to their edited collection, *Memory in an Age of Globalization*, Aleida Assmann and Sebastian Conrad write:

> Until recently, the dynamics of memory production unfolded primarily within the bounds of the nation-state; coming to terms with the past was largely a national project. Under the impact of global mobility and movements, this has changed fundamentally. Global conditions have powerfully impacted on memory debates, and, at the same time, memory has entered the global stage and global discourse. Today, memory and the global have to be studied together, as it has become impossible to understand the trajectories of memory outside a global frame of reference.[22]

In the age of globalization, we have been living and thinking on two levels for quite some time. Just as we have learned that one person's remembering may not come at the cost of another being forgotten or wrongfully accused, so we must learn not to justify our own faith by denouncing that of the other as pagan or infidel. That does not mean that all particular, historical religions should be subsumed under an insipidly universal religion of mankind, but rather that, in their very particularity, they should communicate with each other, pay respect to each other and scale back their exclusionary claims with a view to higher categories of civil coexistence grounded in human nature or the need for common survival, without thereby losing their colour and their binding force. Religions must learn to see themselves through the eyes of the other. Ulrich Beck calls this the 'cosmopolitan spirit':

> 'Cosmopolitan' means changing the religious viewpoint, the internalized 'as-if conversion', the practice of 'both/and', the ability to see one's own religion and culture through the eyes of another religion and the culture of other people. How and to what extent can this 'cosmopolitan spirit' of the world society be said to have a *realistic* chance of becoming a reality?[23]

'Both/and': that is the formula of *religio duplex*, and cosmopolitanism is the demand made by Lessing, Mendelssohn and the masonic Enlightenment. The late eighteenth century is closer to us than the nineteenth and twentieth centuries, and the *religio duplex* model shows itself to be more relevant than we might initially have suspected.

In its general and secular reformulation, this model points the way to recognition as well as to mutual tolerance. This point has been emphasized by Aleida Assmann, who in a manner akin to Mendelssohn, although without his guiding interest in matters of faith, distinguishes between 'culture' as any particular system of values and 'civilization' as its universal counterpart. 'Culture' is defined here as the principle of difference ('what distinguishes people from each other'), civilization as the principle of similarity – not in the sense of anthropological universals but of an aspirational commonality. Civilization thus stands for 'the values and practices concerning which people can reach agreement, regardless of their cultural ties [. . .], hence the sum total of [. . .] premises anchored in the principle of human rights':[24]

> In this broader perspective, the limits of cultural respect emerge with new clarity. Paying respect to other cultures means recognizing the

ineradicable differences that exist between cultures. Yet these differences merit our respect only to the extent that they are compatible with the universalistic values we have summarized here under the heading of 'civilization'. Anything that violates these fundamental transcultural values – sexist forms of violence such as honour killing or female circumcision, for example – can lay claim to neither respect nor tolerance. For from attesting to the reputable value of difference, such practices betray a reprehensible lack of 'civilization'. [. . .] Respect for cultural difference has its limits, and these limits can only be determined by common transcultural values. Respect depends on and is regulated by this higher standard, which marks out the framework within which cultural differences are recognized and heeded. Both are needed, then: attitudes and expressive forms of intercultural politeness which respect differences, but also common agreement on basic transcultural values to act as the standard, framework and limit for cultural differences.[25]

'Both are needed': once again, an appeal is made to the model of dual religion in the secular form of co-allegiance or dual membership. Translated into Mendelssohn's terminology, this means that the 'particular religions', however tenaciously they may cling to their respective traditions, should firstly respect each other and secondly temper their zeal with an eye to a general 'religion of mankind'. Applied to Gandhi's problem, it is only by restraining themselves in view of a universal 'Religion' (of truth) that particular 'religions' will make it possible for Muslims and Hindus to coexist in the same 'house'. History has proven that goal to be utopian, but as an aspirational ideal it is by no means obsolete.

Religio duplex is a concept of the seventeenth and eighteenth centuries. It looks to ancient Egypt for its model. It builds on Greco-Egyptian grammatology, on the one hand, and the Platonic tradition and its tendency to elitist esotericism, on the other. In the eighteenth century it undergoes two decisive transformations: the replacement of the Platonic by the political motif, sealed by Warburton (after a long run-up) in the 'priestly fraud' thesis, and the replacement of the mysteries by cosmopolitanism in Lessing, Mendelssohn, Herder and Wieland. Three factors were discussed as catalysts for the emergence of *religio duplex*: philosophy, statecraft and globalization. Philosophy (with the natural sciences at the forefront up to and including the eighteenth century) draws a sharp distinction in religious matters between the people and the elite; statecraft enlists religion for its political purposes and thereby splits it into official and private, external and internal, political and natural religion; and globalization, hurling it into the marketplace of cultures, confronts it with the competing claims of other religions, forcing it to think beyond its absolute truth-claims and to envisage a common framework within which differences can be recognized and discursively worked through. No one could claim that these factors have lost any of their relevance today. The challenge from science (as one will say, instead of philosophy, now that the differentiation processes of the nineteenth century have run their course) is plain to see, and it can only be dealt with if religion sensibly opts for a 'both/and' in the sense of *religio duplex*. Politicization has emerged as the key problem of the last three decades; for it is evident that the so-called return of religion consists, above all, in the strengthened political claims being made on its behalf, while globalization makes it ever more necessary that religions develop cosmopolitan perspectives and learn to exercise a modicum of self-restraint.

Retrospectus
Are There 'Dual Religions'?

Our investigation of the *religio duplex* idea has taken us through four stations:

1. The ancient Egyptian foundations of this idea and the Greek construction of the Egyptian culture of writing, which posited a culture split between exoteric and esoteric communication corresponding to the distinction between several forms of writing.
2. The interpretation of this split in terms of the Platonic distinction between Being and appearance. According to this schema, popular religion belongs on the side of 'appearance'; it rests on the 'opinion' of the unlettered masses, to whom the truth is conveyed only in images and fables. The philosophical religion, by contrast, is devoted to 'Being' as the arcane religion of the initiated few, who have emancipated themselves from the conventional opinions of the masses and set forth on the quest for truth.
3. The political interpretation of this split in terms of the distinction between political and natural theology. Popular religion is conceived here as a political instrument for establishing states and keeping the masses in line. This interpretation appears in two versions: (a) in the positive sense, as a necessary and hence legitimate and useful fiction that provides an indispensable foundation for political and civil order; (b) in the negative sense, as a fraudulent strategy devised to keep rulers in power and to exploit, suppress and discipline the masses.
4. The reinterpretation of the distinction between Being and appearance in terms of the distinction between particularity and

universality, first developed by Lessing and Mendelssohn in the sense of dual membership, and subsequently reconceived by Gandhi in the sense of a dual concept of religion that differentiates between particular religions and a universal, invisible and individually practised religion of truth. This form of *religio duplex* can be linked up to (post)modern conceptions of dual membership such as those elaborated by Michael Walzer, Jonathan Sacks, Ulrich Beck and Aleida Assmann.

What all these manifestations of *religio duplex* have in common is that the principle of division or reduplication was imposed on religion from the outside rather than inhering in it from the first. In the Platonic version of this idea, the division arose with the emergence of philosophy; in the political version, it arose with the emergence of states; and in the cosmopolitan version, if we can call by this name the new twist given the idea by Lessing and Mendelssohn, it arose with globalization.

We might finally ask whether these ideas of an inner-religious dualism, either in the complementary or the antagonistic sense, correlate in any way with what we know today about the history of religion in the ancient world. After all, I have only been discussing ideas about religion in this book, not religion itself; I have investigated the history of ideas, not the history of religion. In concluding, I would therefore like – at least in a brief retrospect – to adopt a different perspective and approach the question of *religio duplex* by going back to the sources themselves.

Noah and Moses

The immediate occasion for my change in perspective from the history of ideas to the history of religion is Jonathan Sacks' thesis that the distinction between a universal and a particular form of religious affiliation is already to be found in the Hebrew Bible itself, specifically, in the distinction between the Noahic covenant with the 'Noahide commandments', on the one hand, and the Abrahamic or Sinai covenant with the Mosaic laws, on the other. In the Jewish tradition, the Noahic covenant is linked to the doctrine of the 'righteous among the gentiles', that is, non-Jewish people who will partake of the world to come if they obey the seven Noahide laws, which apply to all humanity.[1] Similarly, in the seventeenth century they were appealed to as a 'natural law' shared by all mankind and a framework within which the individual religions – Judaism, Christianity, Islam, and so on – could coexist in peace. In Uriel da Costa, the law of all mankind becomes a religion for all mankind. Da Costa was a Portuguese *marrano* who emigrated to Amsterdam in order to convert back to Judaism, only to end up just as dissatisfied with the Mosaic laws as he had once been with Christianity. Having thus fallen between two stools, he pledged his allegiance to the Noahide commandments as the *lex naturae* and the only true, original and genuinely universal *religio*. Nature has instilled these *lex primaria* in all of us, he argued, and inscribed them into our hearts; all later laws are human products masquerading under the guise of religion.[2] It seems to me that Mendelssohn's concept of a universal 'religion of mankind' also stands in this tradition. His signal contribution, to my mind, was to have restricted the concept of revelation with respect to the higher category of this religion of mankind.

What about ancient Judaism itself? Can the religion that stands behind the texts of the Hebrew Bible be understood as a dual religion, in the sense that it encompasses two levels: a particular level valid for Jews alone and a universal level embracing all mankind? If so, we are dealing here with a structural principle of early Judaism, not just an idea of the seventeenth and eighteenth centuries.

According to the Bible, God enters into a formal covenant (*berit*) on three occasions: with Noah after the Flood, when God commits never again to destroy the earth through such a catastrophe; with Abraham, when God promises him that he will father a great nation; and with Moses, when God turns as an ally (in the sense of overlord) to the descendants of Abraham, now become the nation of Israel. The counter-obligations incurred by Noah – to refrain from violence and cruelty – extend to the entire human race, whereas Abraham's commitment to have himself circumcised is binding only for his male progeny. In the case of the covenant with Moses, the entire corpus of 613 commandments and prohibitions, subdivided into ethical rules, legal statutes and ritual laws, holds solely for the community that submits to these laws. The obligations entered into on the human side thus become increasingly particular and demanding. The Mosaic law applies only to Jews, the Abrahamic covenant applies to 'Abraham's seed' – thus, via Ishmael, to the Arabs as well and thence to Islam (in the Christian interpretation, even Christians may claim descent from Abraham) – while the commitment of the Noahic covenant applies to all humanity. When it comes to the history of the texts, the sequence is reversed: the later the covenants were set down in writing, the more general is their scope. The codification of the 613 commandments and prohibitions in the 'Book of the Covenant' and the 'Book of the Torah' essentially goes back to the exilic period.

The idea of the Abrahamic covenant, meanwhile, can be understood as a post-exilic liberalization of the definition of Judaism. It welcomes all of Abraham's progeny into the fold (including the *'am ha-'ārets*, those who stayed behind in the land, were not deported to Babylon and accordingly do not live by the law).[3] The idea of the Noahic convenant is of particular interest to us here, since it appears to imply the concept of a 'religion of mankind'; it undergoes a crucial transformation in antiquity. In the biblical account (Gen. 9:4–6), we hear of only two prohibitions:

> But flesh with the life thereof, which is the blood thereof, ye shall not eat.
>   And surely your blood of your lives will I require; at the hand of every beast will I require it, and at the hand of man; at the hand of every man's brother will I require the life of man.
>   Whoso sheddeth man's blood, by man shall his blood be shed: for in the image of God made he man.

These prohibitions refer back to God's decision to send a flood to wipe out life on earth:

> And God said unto Noah, The end of all flesh is come before me; for the earth is filled with violence through them; and, behold, I will destroy them with the earth. (Gen. 6:13)

God agrees to undertake no further campaigns of extermination provided humans abstain from violence *(hamas)*. The motif of human dignity resonates in the ban on killing: God made man in his own image and as an image of God, man is sacred and inviolable. In this form, the Noahide commandment still provides the best foundation for a global ethos today.

In the post-biblical era, in the rabbinical interpretation of this passage, the ban on violence was expanded to the canon of the seven Noahide laws: '1. Prohibition of idolatry; 2. Prohibition of Blasphemy; 3. Prohibition of bloodshed; 4. Prohibition of sexual immorality; 5. Prohibition of Theft; 6. Prohibition of cruelty to animals – archaically formulated: prohibition of eating flesh taken from an animal while it is still alive; 7. Establishment of courts of law.'[4] With that we are in late antiquity, which we have already recognized in another context as an early age of globalization. The seven Noahide laws formulate the basis on which Judaism can imagine a peaceful coexistence with other, non-Jewish peoples. During the seventeenth century the concept of natural law with reference to the Noahide

commandments was developed.[5] The textual history of these covenants thus suggests that the early Jewish religion evolved towards the
dual-level structure of *religio duplex* in just the way that Jonathan
Sacks refers to this tradition. Under the conditions of diaspora, the
Jews relied on this dual-level structure to reach an accommodation,
based on mutual recognition, with their host countries and their
religions.

In fact, a similar dualism runs through the entire Hebrew Bible. It
is already expressed in the two names given to God, Elohim and
Jahwe, the first of which relates to the universal God, the second to
the God of the covenant.[6] Through the technique of gematria, the
assignation of numerical values to words in Hebrew based on the
numerical value of their letters, the medieval rabbis and kabbalists
found out that the divine name 'Elohim' and the Hebrew word for
nature, *teva'*, add up to the same number (86). Maimonides appears
to be drawing on this tradition when, in the passage from the *Guide
for the Perplexed* I cited in Part Two, he equates 'works of God' with
'works of nature'.[7] If we assume that the kabbalists identified Elohim
with nature, then we are not at all far from the god of Spinoza, the
philosophers' god in whom Lessing – in however playful and ironic
a fashion – also placed his faith.[8]

The strained juxtaposition of the two most important redactional
strands in the Bible, the Deuteronomist and the Priestly Source, can
also be interpreted in this way. Perhaps the juxtaposition of a monotheism (or more precisely, a monolatry) of *fidelity* with a monotheism
of *truth* – the juxtaposition, that is to say, of a religion that acknowledges and even presupposes the existence of other gods (and hence
the religions affiliated with those gods) and demands that Israel
remain faithful to its god under these circumstances, with a monotheism that denies the existence of other gods and knows only the One
God, as expressed most clearly in Deutero-Isaiah (Isa. 45) – is to be
understood not in the sense of a development from one to the other,
but in the sense of an intentional 'both-and' within the framework
of the *religio duplex* structure. To be sure, Deuteronomy, which
heralds the monotheism of fidelity, was in all likelihood composed
before exile, at least in its original version (seventh century BCE),
whereas Deutero-Isaiah belongs in the post-exilic period (end of the
sixth century BCE) and quite obviously already responds to the
encounter with Zoroastrianism and its more abstract conception of
a Supreme Being. Yet the particularistic monotheism of the Deutero-
nomic tradition was in no way driven out or eclipsed by the universalistic monotheism of the Priestly and Deutero-Isaian tradition. In
his book on Moses, Sigmund Freud traced this dualism back to the

twin origins of biblical monotheism postulated by him: the universalistic monotheism of Akhenaten, as whose follower he identifies his Egyptian Moses, and the particularistic monotheism of the Midianite priest of Yahweh, who following the murder of the Egyptian Moses assumed his leadership role and falsified his theology. This all-too-fantastic construction need not detain us any further here; it is interesting only to the extent that, along with the many astute observations Freud makes in support of it, it appears to confirm the structure of *religio duplex*.[9]

It is perhaps more than an alluring thought experiment to interpret the tension between Elohim and Yahweh, the creator God and the God of the covenant, Priestly Source and Deuteronomist, particularistic and universalistic monotheisms in the sense of *religio duplex*. We then find ourselves dealing with a different form of dual religion, however. The two trends within the Hebrew Bible certainly do not lend themselves to being understood in terms of an esoteric elite religion and an exoteric popular religion. Both trends may well have had their own support bases. Deuteronomism is clearly linked to the intellectual (lay) elite of the *soferim*, the 'scribes', whereas the Priestly Source and the tradition associated with it looks to the Temple in Jerusalem and the sacerdotal elite. Both trends thus belong at the apex of Jerusalem society without having the least to do with secrecy and esotericism.[10]

Still, this is where the roots may lie of that version of *religio duplex* into which Judaism evolved in late antique and early medieval times. This *was* clearly split between exoteric and esoteric communication: the former in the form of rabbinical instruction, the latter in that of the mystical and magical kabbalah. From the fifteenth century onwards, the kabbalah played a central role in Christian philosophical discourse,[11] and the formation of the *religio duplex* idea in its classical phase in the seventeenth and eighteenth centuries was undoubtedly influenced by it. The Hebraists Spencer and Cudworth were familiar with kabbalistic sources and Knorr von Rosenroth had introduced readers to the main features of the Kabbalah in his *Cabbala denudata*,[12] so seventeenth- and eighteenth-century theorists could connect the abstract idea of dual religion with particular instantiations.

I am not a scholar of Judaism and must therefore leave it to the experts to judge whether, and in what sense, Judaism can be understood as a *religio duplex*. Since I began this book with Egypt, I would like to conclude by returning there to inquire of a specific ancient Egyptian tradition whether, and to what extent, the *religio duplex* structure finds expression in it. The sources we discussed earlier in relation to the idea's 'ancient Egyptian foundations' will hardly qualify as evidence for a religion practised on two levels. Although the distinction between two spheres of meaning in Egyptian ritual comes astonishingly close to later theories of the dual meaning of signs developed in Platonic allegoresis, in Egypt that distinction remained confined to closely circumscribed realms of cultic activity and speech. Egyptian religion was nonetheless marked by a pronounced distinction that seems worth investigating in the light of the *religio duplex* question. I refer to the distinction between a broad and a narrow concept of religion, which a number of years ago I brought into connection with Thomas Luckmann's idea of 'invisible religion' and the distinction it presupposes between visible and invisible religion.[13]

Visible and Invisible Religions

By 'invisible religion', Luckmann means the ultimately validating framework of meaning for the various fields of cultural practice, communication and reflection that have emerged as distinct forms within this framework or 'world picture', and to which the 'visible religion' belongs as one field among others specific to this culture. Invisible religion is the higher 'universe of meaning' that determines the individual's relationship to society and the 'world'. Visible religion is the religion manifested in specific institutions of the cult and the priesthood. It is responsible for the tasks involved in transactions with the sacred and the administration of the sacred goods associated with them.

In ancient Egypt we come across a model that explicitly formulates Luckmann's distinction between invisible and visible religion. Luckmann's 'invisible religion' comes surprisingly close to the Egyptian concept of *ma'at*. Ma'at signifies the principle of a universal harmony that manifests itself in the cosmos as order and in the world of human beings as justice.[14] Such concepts also exist in other cultures to describe the totality of meaningful order on the highest plane of abstraction. Examples are the Greek concept *kosmos*, the Iranian *ascha*, the Indian *dharma* and the Chinese *tao*. What distinguishes the ancient Egyptian idea of *ma'at* is its coupling with political power. The king is responsible for ensuring that *ma'at* rules on earth. Without the state, the symbolic universe would collapse. However, the state is not the institutionalization of *ma'at*. As a principle, *ma'at* is not capable of being institutionalized or objectified, that is, codified. What we are confronted with is a hidden theme that manifests itself in its success, not a fully articulated norm. What *ma'at* is can be gleaned from the texts of the wisdom literature where it is presented casuistically, not apodictically; it is not found in a code of religious or juridical rules in the narrower sense.

This framework for a meaningful order that the king is supposed to uphold breaks down into the two opposing cultural spheres of 'law' and 'cult'. These are the spheres in which *ma'at* – otherwise a higher, invisible form and as such incapable of being institutionalized – is made visible. Here one may speak of state institutionalization. The text that unfolds this conception deals in a very fundamental way with the relationship between Re, the sun god and god of creation, and the king:

> Re has installed the king
> on the earth of the living
> so that he may give justice to mankind,
> and please the gods,
> so that he may realize *ma'at* and drive out *isfet*.
> He [the king] brings divine sacrifices to the gods
> and offerings to the dead.[15]

This text distinguishes between 'law' and 'cult', the 'moral and legal' cosmos and the 'religious cosmos' as the two spheres through which the kings uphold the world, both of which are brought together in the higher concept of making *ma'at* a reality. The king – the political order, the 'state' – has been placed on earth by the creator himself with the general task of bringing *ma'at* – justice, truth, order – into being and expelling its opposite, *isfet* – violence, lies and chaos – which normally reigns supreme on earth. It is this that I would like to call religion in the broader sense, Luckmann's 'invisible religion'. Here religion is not contrasted with some 'secular' order or other, but rather stands for order as opposed to all forms of disorder. On this plane religion can be equated with order in a universal sense encompassing all other orders.

Within this broad concept of religion, however, we now see a second distinction introduced: 'administering justice to humans and satisfying the gods'. Here a line is drawn between the sphere of the social and political order, that is, 'justice' and – once again – 'religion' (for after all that is what is meant by 'satisfying the gods'), but now in a much narrower, more specific sense.[16] That is 'visible religion', divided once again into cults of the gods and the dead. This

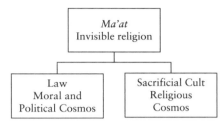

Figure 5

'religious cosmos' is contrasted with the 'moral and political cosmos' as its own 'sub-universe of meaning'.[17] I called this structure the 'Egyptian triangle', as shown in figure 5. The model shown in this figure has the advantage of being formulated in the language of the sources, and thus makes a twofold distinction: between the generalized level of royal activity ('realizing *ma'at*') and the level of specific royal actions, where a further distinction is made between dispensing 'law' (to the people) and directing the 'cult' (for the gods and the dead). This is clearly recognizable as a version of the *religio duplex* structure.

It is very instructive to observe how Egyptian texts refer to gods and goddesses in many different ways, depending on whether these texts are grounded in cultic practice, operate within the framework of visible religion, and set out to 'appease the gods', or whether they are anchored in extra-cultic forms of Egyptian writing and deal in a general way with the fundamental questions of existence, including and especially the divine. Cultic texts are addressed to individual deities or refer to them by their names and epithets; extra-cultic texts, by contrast, speak simply of 'God', as if there were only one. As one example among many I will quote the concluding section of an instructional document, the *Instruction for Merikare*.[18] This is a text that Egyptology places in the genre of 'wisdom literature'. Wisdom literature has to do with questions of right conduct, that is, with 'justice'; we are thus dealing with a genre that stands very far removed from cultic practice. Wisdom literature is a profane or secular discourse. That is not to say that all talk of gods or the divine is banished from it, for these things belong to the fundamentals of human existence as well. But it is not a question here of communicating with the gods, something that is only possible in a cultic setting.

Egyptian instructional texts are all dictated by a father speaking to his son, and they all have a testamentary character. That is especially true of the *Instruction for Merikare*; for here a dead father, King Cheti, speaks from beyond the grave to his son and successor, King Merikare. This framing device sets up the universal, essential, transcendent perspective from which the instruction is delivered. The text concludes with a section on god and mankind:

> Humans are well cared for,
> the livestock of God;
> he made heaven and earth for their sake.
> He pushed back the greediness of the waters
> and created the air so that their nostrils might live.
> His images are they, having come forth from his body.
>
> For their sake he rises to heaven.
> For them he made plants and animals,
> birds and fish,
> so that they might have food.
> If he killed his enemies and went against his children,
> this was only because they thought of rebellion.
>
> For their sake he causes there to be light.
> To see them he travels [the heavens].
> He established for himself a chapel at their back.
> When they weep, he hears.
> He created for them a ruler 'in the egg'
> and commander to strengthen the backbone of the weak.
>
> He made for them magic as a weapon
> to ward off the blows of happenings.
> Watching over them night and day,
> he thrashed the crooked-hearted among them
> as a man beats his son for the sake of his brother.
> God knows every name.[19]

Here the talk is of 'God', as if there were only one, even though the Egyptians knew dozens of important and thousands of lesser deities. This shows once again that we are operating here, outside the cultic setting, at a very high level of generalization and reflection. That is the customary form for speaking about the divine in wisdom literature. It is also clear, however, that a particular god is intended here rather than 'the divine' as such. This god is certainly not, as

Posener still believed, whichever god has jurisdiction in the case to hand ('to whom it may concern'), but rather the One God from whom everything originated, the source and creator of the universe and hence of all the many other gods. The concluding passage of the *Instruction for Merikare* makes clear to the royal pupil that the kingdom he will rule was established for the sake of humans, 'the livestock of God', and represents nothing other than the extension into the social realm of God's creating, preserving and nurturing activity.

The *Book of Two Paths*, a kind of guidebook to the beyond, dates from roughly the same time as the *Instruction for Merikare*. It belongs to the Middle Kingdom literature of the dead, the coffin texts, which were written on the interior sides of coffins. Here we find the following remarkable text, which was surely interpolated into this textual composition from another, extra-cultic source:

Words spoken by Him whose names are hidden.
The Lord of All says [. . .]:
I did four deeds within the portals of the horizon.

I made the four winds,
that every man might breathe, wherever he may be.
That is one deed.

I made the great inundation,
that the bereft might share in it like the great.
That is one deed.

I made every man like his fellow;
I did not command them to do Isfet [i.e., evil],
but it was their own hearts which overthrew what I devised.
That is one deed.

I made their hearts stop forgetting the West,
so that offerings might be made to the gods of the nomes.
That too is one deed.
I created the gods from my sweat,
and men are the tears of my eye.
I shine and am seen every day in my dignity as Lord of All,
and I made night for the Weary-hearted [Osiris].

I will sail really and truly in my bark,
for I am Lord of flood when crossing the sky,

I am not rejected because of any limb of mine.
Hu is with Heka felling that 'Ill-disposed One' for me,
I see the horizon,
I sit before it,
I judge between the wretched and the strong
and repay evil-doers like with like.
Life is mine,
for I am its lord,
and the sceptre will not be wrested from my hand.[20]

The speaker here may be called 'He whose names are hidden' and the 'Lord of All' rather than 'god', yet he is without doubt the same anonymous deity talked about in the *Instruction for Merikare*. Moreover, both texts deal with a very similar theme: the justification of creation. They attempt nothing less than a theodicy of the creator. The *Instruction for Merikare* finds him not guilty of failing to look after his herd of human 'livestock'. Behind the sentence, 'If he [. . .] went against his children', stands the unspoken question: 'How could he go against his children, how could he authorize the violence that claimed so many victims?' The two questions, or rather reproaches, to which the Lord of All responds in the coffin text may be reconstructed as follows:

1. How could the creator permit injustice in his creation?
2. Why does he not take steps to put a stop to it?

The creator's answer to the first question is that he created nature in such a way that everyone is granted an equal share in its life-giving gifts, air and water. Humans, too, he created equal, 'every man like his fellow', and 'made their hearts' know death ('the West') so that they might be pious and God-fearing. He forbade[21] them from doing each other wrong, which in this context can only mean the emergence of inequality and the power wielded by the strong and rich over the poor and weak. Their hearts – their minds and their planning volition – led them to disobey this commandment. Finally he made sure that, as it states literally, their hearts would 'stop forgetting the West' – that is, death and what comes after it. The double negation – 'stop forgetting' – amounts to an emphatic affirmation: 'always think of it, constantly recall it'. God created humans so that they would always be aware of their own mortality and never be able to drive it out of their minds. The advantage of this set-up is that it means they will live in piety and sacrifice to the 'gods of the nomes', that is, the gods of their religion. Admittedly, this works more to the gods' advantage than that of those sacrificing to them, but it also helps humans come to terms with this knowledge or this inability to forget.

God flatly denies the second reproach. He is no *deus otiosus* who retreats to the highest heaven and leaves his creation to its own devices. He incessantly crosses the sky in his 'bark', and just as he gives battle to the cosmic enemy, so too he will rescue the wretched from the clutches of the strong and see that right and justice triumph on earth.[22]

This text, the *Instruction for Merikare* and a number of other 'wisdom literature' texts were written in an era that looked back to a catastrophic experience: the collapse of the Old Kingdom, which was evidently accompanied by paroxysms of violence that claimed a great many victims.[23] In the Merikare text, that catastrophe results from a divine punitive action, just as the catastrophe of Babylonian conquest in the Old Testament, attended by the destruction of the Temple and the downfall of the kingdom, is explained as God's punishment for the disloyalty shown him by his people. The coffin text even more radically absolves the creator of any responsibility for evil in the world. The heart of man – his free will, in other words – is what brings evil into the world, but God will take up arms against it. Both texts are informed by an underlying uncertainty over whether the same God from whom all things proceed also looks after his creation and cares for the individual, or whether his all-encompassing majesty lifts him above such mundane concerns. Those are questions of ultimate meaning which refer to the level of invisible religion. Characteristic of these texts is the high level of abstraction they demonstrate when talking about God as well as the profundity with which they tackle the question of God's justice. This profundity and the reference to god, rather than particular gods, remain typical for Egyptian wisdom literature throughout all epochs of Egyptian literary history.

With the distinction between religion in a broad, extra-cultic sense and a cultic sense, ancient Egyptian culture developed two quite different perspectives for thinking and talking about the relationship between god and man. So far as cultic contact with the divine world is concerned, everything depends on ritual precision, and hence the specific 'profile' of whichever god happens to be worshipped by that particular cult. So far as the essential matters of existence discussed in wisdom literature are concerned, however, only 'god' is spoken of, since here attention is directed to the One God to whom all things, both human and divine, owe their being.

Ancient Egypt left behind a wealth of texts that thematize god and the universe, meaning and justice in this comprehensive sense. Although 'philosophy' has not yet emerged in this discourse as a distinct form, many of these texts – most of them hymns to the Supreme God – could be labelled 'philosophical hymns' owing to their general and wide-ranging connection to the fundamental questions of invisible religion. All of them praise the Only One from whom all things proceed, and they unambiguously confirm Cudworth's thesis that even Egyptian polytheism is undergirded by a monotheism of sorts, an inclusive monotheism that traces all gods back to the One. A Leiden papyrus from the thirteenth century BCE contains a cycle of hymns to Amun.[24] One of them juxtaposes the aspects of encosmic manifestation and hypercosmic hiddenness, or immanence and transcendence. The first part praises god in his inner-worldly manifestations:

> Secret of transformations and sparkling of appearances,
> marvellous god, rich in forms!
> All gods boast of him
> to make themselves greater with his beauty to the extent of his
>   divinity.

> Re himself is united with his body.
> He is called the Great One in Heliopolis.
> He is called Tatenen/Amun, who comes out of the primeval waters
>   to lead the 'faces'. [. . .]

> His *ba* is in heaven, his body in the west,
> his image is in southern Heliopolis and wears his diadem.

The second part now confronts this theology of immanence with a theology of the Hidden God, which seems already to display characteristics of negative theology:

> One is Amun, who keeps himself concealed from them,
> who hides himself from the gods, no one knowing his nature.
> He is more remote than heaven,
> he is deeper than the underworld.

None of the gods know his true form;
his image is not unfolded in books;
nothing certain is testified about him.

He is too secretive for his majesty to be revealed;
he is too great to be inquired after,
too powerful to be known.

People fall down immediately for fear
that his name will be uttered knowingly or unknowingly.
There is no god able to call him by it.
He is *ba*-like, hidden of name like his secrecy.[25]

The following hymn from the same collection is also based on the dialectic of manifestation and hiddenness:

All gods are three:
Amun, Re and Ptah, whom none equals.
He who hides his name as Amun,
he appears to the face as Re,
his body is Ptah.
Their cities on earth,
Thebes, Heliopolis and Memphis,
will last forever. [. . .]
He alone, Amun, together with Re
[and Ptah], united in three.[26]

All gods are three, but these three are also only inner-worldly manifestations of the One Hidden God, who here remains nameless, referred to only as 'he'. This Hidden One manifests himself in the world as name (Amun), sun (Re) and cult image (Ptah), and this trinity in turn provides the basis for all other gods. I can detect traces of a dual religion in this theology, a religion which, beyond concrete cultic, cosmic and mythological forms of visibility, approachability and inner-worldly divine efficacy, recognizes a dimension of hiddenness and divine withdrawal in which certain features of a genuinely philosophical theodicy are already apparent.

The following text comes from the twenty-second dynasty (tenth/ninth century BCE):

Hail, creator of all that is,
producer of all beings,

father of gods, bearer of goddesses,
who appointed them with cities and nomes;
who sired men and bore women,
who creates life for all faces!

The breath of life,
the breeze of the north wind;
a high Nile on whose *ka* one lives,
who provides for gods and mortals.
Sun of the daytime, moon of the night,
who crosses the sky without tiring.

Mighty in display of power, mightier than Sachmet,
like a fire raging;
Great of grace, who cares for the one who adores him,
who turns to heal suffering.
For he gazes on humankind, there is no one he does not know,
and he heeds millions of them.
Who can withstand your wrath,
who can avert the rage of your might?[27]

This god, who once again is not addressed by name, has three faces: he is the creator of the universe with gods and mortals, he animates and maintains the world as air, water and light, and he helps the individual in his hour of need. The personal union of universalistic cosmic god and personal helper is repeatedly emphasized in the Egyptian texts. These texts appear to make the 'salto mortale' referred to by Jacobi within the confines of a single text.

In terms of relating to the distinction between invisible and visible religion, the model of *religio duplex* may be applied to ancient Egypt with some justification. In this case, to be sure, it has nothing to do with exotericism and esotericism, public and arcane religion, political and natural theology, even if the 'visible religion' is a state institution. But if mysteries, initiations, occult secrets or anything of the kind did exist in ancient Egypt, they had their place precisely in the realm of the cult, the 'visible religion', in which 'secrets' (*seshta'u*) are constantly mentioned.

The distinction between invisible and visible religion is not specific to ancient Egyptian religion; it is, rather, a (presumably) universal structure that expresses itself differently in individual religions. It may be the case, however, that the monotheistic religions tend to overturn this distinction, at least to the extent that it is in their power to do so. Even within the narrow limits of our investigation it has become apparent that several authors – John Toland and William Warburton, for example – expressly excluded Christianity from the *religio duplex* structure.[28] To take one example, the Old Testament systematically annuls the distinction, so fundamental to the Egyptian model, between 'cult' and 'justice'. God cannot be assuaged by cultic practice alone; he demands first and foremost that justice be done. Justice becomes the basis for one's relationship with God. Life itself is now placed in the framework of the relationship between God and mankind – religion in the narrower sense of the term – and subordinated to the requirements of justice. The concept of justice thereby ceases to found a sphere that exists outside of specific relations with the divine. Instead, it is drawn into the relationship with God and in this sense theologized. Where this level is attained, we are dealing with a new form of religion, a 'secondary' religion.[29] Secondary religions arise from a process of de-differentiation. What was previously kept apart by the border between cult and justice now falls together. That is why – so we might suppose – secondary religions like Judaism, Christianity and Islam also tend to abolish the distinction between invisible and visible religion, to understand themselves as institutionalized invisible religions and to recognize no level of religious allegiance and orientation beyond their institutionalized creeds and rules for living. This very de-differentiation was what Mendelssohn sought to cancel with his distinction between particular religions and a universal religion of mankind. With that, the concept of invisible religion has also acquired a new, trans-religious meaning.

The 'Mosaic distinction' between true and false in the religious realm belongs at any event on the level of particular, concrete, historical and 'visible' religions, where there can and only ever will be religions in the plural. On this level they are perfectly entitled to insist on this distinction, and no one would want to dispute the gains in clarity and depth of theological thought, or in practical orientation in everyday life, that the transition to religions based on this distinction entails. They only become problematic when the other dimension escapes from view, religion is reduced to a single dimension, and absolute and exclusive religious truths are elevated to the status of universal truths. If it is correct that the two-level structure of *religio duplex* represents the normal form of religion, its origin and future, then a form of religion that confines itself to this one level proves to be a constriction that does justice neither to God nor to humans. This constriction brings with it what was identified as the potential for violence inherent in monotheism or in the Mosaic distinction, which stirred up so much apologetic dust.

However, a one-dimensional monism or cosmotheism that rejects every personal notion of God as idolatrous would be no less problematic than a one-dimensional monotheism that not only posits its own truth as absolute but universalizes it as well, thereby proving incapable of thinking God and religion other than in the singular.

Notes

Introduction

1   'An non diceres, Spinozam sua ab hisce Aegyptiis mutuatum esse?' (P. E. Jablonski, *Pantheon Aegyptiorum*, Frankfurt/Oder 1750, Book 1, chapter 2, 36, s. v. Phthas).
2   *Great Shorter Works of Pascal*, trans. E. Cailliet and J. Blankenagel, Westport, CT, 1974, 117.
3   G. Vallée, *The Spinoza Conversations between Lessing and Jacobi: Texts with Excerpts from the Ensuing Controversy*, New York, 1988, 85. Several weeks after the conversation with Jacobi, Lessing wrote the formula *Hen kai pan* in Greek script on the wallpaper used as a visitors' book in Johann Wilhelm Ludwig Gleim's garden-house in Halberstadt. He also noted it in a guest book. See W. Albrecht (ed.), *Lessing*, Kamenz, 2005, 517–18; R. Daunicht (ed.), *Lessing im Gespräch*, Munich, 1971, 539–40. See also H. B. Nisbet, *Lessing*, Munich, 2008, 821–31.
4   Jacobi, *Über die Lehre des Spinoza*, p. 26.
5   *Hen panta einai* (Frgm. B.50).
6   See my *Moses the Egyptian*, Cambridge, MA, 1997, 139–43. Lessing apparently envisaged the formula as an inscription on an ancient temple; see Albrecht (ed.), *Lessing*, 505. My derivation of the formula from the work by Ralph Cudworth cited in note 7 of this chapter has been contested by St. Eberle, 'Lessing und Zarathustra', in *Rückert-Studien* 17 (2006/07): 73–130, esp. 99–103, with some remarkable arguments. First, according to Eberle, Lessing was thinking of Zoroaster rather than Hermes Trismegistos when he imagined a religion of all-oneness; and, second, he had no doubt read Cudworth in the Latin translation of Johann Lorenz von Mosheim, who distances himself very energetically from Cudworth precisely on the matter of an arcane theology. As

far as the first argument is concerned, Eberle has cited such striking passages from Lessing's writings that his intensive interest in Zoroaster cannot be doubted. However, it should be remembered that Lessing could have stumbled across the formula *Hen kai pan* in very few of the treatises on Zoroaster available to him at the time, whereas this formula is cited dozens of times by Cudworth in numerous Greek and Latin variations. It is beside the point that the formula ought correctly to be read with the definite article (*to hen kai to pan*) or as the sentence *hen to pan* ('All is One'); what matters is that we are dealing everywhere with different predicative connections of the two keywords *hen* and *pan* (or *unus* and *omnia*). Be that as it may, the other objection seems to me to be the more important. The footnote from Mosheim quoted by Eberle in which Mosheim emphatically repudiates the idea of an arcane theology, and with it the model of *religio duplex*, certainly stands in sharp contradiction to the tradition I am pursuing here. The great Mosheim cannot be numbered among the spokesmen of *religio duplex*. On the other hand, the freemason Lessing would have known enough about the importance of esoteric traditions for him not to be put off by a single footnote.

7 R. Cudworth, *The True Intellectual System of the Universe*, London, 1678, 2nd edn, 1743.

8 R. Cudworth, *Systema intellectualis huius universi*, Jena, 1733. On Mosheim's translation and the sometimes very critical footnotes he added to Cudworth's text, see S. Hutton, 'Classicism and Baroque', in M. Mulsow et al. (eds), *Johann Lorenz Mosheim (1693–1755)*, Wiesbaden, 1997, 211–27.

9 *Meditationes, Theses, Dubia philosophico-theologica [Freistadt 1719]. Dokumente.* Ed. with an introduction by M. Pott, Stuttgart-Bad Cannstatt, 1992. On Lau, see M. Mulsow, *Moderne aus dem Untergrund*, Hamburg, 2002, 432–8 (see also the index, p. 505), and E. Feil, *Religio*, vol. 4, Göttingen, 2007, 129–33.

10 'Veritas & Religio una est: quia Ratio una: quia Deus unus' (Thesis IX). The Latin citations from Lau's text follow his own idiosyncratic orthography and punctuation.

11 'Prima, antiquissima, generalissima & Religio maxime rationalis: est Deismus' (Thesis X). The expression *Deismus* here designates the opposition to atheism and not yet – as later – the belief in an impersonal supreme being, in opposition to theism as the belief in a personal God.

12 'Deus fuit, nec fuit Religio. Deus enim, ab aeterno. Religio, in Tempore demum introducta, Accidens est Deitatis.'

13 'Colit vero Ratio: Deum, ceu Universi totius Creatorem: Conservatorem: Gubernatorem; Cultu maxime interno. Universum hoc, Liber ejus est.'

14 'Nulla hinc Turbatio Mentis ob Peccata & Ignem Aeternum.' Lau thus states with the utmost clarity that consciousness of sin in the strict sense only entered the world with revealed religion, a thesis that can invite theological admonishments even today (as I have had occasion to experience!).

15 'Migratio Animarum ex corporibus: Conglutinatio cum Anima Mundi.'
16 A little later, he calls the *Religio Christiana* the 'Religio Rationalissima'.
17 On the doctrine of God's two books, see R. Groh, 'Theologische und philosophische Voraussetzungen der Rede vom Buch der Natur', in A. Assmann et al. (eds), *Zwischen Literatur und Anthropologie*, Tübingen, 2005, 139–46; D. Groh, 'Die Entstehung der Schöpfungstheologie oder der Lehre vom Buch der Natur bei den frühen Kirchenvätern in Ost und West bis zu Augustin', in the same edited collection, 147–60; and D. Groh, *Göttliche Weltökonomie*, Frankfurt/Main, 2010; also A. Assmann, *Die Legitimität der Fiktion*, Munich, 1980, 39–48, as well as H. Blumenberg, *Die Lesbarkeit der Welt*, Frankfurt/Main, 1981.
18 'Particularis: per Colloquia, Angelos, Apparitiones, Visiones, Inspirationes, Somnia, Oracula, Vaticinia, Prophetias, Miracula, Scripturam Sacram; Fundamenta Religionis Revelatae, certarum & Nationum: Judaeorum praecipue & Christianorum.'
19 'Prior: ex Libro Naturae. Posterior: ex Libro Scripturae.'
20 'Sunt interim omnes, in Complexu Generali & Sensu abstracto: Deistae. Sunt Cultores & Adoratores Dei. Sunt Amatores Religionum!'
21 Th. Sundermeier, 'Religion, Religionen', in K. Müller and Th. Sundermeier (eds), *Lexikon missionstheologischer Grundbegriffe*, Berlin, 1987, 411–23; see also Th. Sundermeier, *Was ist Religion?*, Gütersloh, 1999; A. Wagner (ed.), *Primäre und sekundäre Religion als Kategorie der Religionsgeschichte des Alten Testaments*, Berlin, 2006.
22 Hildesheim, 1718. I likewise owe my acquaintance with this work to Martin Mulsow.
23 Ibid., 13: 'sifficiat notasse, Philosophiam Aegyptiorum fuisse omnino duplicam Exotericam et Esotericam.'
24 In his masterful book, *The Eighteenth Century Confronts the Gods*, Cambridge, MA, 1959, Frank Manuel devotes a short section to 'Twofold Philosophy' (65–9), which he takes to mean the truths of the natural religion of an ur-monotheism, handed down, in the midst of polytheisms and idolatries, under the veil of mysteries, hieroglyphs and symbolic language (65). As representatives of the 'double-truth doctrine', Manuel names William Warburton, John Toland, David Hume, Henry St John Bolingbroke, Le Batteux, Baron de Sainte-Croix, Julien Offray de La Mettrie, Abbé Pluche and Charles Dupuis, although he only discusses Toland and Warburton.

Chapter 1 Egyptian Foundations: The Dual Meaning of Signs

1 See J. Assmann, M. Bommas (ed.), *Ägyptische Mysterien?*, Munich, 2002, esp. the chapter by W. Burkert, 'Mysterien der Ägypter in griechischer Sicht', 9–26.

2   Chr. Froidefond, *Le mirage égyptien dans la littérature grècque d'Homère à Aristote*, Gap, 1971; F. Hartog, 'Les Grecs égyptologues', in *Annales. Économies, Sociétés, Civilisations* 41 (1986): 953–67; F. Hartog, 'Voyages d'Egypte', in F. Hartog, *Mémoire d'Ulysse*, Paris, 1996, 49–86.

3   Diodorus Siculus, *Bibliotheca historica: Diodorus of Sicily*. In 12 vols, ed. and trans. C. H. Oldfather, Cambridge, MA, 1946–7.

4   H. L. Jones, *The Geography of Strabo*, 8 vols, Cambridge, MA, and London, 1932–5; J. Yoyotte, P. Charvet, St Gompertz, *Strabon: Le Voyage en Egypte*, Paris, 1997.

5   Diodorus, *Bibliotheca historica* I.70–1.

6   See J. Assmann, *Weisheit und Mysterium*, Munich, 2000, 44–51.

7   J. Griffiths, *Plutarch. De Iside et Osiride*, Cardiff, 1970.

8   See below, note 32 of this chapter.

9   Porphyry, *Epistola ad Anebonem*, ed. A. R. Sodano, Naples, 1958.

10 *Manetho*, ed. and trans. W. G. Waddell, Cambridge, MA, 1964.

11 P. W. van der Horst, *Chaeremon*, Leiden, 1984; P. W. van der Horst, 'Hieroglifen in de ogen van Grieken en Romeinen', in *Phoenix ex Oriente Lux* 30 (1984): 44–53; P. W. van der Horst, 'The Secret Hieroglyphs in Classical Literature', in J. den Boeft and A. H. W. Kessels (eds), *Actus. Studies in Honour of H. L. W. Nelson*, Utrecht, 1982, 115–23.

12 K. Preisendanz, A. Heinrich, *Papyri Graecae Magicae*, 2 vols, Stuttgart, 2nd edn 1973–4; H. D. Betz et al., *The Greek Magical Papyri in Translation*, Chicago, IL, 1986. See also the 5 vols edited by R. Merkelbach and M. Totti: *Abrasax. Ausgewählte Papyri religiösen und magischen Inhalts*, Opladen, 1990–2001. On the Egyptian background of the Greco-Egyptian magical literature, see especially J. Dieleman, *Priests, Tongues, and Rites*, Leiden, 2005.

13 *Corpus Hermeticum*, ed. and trans. A. D. Nock and A.-J. Festugière, 4 vols, Paris, 1945–54. There is a more recent commented translation by B. P. Copenhaver, *Hermetica: The Greek Corpus Hermeticum and the Latin Asclepius in a New English Translation with Notes and Introduction*, Cambridge, 1992.

14 A.-J. Festugière, *La révélation d'Hermes Trismégiste*, 4 vols, Paris, 1944–54, disputes that the Hermetic writings have any Egyptian background at all, instead placing them squarely in the context of Neoplatonism.

15 Iamblichos, *De mysteriis Aegyptiorum* VIII.3.

16 G. Fowden, *The Egyptian Hermes*, Cambridge, 1986. Of decisive importance for this new estimation was the discovery of Hermetic scripts in Coptic at Nag Hammadi; see J.-P. Mahé, *Hermès en Haute Égypte*, 2 vols, Quebec, 1978–82.

17 On the social relations in Ptolemaic and Roman Egypt, see D. Frankfurter, *Religion in Roman Egypt*, Princeton, NJ, 1988; K. Goudriaan, *Ethnicity in Ptolemaic Egypt*, Amsterdam, 1988, and R. S. Bagnall, *Hellenistic and Roman Egypt*, Oxford, 2005. Burial rites show that the

class division between Greeks and non-Greeks was not rigorously maintained; rather, there was a certain social mobility, leading to hybridized cultural forms.

18 See J. Yoyotte, 'Les pèlerinages dans l'Égypte ancienne', in J. Yoyotte et al. (eds), *Les pèlerinages*, Paris, 1960, 19–74.

19 M. Douglas, *In the Wilderness*, Sheffield, 1993, chapter 2, 'The Politics of Enclaves', 42–62.

20 A. I. Baumgarten, *The Flourishing of Jewish Sects in the Maccabean Era*, Leiden, 1997.

21 T. Mann, *Joseph und seine Brüder*, Frankfurt/M., 1964, 1089.

22 The Egyptian term for 'mysteries', predominantly used in relation to cultic mysteries, is *sšt3.w*, or *seschta'u* in the conventional Egyptological pronunciation. Since the aleph was often used to reproduce the foreign 'r', the word might have been pronounced *stēraw* and thus come astonishingly close to the Greek *my-stērion*, for which no Greek etymology exists.

23 The Hebrew expression is *ḥartummim*, in which an equivalent of the Egyptian title *ḥrj-tp* can be seen (demotic: *phritob*, with article; Akkadian: *ḥar-tibi*). *Ḥrj-tp* actually means 'supreme' and is the abbreviation of the title 'supreme priest' (just as 'chef' is an abbreviation of 'chef de cuisine'). J. Quaegebeur, 'On the Egyptian Equivalent of Biblical Hartummim', in S. Israelit-Groll (ed.), *Pharaonic Egypt*, Jerusalem, 1985, 162–72; J. Quaegebeur, 'La désignation *(P3) Ḥry-tp*: PHRITOB', in J. Osing and G. Dreyer (eds), *Form und Maß*, Wiesbaden, 1987, 368–94.

24 See J. Assmann, *Ägypten. Theologie und Frömmigkeit einer frühen Hochkultur*, Stuttgart, 2nd edn 1991, chapter 4; J. Assmann, 'Verklärung', in *Lexikon der Ägyptologie*, vol. 6, Wiesbaden, 1986, 998–1006.

25 On the 'performative' use of language, see the classic studies by J. L. Austin, *How To Do Things with Words*, Oxford, 1962, and J. R. Searle, *Speech Acts*, Cambridge, 1969. A type of language use is to be called 'transformative', meanwhile, if it not only produces a state of affairs (e.g., when a judge declares the accused to be guilty) but intervenes to alter an existing state of affairs (e.g., when Jesus says to the cripple: 'Take up your bed and walk!').

26 J. Assmann, *Tod und Jenseits im Alten Ägypten*, Munich, 2001, 453–76.

27 I have attempted to reconstruct the 'implicit theory of language' of Egyptian cultic recitation in *Ägypten. Theorie und Frömmigkeit einer frühen Hochkultur*, 102–35.

28 J. Assmann, 'Altägyptische Kultkommentare', in J. Assmann and B. Gladigow (eds), *Text und Kommentar*, Munich, 1995, 93–110. On these texts, see also H. W. Fischer-Elfert, 'Das verschwiegene Wissen des Irtisen', in J. Assmann and M. Bommas (eds), *Ägyptische Mysterien?*, 27–35, esp. 30–3. See also A. von Lieven, 'Im Schatten des Goldhauses', in *Studien zur Altägyptischen Kultur* 36 (2007): 147–55.

29   D. Bidoli, *Die Sprüche der Fangnetze in den altägyptischen Sargtexten*, Glückstadt, 1976, 30–1.

30   G. Simmel, 'Das Geheimnis und die geheime Gesellschaft', in G. Simmel, *Soziologie*, Frankfurt/M., 1992, 383–455. See also B. Nedelmann, 'Geheimhaltung, Verheimlichung, Geheimnis – einige soziologische Vorüberlegungen', in H. G. Kippenburg and G. G. Stroumsa (eds), *Secrecy and Concealment*, Leiden, 1995, 1–16.

31   On the expression *b3.w-R'w* ('power of the sun god') as a term for ritual texts, see A. H. Gardiner, 'The House of Life', in *JEA* 24 (1938): 157–79, here pp. 166, 168; A. M. Blackman, 'The Myth of Horus at Edfu II', in *JEA* 29 (1943): 2–36, here p. 22, note 7; J. Assmann, *Liturgische Lieder an den Sonnengott*, Berlin, 1969, 222, note 171; B. H. Stricker, *De bref van Aristeas*, Amsterdam, 1956, 52–3; D. B. Redford, *Pharaonic King-lists, Annals, and Yearbooks*, Mississauga, 1986, 92 and 215–16, note 52.

32   Iamblichus, *De mysteriis Aegyptorium* VI.5; *Iamblichus or The Mysteries*, trans. T. Taylor, London 1821 (translation modified in the quotations that follow).

33   I borrow the concept of 'presentification', in the sense of a magical evocation, from J.-P. Vernant, 'De la présentification de l'invisible à l'imitation de l'apparence', in J.-P. Vernant, *Entre mythe et politique*, Paris, 1996, 359–77.

34   On this, see the apt comments of H. te Velde, 'Some Remarks on the Mysterious Language of the Baboons', in J. H. Kamstra (ed.), *Funerary Symbols and Religion*, Kampen, 1988, 129–36, esp. 134f.

35   L. Simonis, *Die Kunst des Geheimen*, Heidelberg, 2002, 34; see also the reference on 37f. to Henri-Jean Martin, *Histoires et pouvoirs de l'écrit*, Paris, 1988, 91.

36   N. Luhmann, 'Form der Schrift', in H.-U. Gumbrecht and K. L. Pfeiffer (eds), *Schrift*, Munich, 1993, 353.

37   J. Sacks, *The Dignity of Difference*, London, 2002, 125–41.

38   E. A. Havelock, *The Literate Revolution in Greece and its Cultural Consequences*, Princeton, NJ, 1981.

39   In 1738, William Warburton had already made this point against Athanasius Kircher.

40   Herodotus, *Historiae* II.36.

41   R. Merkelbach, *Isis Regina – Zeus Sarapis*, Stuttgart and Leipzig, 1995, 115–18; W. Peek, *Der Isishymnus von Andros und verwandte Texte*, Berlin, 1930. Greek text: J. Bergman, *Ich bin Isis*, Uppsala, 1968, 301ff.; M. Totti, *Ausgewählte Texte der Isis- und Sarapisreligion*, Hildesheim, 1985, 1ff.; L. V. Žabkar, *Hymns to Isis in Her Temple at Philae*, Hanover, 1988, 140–2.

42   *Bibliotheca historica* III.3; see A. and J. Assmann (eds), *Hieroglyphen*, Munich, 2003, 33.

43   L. Simonis, *Die Kunst des Geheimen*, 11–14.

44   See chapter 3.

45   Clement of Alexandria, *Stromata* V.4.20.3 (*Stromata* I–VI, ed.
      O. Stählin, Berlin, 1985, 339). See P. Derchain, 'Les hiéroglphes à
      l'époque ptolémaïque', in C. Baurain et al. (eds), *Phoinikeia Grammata*,
      Liège, 1991, 243–56.
46   See T. Todorov, *Symboltheorien*, Tübingen, 23–6.
47   See E. Winter, article 'Hieroglyphen' in *RAC* 15, 113, Stuttgart, 1989,
      83–103, here 94f. with reference to Plutarch's statement (*De Iside et
      Osiride* 56 [374A]: 'The letters in the Egyptian alphabet number the
      square of five'); A. Volten, 'An "Alphabetical" Dictionary and Grammar
      in Demotic', in *Archiv Orientalni* 20 (1952): 496–508; R. Eisler, 'Platon
      und das ägyptische Alphabet', in *Archiv für die Geschichte der Philoso-
      phie* 34 (1922): 3–13.
48   'The unlimited variety of sound was once discerned by some god, or
      perhaps some godlike man; you know the story that there was some
      such person in Egypt called Theuth. He it was who originally discerned
      the existence, in that unlimited variety, of the vowels – not "vowel" in
      the singular but "vowels" in the plural – and then of other things which,
      though they could not be called articulate sounds, yet were noises of a
      kind; there were a number of them too, not just one; and as a third
      class he discriminated what we now call the mutes. Having done that,
      he divided up the noiseless ones or mutes until he got each one by itself,
      and did the same thing with the vowels and the intermediate sounds;
      in the end he found a number of the things, and affixed to the whole
      collection, as to each single member of it, the name "letter". It was
      because he realized that none of us could ever get to know one of the
      collection all by itself, in isolation from all the rest, that he conceived
      the "letter" as a kind of bond of unity, uniting as it were all these
      sounds into one; and so he gave utterance to the expression "art of
      letters", implying that there was one art that dealt with the sounds.'
      Plato's Philebus, trans. with commentary by R. Hackforth, Cambridge,
      1972, 28.
49   Porphyry, *De vita Pythagorae*, 11–12.
50   N. Luhmann, 'Das Kunstwerk und die Selbstreproduktion der Kunst',
      in H. U. Gumbrecht and K. L. Pfeiffer (eds), *Stil*, Frankfurt/M., 1986,
      620–72, here 627. See also I. Berger, 'Literatur als Kompaktkommuni-
      kation', in I. Berger, *Musil mit Luhmann*, Munich, 2004, 71–91.
51   *Horapollonis Nilotici Hieroglyphica Libri II*, ed. F. Sbordone, Naples,
      1940; English: G. Boas, *The Hieroglyphics of Horapollo*, Princeton, NJ,
      1993.
52   Chaeremon lived in the first century CE. He officiated as an Egyptian
      priest before moving to Rome to tutor Nero. See P. W. van der Horst,
      Chaeremon; P. W. van der Horst, 'The Secret Hieroglyphs in Classical
      Literature'.
53   This is also how Rabelais understood the hieroglyphs: 'Far otherwise
      did heretofore the sages of Egypt, when they wrote by letters, which
      they called hieroglyphics, which none understood who were not skilled
      in the virtue, property, and nature of the things represented by them.'

F. Rabelais, *The Works of Francis Rabelais*, trans. Du Chat et al., vol. 1, 160.

54 Diodorus Siculus, *Bibliotheca historica* III.3–4.

55 G. Bruno, *De Magia* (Opera latina, vol. 3, 411–12). See F. Yates, *Giordano Bruno and the Hermetic Tradition*, London, 2002, 289.

56 See A. Assmann, *Die Legitimität der Fiktion*, 57–77.

57 Plotinus, trans. S. MacKenna, *The Enneads*, London, 1991, 416–17 (V.8.6). See D. Stolzenberg, 'Lectio Idealis', in L. Morra and C. Bazzanella (eds), *Philosophers and Hieroglyphs*, Turin, 2003, 74–97.

58 Marsilio Ficino, *In Plotinum V, vii* (Paul O. Kristeller, *Supplementum Ficinianum. Marsilii Ficini Florentini philosophi Platonici Opuscula inedita et dispersa*, 2 vols, Florence, 1937–45, 1768).

59 On the Egyptian background of Iamblichus's text, see Ph. Derchain, 'Pseudo-Jamblique ou Abammon?', in *Chronique d'Egypte* 38 (1963): 220–6; M. Broze, 'La reinterpretation du modèle hiéroglyphique chez les philosophes de langue grecque', in Bazzanella Morra (ed.), *Philosophers and Hieroglyphs*, 35–49.

60 See H. A. Schlögl, *Der Sonnengott auf der Blüte*, Basel and Geneva, 1977.

61 See J. Assmann, 'Hierotaxis', in J. Osing and G. Dreyer (eds), *Form und Maß*, Wiesbaden, 1987, 18–42.

62 M. Barasch, 'Renaissance Hieroglyphics', in A. and J. Assmann (eds), *Hieroglyphen*, 165–90; L. D. Morenz, 'Neohieroglyphs of the Italian Renaissance', in Bazzanella Morra (ed.), *Philosophers and Hieroglyphs*, 50–73.

63 O. Goldwasser and M. Müller, 'The Determinative System as a Mirror of World Organization', in *Göttinger Miszellen* 170 (1999): 49–68; O. Goldwasser and M. Müller, 'The Building Blocks of a Conceptual Category', in Bazzanella Morra (ed.), *Philosophers and Hieroglyphs*, 219–36; O. Goldwasser and M. Müller, *Lovers, Prophets and Giraffes*, Wiesbaden, 2002.

64 J. Assmann, 'Etymographie', in A. and J. Assmann (eds), *Hieroglyphen*, 37–64.

65 A. Loprieno, in *Texte aus der Umwelt des Alten Testaments*, vol. 3/5, Gütersloh, 1995, 1054.

66 Solar eye (Leiden I.384 rto IX.10–11), see Loprieno, ibid., 1057; B. van de Walle, 'Le Décret d'Horemheb', in *Chronique d'Égypte* 22 (1947): 230–8; M. J. Smith, art. 'Sonnenauge', in *Lexikon der Ägyptologie 5* (1984): 1082–7; Winter, art. 'Hieroglyphen', in *RAC* 15: 92.

67 W. Spiegelberg, *Der demotische Text der Priesterdekrete von Kanopus und Memphis*, Heidelberg, 1922, 74 and 91.

68 Papyrus Jumilhac VI.7. See also J. Vandier, *Le Papyrus Jumilhac*, Paris, 1960, 155 n.133.

69 Papyrus Jumilhac XIV.20.

70 F. Bacon, *The Advancement of Learning* (1605), Oxford, 1974, 98.

71 G. Vico, *La Scienza Nuova Seconda*, Naples 1744, II.2.4; P. Rossi, 'La religion dei geroglifi e le origini della scritura', in P. Rossi, *Le terminate*

antichitè, Pisa, 1969, 81–131; P. Burke, *Vico*, Oxford, 1985; U. Eco, *The Search for the Perfect Language*, Oxford, 1997.

72 Here and elsewhere, I cite the translation by M. Samuels, *Jerusalem: A Treatise on Ecclesiastical Authority and Judaism*, London, 1838; here vol. 2, 114. I have on occasion cautiously modernized Samuels' diction and orthography.

73 W. F. Albright, *The Protosinaitic Inscriptions and their Decipherment*, Cambridge, MA, 1966. Towards the end of the 1990s, John and Deborah Darnell discovered protosinaitic inscriptions dating back to the nineteenth century BCE in Wadi el-Hol, located west of the Nile between Luxor and Abydos.

Chapter 2   From the Dual Meaning of Signs to Dual Religion

1 Spencer, *De legibus Hebraeorum*, Book 1, 155.

2 See S. D. Benin, 'The Cunning of God and Divine Accommodation', in *The Journal of the History of Ideas* 45 (1984): 179–92. Amos Funkenstein traces the general path from the idea of the cunning of God (or Reason) from Maimonides to Hegel in his book, *Theology and the Scientific Imagination from the Middle Ages to the Seventeenth Century*, Princeton, NJ, 1986, 222–71; see also his older work, *Heilsplan und natürliche Entwicklung*, Munich, 1965, and his essay, 'Gesetz und Geschichte', in *Viator* 1 (1970): 147–78.

3 On the 'Sabians', see note 14 of this chapter, below.

4 M. Halbertal, *People of the Book*, Cambridge, MA, 1997, 34.

5 See S. Stroumsa, 'Entre Harran et al-Maghreb', in M. I. Fierro (ed.), *Judíos y musulmanes en al-Andalus y el Magreb*, Madrid, 2002, 153–64.

6 Here I follow D. Krochmalnik, 'Der Sinn der Opfer', in *Der Landesverband der Israelitischen Kultusgemeinden in Bayern* 11/73 (June 1997): 21–4.

7 I thank G. Stroumsa for directing me to F. Dreyfus, 'La condescendence divine (synkatabasis) comme principe herméneutique de l'Ancien Testament dans la tradition juive et dans la traditon chrétienne', in J. A. Emerton (ed.), *Congress Volume Salamanca 1983*, Leiden, 1985, 96–107.

8 G. G. Stroumsa, 'John Spencer and the Roots of Idolatry', in *History of Religions* 40 (2001): 1–23, points out Maimonides' central importance for seventeenth-century research into religion, and particularly for Spencer.

9 On Spencer, see J. Assmann, *Moses the Egyptian*, 55–90; J. Assmann, 'Das Geheimnis der Wahrheit', in ARG 3 (2001), 108–34; G. G. Stroumsa, 'John Spencer and the Roots of Idolatry'.

10 G. G. Stroumsa, ibid., 20, speaks of a 'literary genre' in the rabbinical tradition into which Spencer's book inscribes itself.

11 'The primary meaning was that the law should be the medium of the measures taken by God to abolish idolatry and to preserve the Israelites in His faith and cult; the secondary meaning was that the rites and institutes of that law should serve to prefigure certain mysteries.' ('PRIMARIA erat, ut Lux ea medium esset Ordinarium, quo Deus, ad idololatrium abolendam, & Israelitas in Ipsius fide cultuque retinendos, uteretur; SECUNDARIA erat, ut Legis illius ritus & institute mysteriis quibusdam adumbrandis inservirent'; *De legibus Hebraeorum*, Book 1, 153).

12 Ibid., 155 (1732 edition, 209), with reference to Maimonides and the Babylonian Talmud, treatise *Berakhot*, end of chapter 5 (according to Spencer). He explains *verba duplicata* as *sensu duplici, literali & mystic gravida* ('heavy with double meaning, both literal and mystical'). In this context, Spencer refers to Hugo Grotius, who derives the rabbinical distinction between a written and an oral Torah from the double meaning of the Jewish law, identifying the oral Torah with the Kabbalah (*Commentarius in Matthaeum* 5:20; there is a 'Brevis in Novum Testamentum Commentarius' by Grotius, whose first part deals with the Gospel of Matthew, and *Annotationes in libros evangeliorum*, Amsterdam, 1641, therein 'Ad Matthaeum').

13 'Adeo ut lex Mosis, sensu literali sumpta, paedagogus esset ad Deum; sensu vero mystico spectata, non raro ad Christum et Evangelium' (Book 1, 165 [1732 edition, 218]). Spencer alludes here to Gal. 3:24.

14 On the 'Sabaeans', Maimonides' term for 'heathens', see S. Stroumsa, 'Sabéens de Harran et Sabéens de Maïmonide', in T. Lévy and R. Rashed (eds), *Maïmonide*, Leuven, 2004, 335–52.

15 As far as the number of sources used is concerned, Spencer is surpassed only by Athanasius Kircher, particularly in his *Oedipus Aegyptiacus*, 3 vols, Rome, 1652–4.

16 Spencer, *De legibus Hebraeorum*, Book 1, 157: '[. . .] Deum voluisse ut Moses mystica rerum sublimiorum simulacra scriberet, eo quod huiusmodi scribendi ratio, literaturae, qua Moses institutus erat, hieroglyphicae non parùm conveniret.'

17 As far as I can see, Spencer does not use this concept; however, something like it underpins his description of Egyptian religion. Jacob Friedrich Reimmann extensively discusses the *duplex philosophia* of the Egyptians, namely *exoterica et esoterica*, in his work, *Idea Systematis Antiquitatis Literariae Specialioris sive Aegyptiacae Adumbrati*, Hildesheim, 1718. I have Martin Mulsow to thank for drawing my attention to this work.

18 *Talattuf* in Arabic corresponds to the Greek concept *synkatabasis* = *condescensio*.

19 Ibn Tibbon translates as ʿ*ormah* ('cunning') and *taḥbulah* ('artifice', 'strategy') the Arabic *talattuf*, which actually means 'goodwill, courtesy'.

20 Spencer, *De legibus Hebraeorum*, Book 3, 28.

21 Ibid., Book 1, 157: 'aequum est opinari, Deum religionem, carnalem quidem in frontispicio, sed divinam et mirandam in penetrali, Judaeis tradidisse, ut institute sua ad seculi gustum et usum accomodaret, nec quicquam sapientiae nomina commandatum, Legi vel cultui suo deesse videatur.'

22 'Judaeorum plebem quidem, ritibus omnibus quomodo Legum ipsarum verbis concepti erant, Moses obstrictam, teneri iussit. Caeteros autem, quorum mens esset virtusque firmior, cùm eo cortice liberatos esse, tum ad diviniorem aliquam et hominum vulgo superiorem Philosophiam assuescere, & in altiorem Legum earum sensum mentis oculo penetrare, voluit' (*Praeparatio evangelica* VIII.10, p.m. 378, cited in Spencer, *De legibus Hebraeorum*, Book 1, 156; see n. 24).

23 That is, the *verbum Dei* revealed in the law, not Moses, as Spencer writes.

24 Eusebius, *Praeparatio evangelica* VIII.10.18.

25 Isidore of Pelusiota, *Epistulae* II, *Ep.* 133 (J.-P. Migne, ed., *Patrologia Graeca*, vol. 78, Paris, 1864, 575–6). Spencer omits *kai prosphoros* after *sophos*, presumably because its meaning escaped him; the Patrologia Graeca translates 'et consentanee'. *Prosphoros* means 'fitting, appropriate, seemly'.

26 R. Cudworth, *The True Intellectual System of the Universe*, London, 1678. See J. Assmann, *Moses the Egyptian*, 80–90.

27 E. Cassirer, *Die platonische Renaissance in England und die Schule von Cambridge*, Leipzig, 1932.

28 R. H. Popkin, 'Newton and Maimonides', in J. E. Force and R. H. Popkin, *The Third Force in Seventeenth Century Thought*, Leiden, 1992, 189–202; S. Mandelbrote, 'Isaac Newton and Thomas Burnet', in R. H. Popkin and J. E. Force (eds), *The Books of Nature and Scripture*, Dordrecht, 1994, 149–78.

29 'Appendix: Newton's Out of Cudworth', in R. H. Popkin and J. E. Force, *Essays on the Context and Influence of Isaac Newton's Theology*, Dordrecht, 1990, 207–13.

30 Cudworth uses the terms 'Monarchy' and 'Polyarchy' for the concepts 'monotheism' and 'polytheism', which were not in circulation at the time.

31 Iamblichus, *De mysteriis Aegyptiorum*, VIII.1–6.

32 A.-J. Festugière, *La revelation d'Hermès Trismégiste*, vol. 3, Paris, 1990, 49–50.

33 See J. Assmann, 'Kosmogonie, göttliche Schöpfung und menschliche Kreativität', in J. Assmann, *Theologie und Weisheit im Alten Ägypten*, Munich, 2005, 13–34.

34 Eusebius, *Praeparatio evangelica* III.9.12.

35 Ibid., I.6.1.

36 Jablonski, *Pantheon Aegyptiorum*, 36.

37 'Est nempe Vulcanus ipse, aether supremus, ignis subtilissimus et purissimus, luce perpetua et semper eadem immutabiliter fulgens, qui

omnibus praeest, omniaque regit, qui totum mundum permeat, animat, vivificat' (ibid., 82).

38   Ibid., 83–4. For Jablonski, 'Tithrambo vel Termuthis' is the Egyptian equivalent to the Greek Hecate; see vol. 1, 103–21. The two-faced goddess, Tefnut, appears to stand behind the divine couple Kneph and Tithrambo: her benevolent, feline, mild-mannered form is worshipped under the name of Bastet, while her evil, leonine, wrathful form is worshipped under the name of Sachmet.

39   This refers to the cosmogony of Hermopolis, which identifies four male and four female primal gods as personifications of the pre-existing primal state from which the sun god emerged when he created the world.

40   In the understanding of the seventeenth and eighteenth centuries, this is Isis, expressly invoked here as the goddess of nature. Iamblichus may also have been thinking of Isis, who appears as a lunar goddess in Apuleius.

41   The distinction between spirit and matter, however, is completely foreign to Egyptian thought.

42   See G. G. Stroumsa and P. Fredrikson, 'The Two Souls and the Divided Will', in A. I. Baumgarten, J. Assmann and G. G. Stroumsa (eds), *Self, Soul, and Body in Religious Experience*, Leiden, 1998, 198–217.

43   Des Places' 'cycle des naissances' (for *tēs genesiourgou kyklēsiōs*) probably introduces a falsely Buddhistic note into the text.

44   Cudworth, *The True Intellectual System of the Universe*, 314, referring to Clement of Alexandria, *Stromata* V.7.41.1. Cudworth's translator and adapter, Johann Lorenz von Mosheim, a sworn anti-Neoplatonist, distances himself energetically and radically from Cudworth's model of an esoteric theology in a footnote, to which Stephan Eberle draws attention in *Lessing und Zarathustra* (102): 'numquam ego quemquam ratione valentem ita delirasse arbitror, ut dogmata, quorum utilitatem & veritatem noverat, & quae perspicuis & planis verbis declarari posse videbat, imaginibus & nescio quibus symbolius opprimeret, & hominum oculis subduceret.' In English: 'I believe no one of sound mind has ever been mad enough to keep hidden under images and symbols, and to withdraw from the eyes of his fellow men, teachings he knew to be useful and true, and which he realized could be expressed in clear and plain words.'

    This sentence sounds entirely reasonable to present-day ears, but one wonders how this learned translator of Origenes could have so summarily dismissed a key principle of the whole Platonic tradition. In that tradition (and not just in that one), a careful distinction is made between articulation and communication. Much can 'be expressed in clear and plain words' without being communicated by just anyone. Could Mosheim have known nothing of this famous principle? At any rate, one would be advised not to lend too much weight to this footnote. It can be explained by his antipathy towards Neoplatonism.

45 *Contra Celsum* I.12, in *Patrologia Graeca* 11.677–8; Origen, *Against Celsus*, in J. Donaldson and A. Roberts (eds), *Anti-Nicene Christian Library*, vol. I, Edinburgh, 1869, 409–10.
46 Clement of Alexandria, *Stromata* V.3.19.3 and V.6.41.2.
47 Cudworth, *The True Intellectual System of the Universe*, 316.
48 Ibid., 317.
49 *De rebus sacris et ecclesiasticis exercitationes* XVI, London, 1614, 70ff. See Yates, *Giordano Bruno*, 398–403; A. Grafton, *Defenders of the Text: The Tradition of Scholarship in an Age of Science, 1450–1800*, Cambridge, MA, 1991, 145–61.
50 Cudworth criticized Casaubon for having treated all sixteen treatises that make up the *Corpus Hermeticum* as a single coherent text. In doing so, Casaubon made the mistake of applying locally valid observations to the entire corpus: 'Wherefore the Learned Casaubon seems not [to] have reckoned or concluded well, when from the detection of forgery in two or three of those Trismegistick books at most, he pronounces of them all universally, that they were nothing but Christian Cheats and Impostures. And probably he was led into this mistake, by reason of his too securely following that vulgar Error (which yet had been confuted by Patricius) that all that was published by Ficinus under the name of Hermes Trismegist, was but one and the same Book Poemander, consisting of several chapters, whereas they are all indeed so many Distinct and Independent Books, whereof Poemander is only placed First' (Cudworth, *The True Intellectual System of the Universe*, 320–1).
51 *Corpus Hermeticum*, Treatise XIII.18.1; see Merkelbach, *Abrasax*, vol. 2, 136. See also *Corpus Hermeticum* XIII.17.5.
52 Cudworth, *The True Intellectual System of the Universe*, 339, referring to Plutarch, *De Iside et Osiride* 9.
53 Cudworth, ibid., 337. Cudworth is no doubt referring to Damascius, *De principiis* (*Traité des premiers principes*, ed. L. G. Westerink, trans. J. Combès, vol. 3, Paris, 1991, 167); see note 2 on p. 339 (on *skotos agnōston*) with reference to ch. II, 11, 3–5, and 30, 8–13, as well as to ch. I, 44, 6–13.
54 G. Berkeley, *Siris*, London, 1744, 144–5.
55 P. N. Miller, 'Taking Paganism Seriously: Anthropology and Antiquarianism in Early Seventeenth-Century Histories of Religion', in ARG 3 (2001), 183–209, here 197: 'UNICAM esse supremam omnium causam, UNICUM orbis moderatorem in innumeris illis cultum'; M. Mulsow, 'John Seldens *De Diis Syris*', in ARG 3 (2001), 1–21, here 16.
56 M. Mulsow, ibid.
57 In Egyptian, hieroglyphs can indeed occasionally be characterized as 'gods', and divine symbols could therefore also perhaps be termed hieroglyphs.
58 As Horus of Edfu, the falcon is in fact a sun god, but for different reasons. The goddess Sakhmet has jurisdiction over pestilential diseases, but as the 'solar eye' she is certainly associated with the sun.

59 Again, it is perfectly true that the ibis is the sacred animal of Thoth, and that Thoth is the moon god.
60 Clement of Alexandria, _Stromata_ V.7.43.1–3 (cited in M. Mulsow, 'John Seldens _De Diis Syris_, 21); trans. Roberts-Donaldson in _Anti-Nicene Christian Library_, Edinburgh, 1869, vol. XII, 246.
61 Here I draw on Mulsow, who reproduces Selden's Latin version of the passage in Synesius.
62 _De Diis Syris_, 68–9.
63 Gospel of Philip §67 (M. Krause, _Die Gnosis_, vol. 2, Zurich, 1971, 108). In the opening chapter of _Hidden Wisdom_, Leiden, 1996, 11–26, G. Stroumsa assembles a number of similar passages on the mythological self-concealment of truth.
64 Goethe, 'Aus Makariens Archiv', in Goethe, _Werke_, Hamburg edition, vol. 8, Munich, 1981, 460.
65 K. Müller, 'Über den monistischen Tiefenstrom der christlichen Gottrede', in K. Müller and M. Striet (eds), _Dogma und Denkform_, Regensburg, 2005, 47–84.
66 On the basis of M. Stausberg, _Faszination Zarathustra_, Berlin and New York, 1998, I have retraced the outlines of this story in _The Price of Monotheism_, Stanford, CA, 2009, chapter 3.

Chapter 3   _Religio Duplex_ and Political Theology

1 The concepts 'political theology' and 'natural theology', alongside that of 'poetic theology', make up the _theologia tripertita_ ('threefold theology'), which goes back via Varro to the Greek (Stoic) tradition. The public cultic institutions, temples, churches and their priests preside over the _theologia politikē_ or _civilis_; the _theologia poiētikē_ or _fabularis_ is the poet's affair; and the _theologia physikē_ or _naturalis_ belongs to the philosophers. On the _theologia tripertita_, see G. Lieberg, 'Die theologia tripertita als Formprinzip antiken Denkens', in _Rheinisches Museum_ 125 (1982): 25–53; W. Geerlings, 'Die theological mythica des M. Terentius Varro', in G. Binder and B. Effe (eds), _Mythos_, Trier, 1990, 205–22. On the _theological civilis_, in particular, see H. Cancik, 'Augustinus als constantinischer Theologe', in J. Taubes (ed.), _Der Fürst dieser Welt_, Munich, 1983, 136–52; A. Dihle, 'Die theologia tripertita bei Augustin', in H. Cancik et al. (eds), _Geschichte – Tradition – Reflexion_, vol. 2, Tübingen, 1996, 183–202. On the history of the concept of political theology in antiquity, see E. Feil, 'Von der "Politischen Theologie" zur "Theologie der Revolution"?', in E. Feil and R. Weth (eds), _Diskussion zur Theologie der Revolution_, Munich and Mainz, 1969, 110–32.
2 _Theologiae gentium politicae dissertation prima de Divinitate Principum_, Rostock, 1662; see Mulsow, _Moderne aus dem Untergrund_, 174–80, 190–3.

3 First of all in Lipsius and Campanella; see Mulsow, *Moderne aus dem Untergrund*, 162–3. Political theology, in Morhof's sense of the term, refers to the implicit theology of the political. This is also how the concept was used by Carl Schmitt, who made it famous through his book *Politische Theologie* (Berlin, 1922). Political theology in the critical sense of the term deals, conversely, with the implicit politics of the theological.

4 W. Schröder, *Ursprünge des Atheismus*, Stuttgart-Bad Canstatt, 1998; Mulsow, *Moderne aus dem Untergrund*.

5 There are two treatises of this title: [Johann Joachim Müller], *De imposturis religionum (De tribus impostoribus) – Von den Betrügereyen der Religionen*, critically edited and commented by W. Schröder, Stuttgart-Bad Canstatt, 1999; Anon., *Traktat über die drei Betrüger: Traité des trois imposteurs (L'Esprit de Mr. Benoit de Spinosa)*, critically edited, translated and introduced by W. Schröder, Hamburg, 1992.

6 S. Berti, *Trattato dei tre impostori*, Turin, 1993, 198; Anon., *Traktat über die drei Betrüger* (see previous note, n.5 above).

7 *Historiae* VI.56.6–12; *The Histories of Polybius*, vol. III, trans. W. R. Paton, Cambridge, MA, 1923, 396.

8 H. Diels, *Die Fragmente der Vorsokratiker*, ed. W. Kranz, 6th edn, Hildesheim, 1972, B 25; *Sextus Empiricus. Adversus Mathematicos*, trans. R. G. Bury, Cambridge, MA, 1968, ix, 54.

9 Cited in Schröder, *Ursprünge des Atheismus*, 220.

10 A. Dihle, 'Das Satyrspiel *Sisyphos*', in *Hermes* 105 (1997): 28–42.

11 *De natura deorum* I.42.118: 'Quid? ii, qui dixerunt totam de dis immortalibus opinionem fictam esse ab hominibus sapientibus rei publicae causa, ut, quos ratio non posset, eos ad officium religio duceret, nonne omnem religionem funditus sustulerunt?' ('Take again those who have asserted that the entire notion of the immortal gods is a fiction invented by wise men in the interest of the state, to the end that those whom reason was powerless to control might be led in the path of duty by religion; surely this view was absolutely and entirely destructive of religion'; *De natura deorum*, trans. H. Rackham, Cambridge, MA, and London, 2005, 113).

12 Livius, *Ab urbe condita* I.19.4; cf. Plutarch, *Vitae*, Numa 4.1; 8.10; 15.11; esp. 8. 3–4.

13 Schröder, *Traité des trois imposteurs*, Hamburg, 1992, 72.

14 See J. Assmann, *Moses the Egyptian*, 93.

15 W. Schröder therefore failed to identify the Diodorus citation as such, referring to Naudé instead as its source.

16 'Tous les anciens Législateurs, voulant autoriser, affermir & bien fonder les Loix qu'ils donnoient à leurs peuples, n'ont point eû de meilleur moïen de le faire, qu'en publiant & faisant croire <. . .> qu'ils les avoient reçûës de quelque Divinité: Zoroastre, d'Oromasis, Trismegiste de Mercure, Zalmoxis de Vesta, Charondas de Saturne, Minos de Jupiter, Lycurgue d'Apollon, Drago & Solon de Minerve, Numa de la nymphe Egerie, Mahomet de l'Ange Gabriel; & Moise, qui a été le plus sage de

tous, nous décrit en l'Exode comme il reçût la sienne immédiatement de DIEU' (G. Naudé, *Considérations politiques*, vol. 3, 118–19).

17 Berti, *Trattato de tri impostori*, 198; Anon., *Traktat über die drei Betrüger.*

18 *Adeisidaemon sive Titus Livius a superstitione vindicatus [. . .]*, The Hague, 1709.

19 See Assmann, *Moses the Egyptian*, 93.

20 *Geographika* XVI.2.35–7; cf. P. Schäfer, *Judenhaß und Judenfurcht*, Berlin, 2010, 43–6.

21 Toland, *Origines Judaicae*, 157.

22 A. Ross, *Pansebeia, or, a View of all the Religions of the World*, 6th edn, London, 1696, 362, cited in Schröder, *Ursprünge des Atheismus*, 228.

23 *Tetradymos*, London, 1720, Part 2, 61–100.

24 Toland, *Tetradymos*, 65–6.

25 The citations in cursive type and capital letters draw on Plutarch, *De Iside et Osiride* 9.

26 Toland's 'hood' stands in for *peplos*, a word which Cudworth left in the original and which, since Ficino, has generally been translated as 'veil'. It designates a woollen upper-body garment which women could also draw over their heads.

27 Toland, *Tetradymos*, 71.

28 Ibid.

29 Mulsow, *Moderne aus dem Untergrund*, 123–31, IV.2: 'Idolatry, Superstition, Sacrifice: The History of the Original Religion's Corruption'.

30 W. Warburton, *The divine legation of Moses demonstrated on the principles of a religious deist, from the omission of the doctrine of a future state of reward and punishment in the Jewish dispensation*, London, 1738–41, vol. 2. The work was reviewed by G. E. Lessing in the 'Berlinsche Monatsschrift' in 1751 and more extensively discussed in his fragment 'Über die Elpistiker' (see Nisbet, *Lessing*, 747 n.8).

31 It must be emphasized throughout that in both the atheist and the deist critique of political theology, and even in the representation of political theology as characteristic of paganism, the necessity of theological fictions is almost never called into question. Even most of the atheists do not advocate anarchy (with the exception of Matthias Knutzen and Jean Meslier, who in this regard are forerunners of Bakunin). See Schröder, *Ursprünge des Atheismus*, 228–37.

32 F. Graf and S. Johnston, *Ritual Texts for the Afterlife: Orpheus and the Bacchic Gold Tablets*, London and New York, 2007.

33 See [Abbé Claude Robin], *Recherches sur les initiations anciennes et modernes*, Paris, 1779.

34 Warburton quotes from *Plutarch's Moralia*, vol. 15, *Fragments*, ed. F. H. Sandbach, Cambridge, 1969, Fragment 178. See, among others, P. Scarpi (ed.), *Le religioni dei Misteri*, 2 vols, Milan, 2002, vol. 1, 176; see also Burkert, *Antike Mysterien*, 77.

35   Vol. 1, Book 2, 289–90. Stobaeus ascribes the text to Themistios, and Warburton concurs with this ascription. The fragment was soon afterward recognized as a text by Plutarch, however.

36   *Dissertation on the Ancient Pagan Mysteries*, quoted in W. Hutchinson, *The Spirit of Masonry in Moral and Elucidatory Lectures*, 2nd edn, Carlisle, 1795, 9.

37   *Stromata* V.7.41.1.

38   Plutarch, *De Iside et Osiride* 354 (ch. 8). See also Clement of Alexandria, *Stromata* V.5.31.5: 'Therefore also the Egyptians place Sphinxes before their temples, to signify that the doctrine respecting God is enigmatical and obscure; perhaps also that we ought both to love and fear the Divine Being: to love Him as gentle and benign to the pious; to fear Him as inexorably just to the impious; for the sphinx shows the image of a wild beast and of a man together.'

39   Warburton, *The Divine Legation*, London, 1778, 2nd edn, vol. 1, 190.

40   Clement of Alexandria, *Stromata* V.11.71.1.

41   Warburton, *The Divine Legation*, vol. 1, 234–5.

42   Baron de Sainte-Croix, *Mémoires pour servir à l'Histoire de la religion secrète des anciens Peuples, ou Recherches historiques et critiques sur les mystères du paganisme*, Paris, 1784, VIII.

43   Sainte-Croix, *Mémoires*, 355–7.

44   As an Egyptologist, I cannot help thinking here of a very common epithet of the god Amun which refers to his name (*jmn*, 'be hidden' – *mn*, 'remain'). In its early form, the epithet reads *Jmn mn jḫ.t nb.t*, 'Amun, remaining on all things' (i.e., in lasting possession of all things); in its later, Ramesside form it changed to *Jmn mn m jḫ.t nb.t*, 'Amun, remaining in all things'. This seems to relate precisely to this idea of an all-pervasive presence.

45   J. Assmann, *Moses the Egyptian*, chapter 4. See also my essays 'Hieroglyphen als mnemotechnisches System. William Warburton und die Grammatologie des 18. Jahrhunderts', in J. J. Berns and W. Neuber (eds), *Seelenmaschinen. Gattungstraditionen, Funktionen und Leistungsgrenzen der Mnemotechniken vom späten Mittelalter bis zum Beginn der Moderne*, Vienna, 2000, 711–24, und 'Pictures versus Letters', in J. Assmann and A. I. Baumgarten (eds), *Representation in Religion*, Leiden, 2001, 297–311.

46   Erik Voegelin, *Die politischen Religionen*, ed. Peter Opitz, Munich, 1996, 63.

47   É. Durkheim, *Die elementaren Formen des religiösen Lebens*, Frankfurt/M., 2007.

48   In §24 Lessing writes that Warburton should have limited himself to the claim 'that the lack of those doctrines did not *detract* from Moses' divine mission'. Instead, 'he even saw their absence as proof of it. If only he had tried to base this proof on the suitability of such a law for such a people! But he took refuge instead in a miracle extending without interruption from Moses to Christ, by means of which God supposedly

made each individual Jew just as happy or unhappy as his obedience or disobedience to the law deserved. This miracle, he claimed, made up for the lack of those doctrines, without which no state can subsist; and this substitution, he claimed, proves precisely what that lack seems at first sight to deny.' In the following paragraphs (§25–33) he goes on to develop his counter-thesis of a partial revelation with pedagogic intent. According to Lessing, the Jews only acquired a correct understanding of God's unity and the immortality of the soul upon encountering Zoroastrianism while languishing in Babylonian captivity. In other words, they came to know these doctrines through experience rather than through revelation: 'They became more familiar with it in the schools of the Greek philosophers in Egypt' (§42). The Old Testament is for Lessing the 'primer' for the childhood stage of humanity. Lessing, 'The Education of the Human Race', in H. S. Nisbet, ed., *Philosophical and Theological Writings*, Cambridge, 2005, 223, 228.

49 Friedrich Wilhelm Joseph Schelling, *Sämmtliche Werke*, ed. Karl Friedrich August Schelling, Stuttgart, 1856–61, vol. 13, 492, cited in E. Feil, *Religio*, vol. 4, 872. Schelling explains: 'The gods of the mysteries were recognized as the universal and supreme causes and thus also as the content of the supreme and truly universal religion.'

50 Feil, *Religio*, vol. 4, 872–3.

51 The passage in question appears at the head of chapter 5 below.

52 M. Frank, *Der kommende Gott*, Frankfurt/M., 1982, 245.

53 Ibid., 252.

54 Ibid., 251.

55 Cited in Frank, ibid., 251–2.

56 *Sämmtliche Werke*, vol. 6, 11–70; see the detailed summary in Feil, *Religio*, vol. 4, 840–3. The closeness to masonic ideas is particularly obvious in this text.

57 'The Earliest System-Programme of German Idealism', in M. Baur and D. Dahlstrom (eds), *The Emergence of German Idealism*, Washington, DC, 1999, 310. This text, discovered by Franz Rosenzweig, was composed in 1796, possibly 1797, and was identified by Otto Pöggeler as written in Hegel's handwriting. One thinks here of Goethe's aphorism: 'In natural science, we are pantheists; in poetry, polytheists; morally, monotheists' (*Maximen und Reflexionen*, Hamburg edition, vol. 12, 372).

58 C. Meiners, *Über die Mysterien der Alten, besonders die Eleusinischen Geheimnisse*, Göttingen, 1776.

59 Ibid., 208.

60 Ibid., 261.

61 Ibid., 295–6.

62 Ibid., 298–9.

63 Weishaupt, a product of Jesuit education and professor for canon law and practical philosophy in Ingolstadt, oriented himself mainly towards the Jesuits when setting up his Order. However, the highest level of his three-tiered hierarchy, the 'mysteries class', with its division into 'lesser'

and 'greater mysteries', is unambiguously inspired by Meiners' account of the Eleusinian Mysteries.

64 S. von Moisy,'Von der Aufklärung zur Romantik', in *München*, Munich Exhibition 2.6.–24.8.1984 (exhibition catalogue), 65.

65 'Aus der Korrespondenz des Illuminatenordens', Part 2, 14, cited in M. Neugebauer-Wölk, 'Debatten im Geheimraum der Aufklärung. Konstellationen des Geheimwissens im Orden der Illuminaten', in W. Hartwig (ed.), *Die Aufklärung und ihre Weltwirkung*, special issue of *Geschichte und Gesellschaft* 23, Göttingen, 2010, 32.

66 I. von Born, *Die Mysterien der Aegypter*, in *JF* 1 (1784): 89. See Joseph Uriot, *Les secrets des Francs-Macons mis en Evidence*, Frankfurt and La Haye, 1744 (cited in Koselleck, *Kritik und Krise*, Freiburg, 1959, 67): 'A mesure que le vice s'éléva, la vertu fut abaissée [. . .] et pour n'être point la victime de son cruel antagoniste, elle se fit un azile inaccessible à tout autre qu'à ses fidèles adorateurs.'

67 Koselleck, *Kritik und Krise*, 55–6. See also the important objections voiced by Nisbet, *Lessing*, 773–4, against a construction of the political significance of secret societies in the eighteenth century that lends too much weight to conspiracy theories. I thank Michael Multhammer for this reference. However, with respect to the late eighteenth century and the Illuminati (Koselleck's particular point of reference), Koselleck's analysis still seems convincing to me.

68 In the final chorus of Act I; compare the introductory trio sung by the three boys at the finale of Act II.

69 Koselleck, *Kritik und Krise*, 55.

70 M. Agethen, *Geheimbund und Utopie. Illuminaten, Freimaurer und deutsche Spätaufklärung*, Munich, 1987, 141. W. te Lindert, *Aufklärung und Heilserwartung*, Frankfurt/M., 1998, 22–3, 117–18, and E. Wangermann, *The Austrian Achievement 1700–1800*, London, 1973, 150, speak of 'inner emigration'.

71 See G. Simmel, 'Das Geheimnis und die geheime Gesellschaft', 383–455.

72 See M. Douglas, *In the Wilderness*, Sheffield, 1992, chapter 2: 'The Politics of Enclaves', 42–62.

73 See H. Jordheim, 'Die Hypokrisie der Aufklärer – oder: War Wieland ein Lügner? Eine Untersuchung zu Kosellecks Kritik und Krise', in J. Kurunmäki and K. Palonen (eds), *Time, History and Politics / Zeit, Geschichte und Politik. Zum achtzigsten Geburtstag von Reinhart Koselleck*, Univeristy of Jyväskylä, 2003, 35–54.

74 C. Schmitt, *Der Leviathan in der Staatslehre des Thomas Hobbes*, Hamburg, 1938; reprinted in *Der Leviathan*, Cologne, 1982, 92.

Chapter 4 *Religio Duplex* and Freemasonry

1 Nisbet, *Lessing*, 763.

2 C. Meiners, *Über die Mysterien der Alten*, 271.

3 Schiller, _Die Sendung Moses_ (see footnote 40), 460.
4 _The Travels of Cyrus/Les Voyages de Cyrus_, 2 vols, Paris and London, 1727. In the years that followed, Ramsay's novel went through over thirty French and English reissues and revised editions. Like Terrasson's _Séthos_, it numbered among the century's most widely read books. On the life and work of Andrew Michael Ramsay, see G. D. Henderson, _Chevalier Ramsay_, London, 1952; see also Stausberg, _Faszination Zarathustra_, vol. 2, 838–69. Ramsay lived for years in Fénelon's house in Cambrai, converted to Catholicism, edited Fénelon's writings (including the _Aventures de Télémaque_) and wrote his biography. Ramsay sent his Cyrus on an educational tour that led him to Zoroaster, Hermes Trismegistos and Pythagoras, i.e., the protagonists of _Prisca Theologia_, which Cudworth's _True Intellectual System of the Universe_ had informed him about (Stausberg, _Faszination Zarathustra_, vol. 2, 843).
5 Ramsay was Grand Orator of the Grand Lodge in France. In this capacity, he gave in 1737 a highly regarded speech on the history and goals of freemasonry in which he already adopted a decidedly cosmopolitan standpoint (W. Bergmann, _Andreas Michael Ramsays Rede über die Freimaurerei_, Leipzig, 1907). He demanded, for example, the union of all lodge brothers, irrespective of their traditional national duties, into a 'new people' as a 'spiritual nation', and he saw the task of freemasonry in forming an avant-garde for the education of the human race. See also F. Weil, 'Ramsay et la Franc-Maçonnerie', in _Revue d'histoire de la France_ 63 (1963): 272–8.
6 _Die Reisen des Cyrus_, Breslau, 1780.
7 [J. A. Terrasson], _Séthos_, Paris, 1731, many subsequent editions and reprints; English translation by T. Lediard, _The Life of Sethos_, 2 vols, London, 1732. See R. Nicolai-Haas, 'Die Anfänge des deutschen Geheimbundromans', in R. Ludz (ed.), _Geheime Gesellschaften_, Heidelberg, 1979, 267–92, esp. 272–4, and above all L. Simonis, _Die Kunst des Geheimen_, 187–215. See also J. Assmann and F. Ebeling, _Ägyptische Mysterien. Reisen in die Unterwelt in Aufklärung und Romantik_, Munich, 2011, 48–65.
8 Tamino's initial entrance in _The Magic Flute_ is the exact inverse of this scene: he faints upon catching sight of the snake and first becomes a hero through love (which is absent from Terrasson's novel).
9 For a more detailed summary of the initiation of young Sethos, see my book _Die Zauberflöte_, Munich, 2005, 96–8.
10 G. de Nerval, _Le Voyage en Orient_, Oeuvres II, ed. A Béguin and J. Richer, Paris, 1956, 221–31. See J. Assmann and F. Eberling, _Ägyptische Mysterien_, 303–24.
11 On this point I disagree with Linda Simonis, who traces Terrasson's idea of a 'strict dichotomy in the realm of religion', and hence the idea of _religio duplex_, back to Plutarch and Cudworth (200, note 54).
12 In _Divinae institutions_ I.6, Lactantius refers to the Corpus Hermeticum (_Asclepius_ 20) and emphasizes the correspondence between the hermetic idea of God and the Christian one. See J. Assmann, 'Nachwort',

in C. L. Reinhold, *Die hebräischen Mysterien oder die älteste religiöse Freymaurerey*, Neckargemünd, 2nd edn 2006, 168–9.

13 *Freymäurer-Bibliothek*, ed. J. A. Hermann and J. W. B. von Hymmen, Berlin, 1782, 127–37; I thank F. Ebeling for this reference.

14 Jakob Böhme, *Die Urschriften*, ed. Werner Buddecke, vol. 2, Stuttgart, 1966, 13, cited in W. Schmidt-Biggemann, 'Das Geheimnis des Anfangs. Einige speculative Betrachtungen im Hinblick auf Böhme', in A. and J. Assmann (eds), *Schleier und Schwelle*, vol. 2, Munich, 1998, 47.

15 Paris, 1734. See J. Assmann and F. Ebeling, *Ägyptische Mysterien*, 66–90.

16 R. Selbmann, *Der deutsche Bildungsroman*, Stuttgart, 1994; W. Voss-kamp, 'Der Bildungsroman als literarisch-soziale Institution', in C. Wagenknecht (ed.), *Zur Terminologie der Literaturwissenschaft*, Stuttgart, 1989, 337–52; W. Vosskamp, '*Ein anderes Selbst*', Göttingen, 2004.

17 L. Simonis, *Die Kunst des Geheimen*, with a copious bibliography. This work, to which I am indebted in more ways than one, contains a very comprehensive and detailed chapter on *The Magic Flute* (247–319). On the eighteenth-century secret society novel, see also Nicolai-Haas, *Die Anfänge des deutschen Geheimbundromans*, and especially M. Voges, *Aufklärung und Geheimnis*, Tübingen, 1987.

18 Frankfurt, 1787; see Nicolai-Haas, *Die Anfänge des deutschen Geheim-bundromans*, 271–2.

19 Nicolai-Hass, ibid., 278–84.

20 W. F. Meyern, *Dya-Na-Sore*, 3 vols, Vienna and Leipzig, 1787–91, witheringly reviewed by Schiller in *Allgemeine Literatur-Zeitung* 103 (1788): 204–6. See Nicolai-Haas, *Die Anfänge des deutschen Geheim-bundromans*, 289–90, note 59.

21 Simonis, *Die Kunst des Geheimen*, 215–45.

22 J. H. Jung-Stilling, *Das Heimweh*, ed. M. M. Sam, Dornach, 1994.

23 Jung-Stilling, *Das Heimweh*, 292–5.

24 See Frank, *Der kommende Gott*; Frank, *Gott im Exil*, Frankfurt/M., 1988, 249.

25 Frank, *Gott im Exil*, 250.

26 Simonis, *Die Kunst des Geheimen*, 247–319.

27 J. W. Goethe, *Werke*, Weimar, 1887–1919, vol. IV/5, 149–50.

28 Many blamed the Jesuits for his death.

29 See especially the anonymous text *Ueber geheime Gesellschaften zu populärer Auklärung, von einem Protestanten*, Schweinfurth, 1786, which according to a contemporary review 'presents all secret societies as having been hatched by the Jesuits' (in *Allgemeine Literaturzeitung* 3/165 [1786]: 77–8).

30 Joseph II wanted Bavaria and offered Karl Theodor, who was unhappy there, Austrian Belgium in exchange; the plan was blamed on the Illu-minati and provoked considerable outrage.

31 See the afterword by Matthias Meyer in his edition of F. Schiller, *Der Geisterseher*, Stuttgart, 1996, 219–42, as well as M. Hurst, *Im*

Spannungsfeld der Aufklärung, Heidelberg, 2001; K. H. Kiefer, *Die famose Hexen-Epoche*, Munich, 2004; H. J. Schings, *Die Brüder des Marquis Posa*, Tübingen, 1996.

32 The story first appeared in the *Beyträge zur Geheimen Geschichte des menschlichen Verstandes und Herzens. Aus den Archiven der Natur gezogen*, 2 vols, Leipzig, 1770. The edition I quote from here is *C. M. Wielands sämmtliche Werke*, ed. J. G. Gruber, vol. 15, Leipzig, 1795, 1–66. I thank Florian Ebeling for alerting me to this story.

33 Wieland appropriates this motif from the Hellenistic narrative *The Deception of Nektanebos*.

34 *Herders Briefe*, selected, introduced and annotated by W. Dobbek, Weimar, 1959, 265.

35 Manetho of Sebennytos was a highly educated and well-informed Egyptian priest who wrote his multi-volume work on the history and culture of ancient Egypt at the time of Ptolemy II, in the first half of the third century BCE. The fact that Plutarch quotes him here gives his text a certain authority. We should not forget that the image which the Greeks made of Egypt and passed down to the West did not just rest on travel reports and tour guide anecdotes. There was a rich, solidly founded literature on Egypt, partly written by Egyptians themselves, which we can see reflected in Plutarch.

36 *Egō eimi pan to gegonos kai on kai esomenon* (Plutarch, De Iside et Osiride 9 [354C]).

37 I. Kant, *Critique of the Power of Judgment*, trans. P. Guyer and E. Matthews, Cambridge, 2000, 194.

38 See Introduction, footnote 9.

39 F. Schiller, 'On the Sublime', in Schiller, *Naïve and Sentimental Poetry, and, On the Sublime. Two Essays*, trans. J. Elias, New York, 1967, 198.

40 Kant, *Critique of the Power of Judgment*, 156.

41 Ibid.

42 'Die Sendung Moses', in F. Schiller, *Werke und Briefe*, ed. O. Dann, vol. 6: *Historische Schriften und Erzählungen*, Frankfurt/M., 2000, 451–74.

43 Ibid., 461.

44 C. Colpe, J. Holzhausen, *Das Corpus Hermeticum*, 280.

45 F. Schiller, *Werke und Briefe*, vol. 8, 417.

46 C. L. Reinhold, *Die hebräischen Mysterien oder die älteste Freymaurerey* (1787), ed. and introduced by J. Assmann, Neckargemünd, 2nd edn 2006. Schiller's essay is also reprinted there.

47 W. te Lindert, *Aufklärung und Heilserwartung*, 207.

48 See J. A. M. Snoek, 'What does the word "religious" mean in Reinhold's "religious freemasonry"?', in S. Appel (ed.), *Egypt – Temple of the Whole World*, Leiden and Cologne, 2003, 409–20. At the end of his book on the old and new mysteries, J. A. Starck takes up the cudgels against a 'Magister Pianco' (= H. H. Freiherr Ecker von Eckhofen, author of the book *Der Rosenkreuzer in seiner Blösse*, Amsterdam [= Nuremberg] 1792), who divided the mysteries of the ancients 'into two

kinds of covenant, one concerning religion, the other science'. Starck believes this to be 'quite incorrect, and a mere ideal that he conjured up for himself. All the ancients speak only of greater and lesser mysteries' (355). The polemic against religious freemasonry launched by 'Free Concord' thus evidently concealed a debate with the Asiatic Brothers, the lodge established by Freiherr von Eckhofen (alias Magister Pianco) that was particularly influential in Vienna. The polemical treatise of 'Magister Pianco' is dedicated to a 'venerable brother Phoebron, Supreme Director of the Upper Order of the Rosicrucians in Germany' (Dr Bernhard Joseph Schleiß von Löwenfeld), who for his part responds to this attack with the treatise *Der im Lichte der Wahrheit strahlende Rosenkreuzer, allen lieben Mitmenschen, auch dem Magister Pianco zum Nutzen hingestellt*, Leipzig, 1782. An account of the rituals and ideology of the Asiatic Brothers is given by Anonymous, *Die Brüder St Johannis des Evangelisten aus Asien in Europa oder die einzige wahre und ächte Freimaurerei, von einem hohen Obern*, Berlin, 1803; see also Anonymous, *Der Asiate in seiner Blöße oder gründlicher Beweis: daß die Ritter und Brüder Eingeweihten aus Asien ächte Rosenkreuzer sind; durch wichtige noch unbekannt gebliebene Dokumente erwiesen, welche ihr System, Lehre und Einweihung betreffen. Zum ernsten Nachdenken und Warnung für alle Brüder Freimaurer*, Asia [Leipzig or Bremen], 1790; H. H. Frhr. von Ecker und Eckhofen, *Abfertigung an den ungenannten Verfasser der verbreiteten sogenannten Authentischen Nachricht von den Ritter- und Brüder-Eingeweihten aus Asien*, Hamburg, 1788.

49 E. Rosenstrauch-Königsberg, 'Eine freimaurerische Akademie der Wissenschaften in Wien', in E. Rosenstrauch-Königsberg, *Zirkel und Zentren*, ed. G. Hering, Vienna, 1990, 67–87. The author shows that Born, fearing the influence of former Jesuits, deliberately avoided establishing an official Academy of Sciences at the University, preferring the shelter provided by a secret society instead.

50 Karl Michaeler, Historisch-kritische Abhandlung über die phönicischen Mysterien, Vienna, 1796.

51 A. Giese, 'Freimaurerisches Geistesleben zur Zeit der Spätaufklärung am Beispiel des Journals für Freymaurer', in *Bibliotheca Masonica*, ed. F. Gottschalk, Part 2, Graz, 1988, 11–31; H. Reinalter, 'Ignaz von Born als Freimaurer und Illuminat', in H. Reinalter (ed.), *Die Aufklärung in Österreich*, Frankfurt, 1991, 33–67; D. Lindner, *Ignaz von Born*, Vienna, 1986.

52 He did so on the basis of a legendary tradition which conflated different kings in Egyptian history like Sesostris I, III and Ramses II (and which we already encounter in Herodotus): an ideal character who was not only, as Born writes, 'wise, benevolent and just' but also a military leader whose conquests placed even the exploits of Alexander the Great in the shade.

53 Diodorus writes of a dam being built towards the south, i.e., against the inundation.

54 The footnote refers simply to Plutarch, *De Iside et Osiride*. The famous passage on the 'veiled image at Sais' is presumably intended.

55 P. Hadot, *The Veil of Isis*, Cambridge, MA, 2006, and P. Hadot, *Zur Idee des Naturgeheimnisses*, Wiesbaden, 1982.

56 I.13.1: 'They were mortal, but owing to their wisdom and the blessings they brought to all humankind they had immortality conferred upon them.'

57 Osiris is considered the inventor of music and dance, through which he wins over people and 'brings them into social intercourse'. He is also thought to have introduced agriculture and viticulture. Isis appears as a healer.

58 The transference to Hermes of the legend of the pillars of Seth goes back to the Arab philosophers of the Middle Ages. The legend was handed down by Josephus.

59 Nothing of the sort stands in the passage referred to in Diodorus (I.56). He mentions the famous system of nomes in I.89 but ascribes them to a 'particularly wily' ruler, who introduced this system as a strategy to prevent popular uprisings (according to the principle of 'divide and rule'). Every nome that arose in this way was given its own taboos and quarrelled with its neighbour when they were flouted.

60 G. Naudé, *Considérations politiques sur les coups d'État*, Paris, 1667.

61 Of interest with regard to Schinkel's stage design for *The Magic Flute* is the information: 'the square colonnade was lined by sculpted animals, each sixteen cubits in height, which supported the room in place of pillars', from Diodorus, *Bibliotheca Historica* I.47, 1: 'it is supported, in place of pillars, by monolithic figures in the form of living creatures some sixteen cubits high, wrought in the ancient manner as to shape'. Diodorus is referring to Osiris pillars; Born interprets the 'living creatures' as animals (Hebrew *ḥajjot*).

62 Moses is mentioned in Diodorus, *Bibliotheca historica* I.94.2 among the great legislators to have claimed God as the source of their laws. Just as Menes referred to Hermes, Minos to Zeus, Lycurgus to Apollo, Zarathustra to Ahura Mazda and Zalmoxis to Hestia, so Moses referred to Iao.

63 Diodorus, *Bibliotheca historica* I.96–8.

64 With reference to Porphyry, *De abstinentia* I, from Eusebius, *Praeparatio evangelica* I.9.

65 Here, too, Born refers to Diodorus, who actually says something different in chapters 73 and 74 of Book One. Neither the category of 'freedom' nor that of 'the female sex' plays a role in his work. It goes without saying that there were priestesses in Egypt; see A. M. Blackman, 'On the Position of Women in the Egyptian Hierarchy', in *JEA* 7 (1923): 8ff., 24ff. The claim to the contrary goes back to Herodotus, whom Born cites as his witness here. The question was later to preoccupy Verdi, who urgently needed female voices on musical grounds but was reluctant to challenge Herodotus's authority.

66   J.-B. de Bossuet, tutor of Louis XV and author of the famous *Discours sur l'histoire universelle à Monseigneur le Dauphin* (1682), Paris, 1774, based his representation of Egyptian history on Diodorus's *Bibliotheca* with similar intentions in mind.

67   See Assmann, *Weisheit und Mysterium*.

68   Iamblichus, *De mysteries Aegyptiorum* VIII.2, cited by Born, *Die Mysterien der Aegypter*, in *JF* 1 (1784): 58.

69   See J. Assmann and F. Ebeling, *Ägyptische Mysterien*, 29–47.

70   [C. de Pauw], *Recherches philosophiques sur les Egyptiens et Chinois*, London, Lausanne and Geneva, 1774; *Philosophische Untersuchungen über die Aegypter und Chineser*, 2 vols, trans. J. G. Krünitz, Berlin, 1774; *Philosophical Dissertations on the Egyptians and Chinese*, 2 vols, trans. Capt. J. Thomson, London, 1795.

71   In a footnote, de Pauw cites the passage from Synesius that we have already discussed above.

72   Lucian, *Philopseudes*.

73   Ibid., 33.

74   [Abbé Claude Robin], *Recherches sur les initiations anciennes et modernes*, Paris, 1779; the book was translated into German by Friedrich Gabriel Resewitz, *Ueber die Einweihungen in alten und neuern Zeiten*, Memphis and Braunschweig [St Petersburg], 1782.

75   *Recherches sur les initiations anciennes et modernes*, 13–16.

76   See J. Assmann and F. Ebeling, *Ägyptische Mysterien*, 114–40.

77   Ammianus Marcellinus, *Res gestae* XXII.15.30: 'sunt et syringes subterranei quidam et flexuosi secessus, quos, ut fertur, periti rituum vetustorum, adventare diluvium praescii, metuentesque ne caerimoniarum oblitteraretur memoria, penitus operosis digestos fodinis, per loca diversa struxerunt, et excisis parietibus, volucrum ferarumque genera multa sculpserunt et animalium species innumeras multas, quas hierographicas litteras appellarunt.'

78   See my contribution, 'Das gerettete Wissen. Flutkatastrophen und geheime Archive', in M. Mulsow and J. Assmann, *Sintflut und Gedächtnis*, Paderborn, 2006, 291–301.

79   Dio Chrysostom, *Trojana Oratio XI*, ed. L. Dindorf, Leipzig, 1919, 177.

80   See G. Fowden, *The Egyptian Hermes*, Cambridge, 1986, 29–30.

81   Waddell imprecisely translates the Greek *stēlai* as 'inscriptions'.

82   'Siriadic' from *Sirius*, 'South, Egypt', or within Egypt the Sahîd, the region around Thebes.

83   *Manetho*, ed. W. G. Waddell, Cambridge, MA, 1964, Appendix I, 208–9.

84   (Anonymous, *Athenian letters or, the Epistolary Correspondence of an Agent of the King of Persia, residing at Athens during the Peloponnesian war*, 4 vols, London, 1741–3, vol. 1, 95–100 (letter XXV by Orsames of Thebes). The transcodification of the stelae of Hermes I into the books of Hermes II plays an important role in J. G. Wachter's *Naturae et Scripturae Concordia*, Copenhagen, 1752, §83ff.

85 It is not known when Mozart was promoted to the master's degree. His
    promotion to Fellowcraft took place in 'True Concord' on 1 July 1785.
    If he had not been elevated in the interim to the rank of Master, he
    would not have been allowed to take part in his father's induction, as
    indicated in the protocols. The famous letter to his gravely ill father in
    which Mozart speaks of his having befriended death as 'the true goal
    of our existence' obviously articulates these experiences; it is dated two
    years later, 4 April 1787. See H. Strebel, *Der Freimaurer Wolfgang
    Amadé Mozart*, 41ff. There Strebel also corrects Hildesheimer's fully
    misguided evaluation of this letter.
86 J. F. Reimmann, *Idea Systematis Antiquitatis Literariae Specialiorus*.
    On Reimann, see M. Mulsow and H. Zedelmaier (eds), *Skepsis, Prov-
    idenz, Polyhistorie*, Tübingen, 1998.
87 For an interpretation of *The Magic Flute* as a dualistic opera which
    conceals the esoteric messages of freemasonry in the exoteric form of
    Volkstheater, see Simonis, *Die Kunst des Geheimen*, 262–94 (Mozart)
    and 295–319 (Goethe). In my book, *Die Zauberflöte*, I discuss both
    libretto and music in the light of the masonic theory of mysteries, par-
    ticularly with respect to the dualistic model of *religio duplex*. The opera
    presents this model while at the same time holding out the prospect of
    its imminent overcoming. I refer readers to this publication for further
    details.
88 As an aesthetic adaptation of masonic rituals of initiation, *The Magic
    Flute* has a precursor in Johann Gottlieb Naumann and Caterino Maz-
    zolà's opera *Osiride*, premiered in Dresden in 1781; see F. Eberling,
    'Catarino Mazzolàs Libretto "Osiride" (Dresden 1781)', in *Mozart-
    Jahrbuch*, 1999, 49–69, and D. J. Buch, *Magic Flutes and Enchanted
    Forests*, Chicago, IL, 2008, 199–203. What is missing there, however,
    is the dual character of the piece as *opera duplex*, just as it is missing
    in the French adaptation of *The Magic Flute* as *Les mystères d'Isis*
    (Paris, 1801), in which all the *Volkstheater* elements have been cut in
    order to turn it into a *Grand Opéra* in the French style.
89 Mozart's connections to freemasonry go all the way back to his youth
    in Salzburg and must have become considerably more intensive in the
    years 1773–9, when he wrote or revised the stage music for a play
    written by the prominent freemason Philipp Freiherrn von Gebler,
    Thamos König in Ägypten. However, he did not join a lodge himself
    until he moved to Vienna. On 14 December 1784, he entered the
    'Beneficence' lodge, established by his friend from his days in Mannheim,
    the playwright, dramaturge and theatre theorist Otto Reichsfreiherrn
    von Gemmingen-Hornberg. By 1 January 1785 he had already become
    a Fellowcraft in the sister lodge 'True Concord'; he was promoted to
    Master mason soon after that.
90 See J. Assmann, *Die Zauberflöte*, 100–6.
91 F. Dieckmann, *Orpheus, eingeweiht*, Frankfurt/M. and Leipzig, 2005.
92 See J. Assmann, *Die Zauberflöte*, 89. On the utopian character of the
    programme proposed by the Illuminati, see Koselleck's pathbreaking

study, *Kritik und Krise*. Koselleck sees in the eighteenth-century secret societies the germ-cells of the future bourgeois society, which under the conditions of absolutism must provisionally constitute itself in the underground. On the 'illuminatist utopia', see also Simonis, *Die Kunst des Geheimen*, 14–23.

93 On the near-death experience conveyed in the greater mysteries, see the Plutarch fragment handed down by Stobaeus; see above, n.34 of chapter 3.

94 *JF* 2 (1785): 56.

Chapter 5   In the Era of Globalization: *Religio Duplex* as Dual Membership

1 G. Chr. Lichtenberg, *Sudelbücher*, Book 1, No. 143, in Lichtenberg, *Schriften und Briefe*, vol. 2, Munich and Vienna, 1971, 197. I thank Klaus Müller for alerting me to this passage.

2 W. Mignolo, 'The Many Faces of Cosmo-polis', in *Public Culture* 12 (2000): 721–48.

3 P. Artzi, 'Ideas and Practices of International Co-existence in the 3rd Millennium BCE', in *Bar Ilan Studies in World History* 2 (1984): 25–39; P. Artzi, 'The Birth of the Middle East', in *Proceedings of the 5th World Congress of Jewish Studies*, Jerusalem, 1969, 120–4; M. Rowlands, M. Trolle Larsen and K. Kristiansen (eds), *Centre and Periphery in the Ancient World*, Cambridge, 1987.

4 See J. Assmann, *Moses the Egyptian*, 45–54, and J. Assmann, 'Translating Gods', in S. Budick and W. Iser (eds), *The Translatability of Cultures*, Stanford, CA, 1996, 25–36.

5 V. Haas, 'Eine hethitische Weltreichsidee', in K. A. Raaflaub (ed.), *Anfänge politischen Denkens in der Antike*, Munich, 1993, 135–44.

6 See P. D. A. Garnsey and C. R. Whittaker (eds), *Imperialism in the Ancient World*, Cambridge, 1978; T. M. Larsen (ed.), *Power and Propaganda*, Copenhagen, 1979; M. Duverger (ed.), *Le concept d'empire*, Paris, 1980.

7 K. Jaspers, *Vom Ursprung und Ziel der Geschichte*, Munich, 1949; S. N. Eisenstadt (ed.), *The Origins and Diversity of the Axial Age*, Albany, NY, 1986; B. Schwartz (ed.), *Wisdom, Revelation, and Doubt*, Cambridge, MA, 1975; S. N. Eisenstadt (ed.), *Kulturen der Achsenzeit*, 2 vols, Frankfurt/M., 1987; S. N. Eisenstadt (ed.), *Kulturen der Achsenzeit II*, 3 vols, Frankfurt/M., 1992; J. P. Arnason, S. N. Eisenstadt and B. Wittrock (eds), *Axial Civilizations and World History*, Leiden and Cologne, 2005.

8 J. P. Arnason, S. N. Eisenstadt and B. Wittrock (eds), *Axial Civilizations and World History*.

9 E. Voegelin, *Order and History*, vol. 4: *The Ecumenic Age*, Baton Rouge, LA, 1974.

10   A. Assmann, *Zeit und Tradition*, Cologne and Vienna, 1999; K. Koch, *Europa, Rom und der Kaiser vor dem Hintergrund von zwei Jahrtausenden Rezeption des Buches Daniel*, Hamburg, 1997; M. Delgado, K. Koch and E. Marsch (eds), *Europa, Tausendjähriges Reich und Neue Welt*, Fribourg and Stuttgart, 2003.

11   W. Mignolo has drawn attention to this epochal difference.

12   Abū Bakr Ibn Tufail, *Der Philosoph als Autodidakt, Hayy ibn Yaqzan*, trans. and ed. P. O. Schaerer, Hamburg, 2004. See U. Rudolph, 'Abu Bakr Ibn Tufail', in F. Niewöhner (ed.), *Klassiker der Religionsphilosophie*, Munich, 1995, 126–41.

13   A. Blumauer, 'Ueber den Kosmopolitismus des Maurers', in *JF* 2/3 (1784): 114–20, here p. 118.

14   Strength, beauty and wisdom are the three pillars of freemasonry. They appear in the final chorus of *The Magic Flute*: 'Strength has triumphed, rewarding / beauty and wisdom with an everlasting crown.'

15   E. Krippendorff, *Die Kultur des Politischen*, Berlin, 2009, 207–9; see J. Assmann, *Die Zauberflöte*, 117. A new edition of the cantata with a facsimile of the manuscript (July 1791) and the 1792 first edition appeared in 2010 with Pasticcio-Verlag, Gauting (ed. R. Leptihn). On the life and work of F. H. Ziegenhagen (1753–1806), who was a member of the Regensburg masonic lodge during his years there and, from 1786, even its Worshipful Master, see pp. 35–42.

16   Mixobarbaron Liberi Patris Signo Marmoreo in Villa nostra omnium Deorum Argumenta habenti.

17   H. G. E. White (ed. and trans.), *Ausonius*, 2 vols, Cambridge, MA, 1985, 186–7.

18   J. G. Griffiths, *Apuleius of Madauros: The Isis-Book (Metamorphoses, Book XI)*, Leiden, 1975, 70–1 and 114ff.

19   The Ethiopians are mentioned in this context because Philae, the main cult site of Isis in late Egypt, was located in Nubia.

20   In the ancient cult place of the Egyptian goddess of the harvest, Renenutet or (Th)ermutis, King Ptolemy Soter II built a temple to Isis-Thermutis.

21   Thiouis = Egypt. *t3 w't*, Copt. TIOYI, 'the one'; see A. Vogliano, *Primo rapporto degli scavi condotti dalla missione archeologica d'Egitto della R. universita di Milano nella zona di Madinet Madi*, Milan, 1936, 27–51, esp. p. 34.

22   V. F. Vanderlip, *The Four Greek Hymns of Isidorus and the Cult of Isis*, Toronto, 1972, 18–19; É. Bernand, *Inscriptions métriques de l'Égypte gréco-romaine*, Paris, 1969, Nr. 175, 632ff.; M. Totti, *Ausgewählte Texte der Isis- und Serapis-Religion*, Hildesheim, 1985, 76–82; F. Dunand, 'Syncrétismes dans la religion de l'Egypte Romaine', in F. Dunand and P. Levêque (eds), *Les syncrétismes dans les religions de l'antiquité*, Leiden, 1975, 152–85. On Isidorus, see H. J. W. Drijvers, 'De Hymnen van Madinet-Madi en de hellenistische Isisreligie', in *Vox Theologica* 32 (1962): 139–50.

23   *De Iside et Osiride* 67 (377E–F).

24 Origen, *Contra Celsum* I.24 and V.41 (45). See M. Hengel, *Judentum und Hellenismus*, Tübingen, 1988, 476, where the passage is cited in its broader context.

25 The drama *Nathan the Wise* forms at once the climax and the end-point to the so-called 'fragment dispute' between Lessing and the Hamburg chief pastor Johan Melchior Goeze. The dispute centred on the opposition between 'natural' and revealed religion, enlightenment and Lutheran orthodoxy. The play, written after the Duke of Brunswick had forbidden Lessing the publication of further theological polemics, thus represents the continuation of the theological controversy with other means. See E.-P. Wieckenburg, *Johan Melchior Goeze*, Hamburg, 2007, 186–207, and Nisbet, *Lessing*, 782–810.

26 Mulsow, *Moderne aus dem Untergrund*; Schröder, *Ursprünge des Atheismus*; M. C. Jacob, *The Radical Enlightenment*, London, 1981.

27 See F. Niewöhner, *Veritas sive Varietas*, Heidelberg, 1988, 30–4.

28 B. Lewis and F. Niewöhner, *Religionsgespräche im Mittelalter*, 1992. Ramon Llull must also be mentioned in this context, from whom a rich line of tradition extends via Nicolaus of Cusa and Giordano Bruno to the Modern Age. In his *Book of the Gentile and the Three Wise Men*, in A. Bonner (ed.), *Doctor Illuminatus: A Ramon Llull Reader*, Princeton, NJ, 1985, he also involves 'heathendom' in the interreligious dialogue.

29 See Niewöhner, *Veritas sive Varietas*, as well as K.-K. Kuschel, *Von Streit zum Wettstreit der Religionen*, Düsseldorf, 1998; M. Mulsow, *Die drei Ringe*, Tübingen, 2001.

30 Diodorus Siculus, *Bibliotheca historica* I.21.

31 This 'and' is anything but self-evident. Biblical ethics would suggest that divine and human judgement can diverge widely, and that whoever is cast out and persecuted in this life will be rewarded with love and justice in the next. This principle is central to Christianity, but it already appears in Judaism in connection with the idea of martyrdom (Daniel, Maccabees 1 and 2). The self-evident unity of human and divine approbation, by contrast, is typical for ancient Egyptian ethics, although Lessing could not have known this and it lies far from the present context. Here we are dealing rather with the Protestant (particularly Calvinist and Puritan) principle that the signs of divine blessing can be detected in earthly success.

32 The complete work, *Apologie oder Schutzschrift für die vernünftigen Verehrer Gottes*, was first published in 1972 in the Insel-Verlag, Frankfurt (ed. G. Alexander). The fragments published by Lessing are reprinted, alongside other documents relating to the controversy, in vol. 8 of his works.

33 Lessing, *Werke*, vol. 7, 457–91.

34 On Goeze, see E.-P. Wieckenberg, *Johan Melchior Goeze*, Hamburg, 2007. On the controversy with Lessing, see pp. 186–207 and Nisbet, *Lessing*, 782–810.

35 Lessing, *Werke*, vol. 7, 458; see also 'Axiomata III' and 'IV', *Werke*, vol. 8, 136–8. In her unpublished essay 'Zeiten der Lektüre. Mosaisches und paulinisches Unterscheiden: Schiller, Herder, Mendelssohn', Christiane Frey calls this 'the Pauline distinction'. In referring to the 'letter (*gramma*) that kills', however, Paul certainly did not have historicity and human works in mind, like Lessing, but rather the deadening normativity of the eternally prescribed Law.

36 'Gotth. Ephr. Lessings nötige Antwort auf eine sehr unnötige Frage des Hrn. Hauptpastor Goeze in Hamburg', in Lessing, *Werke*, vol. 8, 309–13.

37 In Lessing, *Werke*, vol. 7, 476–88; Lessing, *Philosophical and Theological Writings*, ed. H. S. Nisbet, Cambridge, 2005, 217–40. The complete work, which Lessing had undoubtedly finished in 1777 (at least in broad outline), finally appeared in 1780 with Voss and Son in Berlin; see Lessing, *Werke*, vol. 8, 489–510 and 706–11.

38 Lessing, *Werke*, vol. 2, 720.

39 Ibid., 719.

40 'On the origin of revealed religion', in Lessing, *Philosophical and Theological Writings*, 35.

41 Ibid., 36.

42 Ibid.

43 Nisbet, *Lessing*, 671. Nisbet relates this 'strategy' not to *religio duplex* but to Leibnizian perspectivism, which sought (in Lessing's words) 'to lead everyone to truth on whatever path it found him on'.

44 M. Samuels, *Jerusalem: A Treatise on Ecclesiastical Authority and Judaism*, London, 1838. On Mendelssohn's *Jerusalem*, see the subtle analysis by C. Hilfrich, *'Lebendige Schrift'*, Munich, 2000.

45 Mendelssohn, *Schriften über Religion und Aufklärung*, ed. M. Thom, Berlin, 1989, 341. Mendelssohn should not be misunderstood. He would have agreed with Georges Bernanos, who wrote: 'God has no arms but our own' to realize the insights and commands of 'spirit and heart' here on earth. What he opposes is the blatant use of compulsion and force to ensure that 'doctrinal opinions', i.e., dogmas, are followed.

46 *Zohar* 2: 98b. Quoted in E. Wolfson, *Through a Speculum That Shines: Vision and Imagination in Medieval Jewish Mysticism*, Princeton, NJ, 1994, 384.

47 See A. Goldberg, 'Der verschriftete Sprechakt als rabbinische Literatur', in A. and J. Assmann and C. Hardmeier (eds), *Schrift und Gedächtnis*, Munich, 1983, 123–40.

48 This point is made explicitly, and in opposition to the 'national religion' of Judaism, by J. F. W. Jerusalem in his *Reflections on the Most Edifying Truths of Religion*, Braunschweig, 1768, 129; see Feil, *Religio*, vol. 4, 396. Jerusalem was closely acquainted with Lessing; Mendelssohn would have known the book.

49 K. Barth, *Kirchliche Dogmatik*, vol. I/2, Zurich, 4th edn 1948, 327.

50 D. Bonhoeffer, *Widerstand und Ergebung*, Munich, 1970.

51 J. Ratzinger, *Truth and Tolerance: Christian Belief and World Religions*, San Franciso, CA, 2004, 170.

52 See K.-P. Jörns, *Notwendige Abschiede*, Gütersloh, 2004, especially Part II, chapter 1: 'Farewelling the Idea that Christianity is a Religion Unlike any Other' (70–101).

53 The first three dialogues appeared in 1778: *Ernst und Falk: Gespräche für Freymäurer*, Wolfenbüttel, 1778; the remaining two were published by Adolph von Knigge, apparently without Lessing's knowledge. I use the English translation in Lessing, *Philosophical and Theological Writings*, ed. Nisbet, 184–216. See also Nisbet, *Lessing*, 763–81; Nisbet, 'Zur Funktion des Geheimnisses in Lessings "Ernst und Falk" ', in P. Freimark (ed.), *Lessing und die Toleranz*, Detroit, 1986, 291–309, and P. Michelsen, 'Die "wahren Taten" der Freimaurer', in P. C. Ludz (ed.), *Geheime Gesellschaften*, Heidelberg, 1979, 293–324. Lessing published the text anonymously, but he had already sent the manuscript to his friend Moses Mendelssohn in 1777 (Nisbet, *Lessing*, 766–7). In 1779, Lessing also sent the manuscript to Ignaz von Born, whom he had already visited in Prague in 1775 during his trip to Vienna; see H. Schneider, *Lessing: Zwölf biographische Studien*, Bern, 1951, 190–1 (cited in Nisbet, *Lessing*, 777). See also M. Frank, *Der kommende Gott*, 140–1.

54 Lessing, 'Ernst and Falk', in *Philosophical and Theological Writings*, ed. Nisbet, 193–7.

55 Ibid., 186.

56 E. H. Erikson, 'Ontogeny of Ritualization in Man', in *Philosophical Transactions of the Royal Society* 251 B, London, 1966, 337–49.

57 As early as 1719, Ludwig Theodor Lau had enumerated seven *Impedimenta Veritatis* or 'impediments to truth' in his *Meditationes*: 'the prejudices of reason, religion, education, authority, region, nation, passion and others besides' ('Praejudicia Rationis, Religionis, Educationis, Autoritatis, Regionis, Nationis, Passionum, aliaque'; Thesis IV).

58 J. G. Herder, *Briefe zur Beförderung der Humanität*, in Herder, *Werke in zehn Bänden*, ed. M. Bollacher, vol. 7, Frankfurt/M, 1991, 132–41. Herder also discusses Lessing's *Ernst und Falk* in his detailed history of freemasonry: 'Historische Zweifel über F. Nicolai's Buch von den Beschuldigungen, welche den Tempelherren gemacht worden, von ihren Geheimnissen und dem Entstehen der Freimaurergesellschaft, 1782', in *J. G. v. Herders Sämmtliche Werke, Zur Philosophie und Geschichte, Dreyzehnter Theil*, Karlsruhe, 1820, 266–360 = *Sämmtliche Werke*, Stuttgart, 1829, 258–345. In this treatise, Herder first critically discusses Lessing's derivation of the concept 'freemasonry' from 'masoney', 'round table', before presenting his own reconstruction of the movement's history.

59 Herder, ibid., 141.

60 Cited in Lessing, *Ernst und Falk: Mit den Fortsetzungen Johann Gottfried Herders und Friedrich Schlegels*, ed. I. Contiades, Frankfurt/M, 1968, 118.

61 Herder, *Philosophical Writings*, ed. M. N. Forster, Cambridge, 2002, 406–7.
62 Ibid., 406.
63 Nisbet, 'Zur Funktion des Geheimnisses'.
64 C. M. Wieland, *History of the Abderites*, trans. M. Dufner, Cranbury, NJ, 1993, 126.
65 Ibid., 126–7.
66 'Das Geheimniß des Kosmopolitenordens', in *C. M. Wielands sämmtliche Werke*, ed. J. G. Gruber, vol. 40, Leipzig, 1826, 441–78.
67 A. Sen, *Identity and Violence: The Illusion of Destiny*, London, 2006.
68 As well as Sen, *Identity and Violence*, see my essay, 'Humanity and Citizenship', in J. Cohen (ed.), *For Love of Country*, Boston, MA, 1996, 111–18, esp. 117–18.
69 W. Mignolo, 'The Many Faces of Cosmo-polis'.
70 A. Assmann, 'Jaspers' Achsenzeit, oder Schwierigkeiten mit der Zentralperspektive in der Geschichte', in D. Harth (ed.), *Karl Jaspers*, Stuttgart, 1989, 187–205, and A. Assmann, 'Einheit und Vielfalt in der Geschichte', in S. N. Eisenstadt (ed.), *Kulturen der Achsenzeit II*, vol. 2, 330–40. See also J. Dittmer, 'Jaspers' Achsenzeit und das interkulturelle Gespräch. Überlegungen zur Relevanz eines revidierten Themas', at <http://www.chairete.de/Beitrag/TA/jaspers_achsenzeit.pdf>.
71 Quoted in N. Schindler, 'Aufklärung und Geheimnis im Illuminatenorden', in P. C. Lodz (ed.), *Geheime Gesellschaften*, Heidelberg, 1979, 203–29, here p. 203.
72 F. Schiller, 'Letters on the Aesthetic Education of Man', in W. Hinderer and D. Dahlstrom (eds), *Essays*, New York, 2005, 118–20.
73 Ibid., 125–6.
74 Ibid., 125.
75 J. Assmann, 'Der Ka als Double', in V. I. Stoichita (ed.), *Das Double*, Wiesbaden, 2006, 59–78.
76 J. Assmann (ed.), *Die Erfindung des Inneren Menschen*, Gütersloh, 1993.
77 R. Weihe, *Die Paradoxie der Maske*, Munich, 2004. See especially the concluding chapter, 'Homo Duplex', 329–54.
78 Ibid., 340–2.
79 Nicolaus of Cusa, *Cusanus-Texte. Proclus Latinus. Die Exzerpte und Randnotes des Nikolaus von Kues zu den lateinischen Übersetzungen der Proklus-Schriften*, vol. 2, ed. K. Bormann, Heidelberg, 1986, 15, cited in Weihe, *Paradoxie*, 341.
80 C. G. Jung, *Die Beziehungen zwischen dem Ich und dem Unbewußten*, Munich, 4th edn 1994, 78.
81 H. Plessner, 'Soziale Rolle und menschliche Natur', in *Gesammelte Schriften*, vol. 10, Frankfurt/M,1985, 227–40.
82 É. Durkheim, 'The Dualism of Human Nature and its Social Conditions', in *Essays on Sociology and Philosophy*, ed. K. H. Wolff, New York, 1964, 325–40. See also D. A. Marshall, 'Durkheimian Dualism

Redux: Homo Duplex and the Origin of Religion', at <http://www
.allacademic.com/meta/p105188_index.html>.
83 Schiller, 'Letters on the Aesthetic Education of Man', Eighteenth Letter.
In the letters twenty to twenty-six, however, Schiller emphasizes that
what matters most is that both these drives be harmonized and inte-
grated. To that end, he posits in the twenty-seventh letter a third drive
in which material and formal drives are reconciled: the play drive.
84 Lessing, 'Ernst and Falk', in *Philosophical and Theological Writings*,
193–4.
85 Ibid.
86 Ibid., 196.
87 See Michelsen, *Die 'wahren Taten'*, 307. Michelsen makes a significant
correction to Koselleck's thesis by pointing out that Lessing's conception
of freemasonry is *not* to be understood as a 'violent' counter-movement
and 'explosive force within absolutism'; rather, Lessing is concerned
precisely with maintaining boundaries.
88 The term coined by Assmann here, *Bindungstrieb*, plays on *Bildung-
strieb*, the 'formative drive' posited by eighteenth-century naturalist J. F.
Blumenbach and expanded to the fields of psychology and sociology in
the contemporary *Bildungsroman*. I take my translation, the 'drive to
bond', from Lawrence and Nohria's four-drive theory of human nature:
P. Lawrence and N. Nohria, *Driven: How Human Nature Shapes Our
Choices*, San Francisco, CA, 2002. – Translator's note.
89 A. Margalit, *The Ethics of Memory*, Cambridge, MA, 2003.

Prospectus: *Religio Duplex* Today?

1 D. Conrad, *Gandhi und der Begriff des Politischen*, ed. B. Conrad-Lütt,
Munich, 2006, 60.
2 Ibid., 55.
3 D. G. Tendulkar, *Mahatma: Life of Mohandas Karamchand Gandhi*,
Delhi 1960–3, vol. 7, 45, cited in Conrad, *Gandhi*, 56.
4 Gandhi, *Collected Works*, Delhi and Ahmedabad 1956ff., vol. 17,
405–6, cited in Conrad, *Gandhi*, 52.
5 Conrad, *Gandhi*, 52.
6 Ibid., 60.
7 Gandhi, *Collected Works*, vol. 39, 3, cited in Conrad, *Gandhi*, 58.
8 Conrad, *Gandhi*, 59.
9 Ibid.
10 J. Sacks, *The Dignity of Difference*, London, 2002.
11 Ibid., 52–3.
12 Ibid., 55.
13 'Religions are about identity and identity excludes' (ibid., 46).
14 Ibid., 55.
15 U. Beck, *Der eigene Gott*, Frankfurt/M and Leipzig, 2008, 202.

16 Sacks, *The Dignity of Difference*, 55.
17 Both etymologies were proposed in antiquity, the first by Lactantius, the second by Cicero. Cicero is probably right, but Lactantius's derivation and definition became authoritative for the self-conception of Christianity, and our present concept of religion has a Christian inflection rather than an ancient Roman one.
18 Sacks, *The Dignity of Difference*, 56.
19 Ibid., 57.
20 Ibid.
21 M. Walzer, *Thick and Thin*, Notre Dame, IN, 1994, 8.
22 See A. Assmann and S. Conrad (eds), *Memory in an Age of Globalization*, London, 2010, 2.
23 U. Beck, *A God of One's Own Religion's Capacity for Peace and Potential for Violence*, Cambridge, 2010, 136.
24 A. Assmann makes clear that this concept of civilization on the basis of human rights does not represent a Western monopoly, even if it arose in the West. 'It is to be detached from its historical origins and reformulated as a global claim' ('Höflichkeit und Respekt', in G. Engel et al. (eds), *Konjunkturen der Höflichkeit in der frühen Neuzeit*, Frankfurt/M, 2009, 173–89, here p. 188, alluding to O. Höffe, *Koexistenz der Kulturen im Zeitalter der Globalisierung*, Munich, 2008). Höffe demands that these principles be de-Europeanized or de-Westernized so that they can be globalized.
25 A. Assmann, *Höflichkeit und Respekt*, 188–9.

Retrospectus: Are There 'Dual Religions'?

1 K. Müller, *Tora für die Völker*, Berlin, 2nd edn 1998.
2 Uriel da Costa, *Exemplar humanae vitae*, in E. Feil, *Religio*, vol. 3, Göttingen, 2001, 410–16, esp. p. 412.
3 See T. Römer, 'Recherches actuelles sur le cycle d'Abraham', in A. Wénin (ed.), *Studies in the Book of Genesis*, Leuven, 2001, 179–211. H. Spieckermann, 'Ein Vater vieler Völker', in *Abraham unser Vater*, ed. R. G. Kratz and T. Nagel, Göttingen, 2003, 8–31, showed that the Abrahamic traditions in the Bible must go back to an earlier textual layer.
4 After K. Müller, 'Das noahidische Tora', in *Freiburger Rundbrief* 3 (1996) (<http://www.freiburger-rundbrief.de/de/?item=397>).
5 J. Selden, *De iure naturali et gentium iuxta disciplinam Ebraeorum*, London, 1640.
6 See A. de Pury, 'Gottesname, Gottesbezeichnung und Gottesbegriff', in J.-C. Gertz, K. Schmid and M. Witte (eds), *Abschied vom Jahwisten*, Berlin and New York, 2002, 25–47. In the classical rabbinical tradition to which Claus-Jürgen Thornton draws my attention, Elohim signifies God in his aspect as judge; this name for God can also be translated as 'judge' in parts of the Old Testament.

7   M. Maimonides, *Moreh Nevuchim* III.32.
8   M. Idel, 'Deus sive Natura', in M. Idel, *Maïmonide et la mystique juive*, Paris, 1991, 105–36.
9   S. Freud, *Moses and Monotheism*, trans. K. Jones, New York, 1967.
10 On the scribal elite as a support base for Deutoronomy and the Deuteronomistic tradition, see D. Carr, *Writing on the Tablets of the Heart*, Oxford, 2005, esp. 111–73; K. van der Toorn, *Scribal Culture and the Making of the Hebrew Bible*, Cambridge, MA, 2007.
11 See W. Schmidt-Biggemann (ed.), *Christliche Kabbala*, Sigmaringen, 2003; M. Idel, 'Reuchlin', in *Studia Universitatis Babes-Bolyai: Studia Judaica*, 2008, 30–55; K. E. Grözinger, 'Reuchlin und die Kabbala', in *Reuchlin und die Juden*, ed. A. Herzig, Sigmaringen, 1993, 175–87; J. Reuchlin, *De Arte Cabbalistica – On the Art of the Kabbala*, trans. M. and S. Goodman, New York, 1983; C. Wirszubski, *Pico della Miandola's Encounter with Jewish Mysticism*, Cambridge, MA, and London, 1989.
12 A. B. Kilcher (ed.), *Die Kabbala Denudata*, Bern, 2006.
13 T. Luckmann, *The Invisible Religion: The Problem of Religion in Modern Society*, New York, 1967; see J. Assmann, *Religion and Cultural Memory*, trans. R. Livingstone, Stanford, CA, 2006. [I draw heavily on Livingstone's translation in the following four paragraphs, which essentially reproduce part of the chapter entitled 'Invisible Religion and Culture Memory', in *Religion and Cultural Memory*, 33–5. – Translator's note.]
14 See J. Assmann, *Ma'at*, Munich, 1990.
15 J. Assmann, *Der König als Sonnenpriester*, Glückstadt, 1970; J. Assmann, *Sonnenhymnen in Thebanischen Gräbern*, Mainz, 1983, 48–9; J. Assmann, *Ma'at*, 205–12.
16 See also J. Assmann, *The Search for God in Ancient Egypt*, trans. D. Loton, Ithaca, NY, 1984, 3–6.
17 P. Berger and T. Luckmann, *The Social Construction of Reality*, New York, 1966.
18 I quote from the edition by J. F. Quack, *Die Lehre für Merikare*, Wiesbaden, 1992.
19 Ibid., 78–81, translated in J. Assmann, *Of God and Gods: Egypt, Israel and the Rise of Monotheism*, Monroe, 2008, 62–3.
20 J. Assmann and A. Kucharek, *Ägyptische Religion*, vol. 1, Frankfurt/M and Leipzig, 2008, 361; partially translated in J, Ray, *Reflections of Osiris: Lives from Ancient Egypt*, Oxford, 2002, 30.
21 Literally, 'not commanded'; in Egyptian, 'to forbid' means 'not to command'.
22 On the motif of chastising god, see E. Otto, *Der Vorwurf an Gott*, Hildesheim, 1951; G. Fecht, *Der Vorwurf an Gott in den 'Mahnworten des Ipuwer'*, Heidelberg, 1972.
23 J. Assmann, *Ägypten. Eine Sinngeschichte*, Munich,1996, 122–31.
24 J. Zandee, *De Hymnen aan Amon van Pap. Leiden I 350*, Amsterdam, 1947.

25 pLeiden I.350, IV.17–19 (Zandee, ibid., 75–86; J. Assmann, *Moses the Egyptian*, 196–7).
26 pLeiden I.350, IV.21–6 (Zandee, ibid., 87–91; J. Assmann, *Of God and Gods*, 64).
27 The hymn of the 'stele of the banished'; see J. von Beckenrath, 'Die "Stele der Verbannten" im Museum des Louvre', in *Revue d'Égyptologie* 20 (1968): 7–36, partially translated in J. Assmann, *The Search for God in Ancient Egypt*, 233.
28 Here the first name that should be mentioned is Augustine, himself an erstwhile follower of esoteric movements like Manichaeism and Neo-platonism, for whom Christianity sounds the death knell for all forms of esotericism. See G. G. Stroumsa, 'Milk and Meat', in Stroumsa, *Hidden Wisdom*, 132–46.
29 On the distinction between primary and secondary religions, see T. Sundermeier, 'Religion, Religions' in K. Müller et al. (eds), *Dictionary of Mission: Theology, History, Perspective*, Maryknoll, 1997, 388–9; J. Assmann, *Ma'at*, 19–20, 279–83; A. Wagner (ed.), *Primäre und sekundäre Religionen als Kategorie der Religionsgeschichte des Alten Testaments*, Berlin and New York, 2006.

Bibliography

Author names in square brackets precede works which were published anonymously but can be attributed with certainty to the named authors.

Abū Bakr Ibn Tufail, *Der Philosoph als Autodidakt, Hayy ibn Yaqzan.* Trans. and ed. Patric O. Schaerer, Hamburg, 2004.

Manfred Agethen, *Geheimbund und Utopie: Illuminaten, Freimaurer und deutsche Spätaufklärung*, Munich, 1987.

Wolfgang Albrecht (ed.), *Lessing: Gespräche, Begegnungen, Lebenszeugnisse. Ein kommentiertes Lese- und Studienwerk*, Kamenz, 2005.

William F. Albright, *The Protosinaitic Inscriptions and Their Decipherment*, Cambridge, MA, 1966.

Ammianus Marcellinus, *Res gestae:* Ammien Marcellin, *Histoire*, vol. 3: *Livres xx–xxii*, ed. and trans. by Jean Fontaine, Paris, 1996.

Anonymous, *Athenian letters or, the Epistolary Correspondence of an Agent of the King of Persia, residing at Athens during the Peloponnesian war. Containing the History of the Times, in Dispatches to the Ministers of State at the Persian Court. Besides Letters on various subjects between Him and His Friends*, 4 vols, London, 1741–3.

Anonymous, *Traktat über die drei Betrüger. Traité des trois imposteurs (L'esprit de Mr. Benoit de Spinosa)*, ed., trans. and introduced by Winfried Schröder, Hamburg, 1992.

Johann P. Arnason, Shmuel N. Eisenstadt and Björn Wittrock (eds), *Axial Civilizations and World History, Jerusalem Studies in Religion and Culture* 4, Leiden and Cologne, 2005.

Peter Artzi, 'The Birth of the Middle East', in *Proceedings of the 5th World Congress of Jewish Studies*, Jerusalem, 1969: 120–4.

Peter Artzi, 'Ideas and Practices of International Co-existence in the 3rd Millennium BCE', in *Bar Ilan Studies in History* 2 (1984): 25–39.

Aleida Assmann, *Die Legitimität der Fiktion. Ein Beitrag zur Geschichte der literarischen Kommunikation*, Munich, 1980.

Aleida Assmann, 'Jaspers' Achsenzeit, oder Schwierigkeiten mit der Zentralperspektive in der Geschichte', in Dietrich Harth (ed.), *Karl Jaspers. Denken zwischen Wissenschaft, Politik und Philosophie*, Stuttgart, 1989, 187–205.

Aleida Assmann, 'Die Weisheit Adams', in Aleida Assmann (ed.), *Weisheit*, Munich, 1991, 305–24.

Aleida Assmann, 'Einheit und Vielfalt in der Geschichte. Jaspers' Achsenzeit neu betrachtet', in Shmuel Noah Eisenstadt (ed.), *Kulturen der Achsenzeit II*, Frankfurt/Main, 1992, vol. 2, part 3, 330–40.

Aleida Assmann, *Erinnerungsräume. Formen und Funktionen des kulturellen Gedächtnisses*, Munich, 1999.

Aleida Assmann, *Zeit und Tradition. Kulturelle Strategien der Dauer*, Cologne and Vienna, 1999.

Aleida Assmann, 'Herder zwischen Nationalkulturen und Menschheitsgedächtnis', in *Saeculum* 52 (2001): 41–54.

Aleida Assmann, 'Höflichkeit und Respekt', in Gisela Engel et al. (ed.), *Konjunkturen der Höflichkeit in der Frühen Neuzeit*, Frankfurt/Main, 2009, 173–89.

Aleida Assmann and Jan Assmann, *Schleier and Schwelle*, vol. 1: *Geheimnis and Öffentlichkeit*, 1997; vol. 2: *Geheimnis and Offenbarung*, 1998; vol. 3: *Geheimnis and Neugierde*, 1999.

Aleida Assmann and Jan Assmann, 'Die Erfindung des Geheimnisses durch die Neugier', in J. and A. Assmann (ed.), *Schleier and Schwelle*, vol. 3: *Geheimnis and Neugier, Archäologie der literarischen Kommunikation* V/3, Munich, 1999: 7–11.

Aleida Assmann and Jan Assmann (ed.), *Hieroglyphen. Stationen einer anderen abendländischen Grammatologie, Archäologie der literarischen Kommunikation* VIII, Munich, 2003.

Aleida Assmann and Sebastian Conrad (ed.), *Memory in an Age of Globalisation*, London: Palgrave Macmillan, 2010.

Jan Assmann, *Liturgische Lieder an den Sonnengott*, Berlin, 1969.

Jan Assmann, *Der König als Sonnenpriester. Ein kosmographischer Begleittext zur kultischen Sonnenhymnik in thebanischen Tempeln und Gräbern, Abhandlungen des Deutschen Archäologischen Instituts* VII, Glückstadt, 1970.

Jan Assmann, *Ägyptische Hymnen und Gebete*. Trans., commentary and introduction, OBO, Fribourg and Göttingen, 2nd edn, 1999 (1st edn 1975).

Jan Assmann, *Sonnenhymnen in Thebanischen Gräbern*, Mainz, 1983.

Jan Assmann, *Ägypten. Theologie und Frömmigkeit einer frühen Hochkultur*, Stuttgart, 1984, 2nd edn, 1991.

Jan Assmann, Article 'Verklärung' in *Lexikon der Ägyptologie*, vol. 6, Wiesbaden, 1986, 998–1006.

Jan Assmann, 'Hierotaxis. Textkonstitution und Bildkomposition in der ägyptischen Kunst und Literatur', in Jürgen Osing and Günter Dreyer (ed.), *Form und Maß. Beiträge zur Literatur, Sprache und Kunst des alten Ägypten. Festschrift für Gerhard Fecht*, Wiesbaden, 1987, 18–42.

Jan Assmann, *Ma`at. Gerechtigkeit und Unsterblichkeit im Alten Ägypten*, Munich, 1990.

Jan Assmann (ed.), *Die Erfindung des Inneren Menschen. Studien zur religiösen Anthropologie*, Gütersloh, 1993.

Jan Assmann, 'Altägyptische Kultkommentare', in Jan Assmann and Burkhard Gladigow (eds), *Text und Kommentar*, Munich, 1995, 93–110.

Jan Assmann, 'Translating Gods: Religion as a Factor of Cultural (In)translatability', in Sanford Budick and Wolfgang Iser (eds), *The Translatability of Cultures. Figurations of the Space Between*, Stanford, CA, 1996, 25–36 (reprinted in Hent de Vries (ed.), *Religion. Beyond a Concept*, New York, 2008, 139–49).

Jan Assmann, *Ägypten. Eine Sinngeschichte*, Munich, 1996.

Jan Assmann, *Moses the Egyptian. The Memory of Egypt in Western Monotheism*, Cambridge, MA, 1997.

Jan Assmann, *Das verschleierte Bild zu Sais. Schillers Ballade und ihre griechischen und ägyptischen Hintergründe*, Lectio Teubneriana VIII, Stuttgart and Leipzig, 1999.

Jan Assmann, 'Hieroglyphen als mnemotechnisches System. William Warburton und die Grammatologie des 18. Jahrhunderts', in Jörg Jochen Berns and Wolfgang Neuber (eds), *Seelenmaschinen. Gattungstraditionen, Funktionen und Leistungsgrenzen der Mnemotechniken vom späten Mittelalter bis zum Beginn der Moderne*, Vienna, Cologne and Weimar, 2000, 711–24.

Jan Assmann, *Religion and Cultural Memory*, trans. Rodney Livingstone, Stanford, CA, 2006.

Jan Assmann, *Weisheit und Mysterium. Das Bild der Griechen von Ägypten*, Munich, 2000.

Jan Assmann, *Das Geheimnis der Wahrheit. Das Konzept der 'doppelten Religion' und die Erfindung der Religionsgeschichte*, in ARG 3 (2001), 108–34.

Jan Assmann, *Tod und Jenseits im Alten Ägypten*, Munich, 2001.

Jan Assmann, 'Nachwort', in Carl Leonhard Reinhold, *Die hebräischen Mysterien oder die älteste religiöse Freymaurerey*, ed. by Jan Assmann, Neckargemünd, 2nd edn, 2006 (1st edn, 2001).

Jan Assmann, 'Pictures versus Letters: William Warburton's Theory of Grammatological Iconoclasm', in Jan Assmann and Albert I. Baumgarten (eds), *Representation in Religion: Studies in Honor of Moshe Barasch*, Leiden, 2001, 297–311.

Jan Assmann, *The Price of Monotheism*, trans. Robert Savage, Stanford, CA, 2009.

Jan Assmann, 'Etymographie. Zeichen im Jenseits der Sprache', in A. and J. Assmann (eds), *Hieroglyphen*, 37–64.

Jan Assmann, 'Die Mosaische Unterscheidung in Schönbergs Moses und Aron', in *Musik und Aesthetik* 9/33 (2005): 5–29.

Jan Assmann, *Die Zauberflöte. Oper und Mysterium*, Munich, 2005.
Jan Assmann, 'Kosmogonie, göttliche Schöpfung und menschliche Kreativität', in J. Assmann, *Theologie und Weisheit im Alten Ägypten*, Munich, 2005, 13–34.
Jan Assmann, 'Der Ka als Double', in Victor I. Stoichita (ed.), *Das Double*, Wiesbaden, 2006, 59–78.
Jan Assmann, 'Das gerettete Wissen. Flutkatastrophen und geheime Archive', in Martin Mulsow and Jan Assmann, *Sintflut und Gedächtnis. Erinnern und Vergessen des Ursprungs*, Paderborn, 2006, 291–301.
Jan Assmann and Martin Bommas (eds), *Ägyptische Mysterien?*, Munich, 2002.
Jan Assmann and Florian Ebeling, *Ägyptische Mysterien: Reisen in die Unterwelt in Aufklärung und Romantik*, Munich, 2011.
Jan Assmann, Andrea Kucharek, *Ägyptische Religion*, vol. 1: *Totenliteratur*, Frankfurt/Main and Leipzig, 2008, 361f.
Ausonius, ed. v. Hugh G. Evelyn-White, 2 vols, Cambridge, MA, 1985.
John L. Austin, *How To Do Things with Words*, Oxford, 1962.
Francis Bacon, *The Advancement of Learning* (1605), Oxford, 1974.
Roger S. Bagnall, *Hellenistic and Roman Egypt. Sources and Approaches*, Aldershot, 2006.
Franz Ballod, *Prolegomena zur Geschichte der zwerghaften Götter in Ägypten*, Moskau: Liessner and Sobko, 1913.
Moshe Barasch, 'Renaissance Hieroglyphics', in A. and J. Assmann (eds), *Hieroglyphen*, 165–90.
Karl Barth, *Kirchliche Dogmatik*, vol. I/2, Zürich, 4th edn, 1948 (1st edn, 1938).
Albert I. Baumgarten, *The Flourishing of Jewish Sects in the Maccabean Era. An Interpretation*, Leiden: Brill, 1997.
Ulrich Beck, *A God of One's Own. Religion's Capacity for Peace and Potential for Violence*, trans. Rodney Livingstone, Stanford, CA, 2010.
Jürgen von Beckerath, 'Die "Stele der Verbannten" im Museum des Louvre', in *Revue d'Égyptologie* 20 (1968): 7–36.
Wilhelm Begemann, *Andreas Michael Ramsays Rede über die Freimaurerei*, Leipzig, 1907.
Stephen D. Benin, 'The Cunning of God and Divine Accommodation', in *The Journal of the History of Ideas* 45 (1984): 179–92.
Ingrid Berger, 'Literatur als Kompaktkommunikation', in I. Berger, *Musil mit Luhmann. Kontingenz, Roman, System*, Munich, 2004, 71–91.
Peter L. Berger and Thomas Luckmann, *Die gesellschaftliche Konstruktion der Wirklichkeit*, Frankfurt/Main, 1970.
Jan Bergman, 'Ich bin Isis. Studien zum memphitischen Hintergrund der griechischen Isis-Aretalogien', in *Historia Religionum* 3, Uppsala, 1968.
George Berkeley, *Siris: A Chain of Philosophical Reflexions and Inquiries Concerning the Virtues of Tar Water*, London, 1744.
Étienne Bernand, *Inscriptions métriques de l'Égypte gréco-romaine*, Paris, 1969.

Silvia Berti, *Trattato dei tre impostori. La vita e lo spirito del Signor Benedetto de Spinoza*, Turin, 1994.

Hans Dieter Betz et al., *The Greek Magical Papyri in Translation. Including the Demotic Texts*, Chicago, IL, 1986.

Dino Bidoli, 'Die Sprüche der Fangnetze in den altägyptischen Sargtexten', in *ADAIK* 9, Glückstadt, 1976.

Rainer Bischof, *Vom europäischen Geist: Gedanken zum Menschen und zur Kunst*, Vienna, 2000.

Aylward M. Blackman, 'On the Position of Women in the Egyptian Hierarchy', in *JEA* 7 (1923): 8ff., 24ff.

Aylward M. Blackman, 'The Myth of Horus at Edfu II', in *JEA* 29 (1943): 2–36.

Hans Blumenberg, *Die Lesbarkeit der Welt*, Frankfurt/Main, 1981.

Dietrich Bonhoeffer, *Widerstand und Ergebung*, Munich, 1970.

Ignaz von Born, 'Ueber die Mysterien der Aegyptier', in *JF* 1 (1784): 15–132.

Ignaz von Born, 'Ueber die Mysterien der Indier', in *JF* 4 (1784): 5–54.

Jacques-Bénigne de Bossuet, *Discours sur l'histoire universelle à Monseigneur le Dauphin. Pour expliquer la suite de la religion et les changements des empires, Première partie: Depuis le commencement du monde jusqu'à l'empire de Charlemagne* (1681), Paris, 1744.

Volkmar Braunbehrens, *Mozart in Wien*, Munich and Zurich, 1986.

Michèle Broze, 'La réinterprétation du modèle hiéroglyphique chez les philosophes de langue grecque', in Lucia Morra and Carla Bazzanella (eds), *Philosophers and Hieroglyphs*, Turin, 2003, 35–49.

David Joseph Buch, *Magic Flutes and Enchanted Forests. The Supernatural in Eighteenth Century Performing Arts*, Chicago, IL, 2008.

Peter Burke, *Vico*, Oxford, 1985.

Walter Burkert, *Antike Mysterien*, Munich, 1990.

Walter Burkert, 'Mysterien der Ägypter in griechischer Sicht. Projektionen im Kulturkontakt', in Jan Assmann and Martin Bommas (eds), *Ägyptische Mysterien?*, Munich, 2002, 9–26.

Hubert Cancik, 'Augustinus als constantinischer Theologe', in Jacob Taubes (ed.), *Der Fürst dieser Welt. Carl Schmitt und die Folgen, Religionstheorie und politische Theologie* I, Munich, 1983, 136–52.

Stephen C. Carlson, *The Gospel Hoax: Morton Smith's Invention of Secret Mark*, Waco/Texas, 2005.

David Carr, *Writing on the Tablets of the Heart: Origins of Scripture and Literature*, Oxford, 2005.

Isaac Casaubon, *De rebus sacris et ecclesiasticis exercitationes XVI: Ad Cardinalis Baronii Prolegomena in Annales*, London, 1614.

Ernst Cassirer, *Die platonische Renaissance in England und die Schule von Cambridge*, Leipzig, 1932.

M. Tullius Cicero, *De natura deorum*, trans. H. Rackham, Cambridge, MA, and London, 2005.

Clemens Alexandrinus, *Stromata: Stromata I–VI*. ed. Otto Stählin, newly ed. by Ludwig Früchtel, 4th edn with addenda by Ursula Treu, Berlin, 1985.

Heinrich Clementz, *Des Flavius Josephus Kleinere Schriften*, Wiesbaden, 1993.
Dieter Conrad, *Gandhi und der Begriff des Politischen. Staat, Religion und Gewalt*, ed. v. Barbara Conrad-Lütt, Munich: W. Fink, 2006.
Brian P. Copenhaver, *Hermetica. The Greek Corpus Hermeticum and the Latin Asclepius in a new English translation with notes and introduction*, Cambridge, 1992.
Corpus Hermeticum. Texte établi par A. D. Nock et traduit par André-Jean Festugière, 4 vols, Paris: Les belles-lettres, 1945–54.
Ralph Cudworth, *The True Intellectual System of the Universe. The first part, wherein All the Reason and Philosophy of Atheism is confuted and its Impossibility demonstrated*, London, 1678; 2nd edn, 1743.
Ralph Cudworth, *Systema intellectualis huius universi*, ed. and trans. by Johann Lorenz von Mosheim, Jena, 1733 (Nachdruck Leiden, 1773).
Damaskios, *De Principiis (Traité des premiers principes*, ed. by L. Gerrit Westerink, trans. by Joseph Combès, Collection Budé, vol. 3: *De la procession*, Paris, 1991.
Richard Daunicht (ed.), *Lessing im Gespräch. Berichte und Urteile von Freunden und Zeitgenossen*, Munich, 1971.
Mariano Delgado, Klaus Koch and Edgar Marsch (eds), *Europa, Tausendjähriges Reich und Neue Welt. Zwei Jahrtausende Geschichte und Utopie in der Rezeption des Danielbuches*, Fribourg and Stuttgart, 2003.
Philippe Derchain, 'Pseudo-Jamblique ou Abammon? Quelques observations sur l'égyptianisme du "De mysteriis"', in *Chronique d'Égypte* 38 (1963): 220–6.
Philippe Derchain, 'Les hiéroglyphes à l'époque ptolémaïque', in Claude Baurain et al. (eds), *Phoinikeia Grammata. Lire et écrire en Méditerranée*, Liège, 1991, 243–56.
Friedrich Dieckmann. *Orpheus, eingeweiht. Eine Mozart-Erzählung*, Frankfurt/Main and Leipzig, 2005.
Liselotte Dieckmann, *Hieroglyphics. The History of a Literary Symbol*, St Louis: Washington University Press, 1970.
Jacco Dieleman, 'Priests, Tongues, and Rites. The London-Leiden Magical Manuscripts and Translation in Egyptian Ritual (100–300 CE)', *Religions in the Graeco-Roman World* 153, Leiden: Brill Academic Publishers, 2005.
Hermann Diels, *Die Fragmente der Vorsokratiker. Griechisch und deutsch*, ed. by Walther Kranz, unaltered reprint of the 6th edn, Hildesheim, 1972.
Albrecht Dihle, 'Das Satyrspiel "Sisyphos"', in *Hermes* 105 (1977): 28–42.
Albrecht Dihle, 'Die Theologia tripertita bei Augustin', in Hubert Cancik et al. (eds), *Geschichte – Tradition – Reflexion. Festschrift für Martin Hengel*, vol. 2, Tübingen, 1996, pp. 183–202.
Diodorus Siculus, *Bibliotheca historica: Diodorus of Sicily*. In 12 vols, ed. and trans. C. H. Oldfather, Cambridge, MA, 1946–7.
Dion Chrysostomus, *Trojana Oratio XI*, ed. by Ludwig Dindorf, Leipzig, 1919.

Jörg Dittmer, *Jaspers' Achsenzeit und das interkulturelle Gespräch. Überlegungen zur Relevanz eines revidierten Themas*, <http://www.chairete.de/Beitrag/TA/jaspers_achsenzeit.pdf>.

Mary Douglas, *In the Wilderness: The Doctrine of Defilement in the Book of Numbers*, Sheffield, 1993.

Alexander Dow, *Abhandlung zur Erläuterung der Geschichte der Religion, und Staatsverfassung von Hindostan: Aus dem Englischen übersetzt*, Leipzig, 1773.

François Dreyfus, 'La condescendance divine (synkatabasis) comme principe herméneutique de l'Ancien Testament dans la tradition juive et dans la tradition chrétienne', in John A. Emerton (ed.), *Congress Volume Salamanca, 1983, Supplements to Vetus Testamentum* 36, Leiden, 1985, 96–107.

Han J. W. Drijvers, 'De Hymnen van Madinet-Madi en de hellenistische Isisreligie', in *Vox Theologica* 32 (1962): 139–50.

Richard van Dülmen, *Der Geheimbund der Illuminaten. Darstellung, Analyse, Dokumentation*, Stuttgart-Bad Cannstatt, 1975.

Françoise Dunand, 'Syncrétismes dans la religion de l'Egypte Romaine', in F. Dunand and Pierre Levêque (eds), *Les syncrétismes dans les religions de l'antiquité*, Colloque de Besançon, Bibliothèque des Centres d'Études supérieures spécialisés, Leiden, 1975, 152–85.

Charles Dupuis, *Origine de tous les Cultes, ou la Religion Universelle*, 12 vols, Paris, 1795.

Émile Durkheim, *The Dualism of Human Nature and its Social Conditions*, in Kurth H. Wolff (ed.), *Essays on Sociology and Philosophy*, ed. by Kurt H. Wolff, New York: Harper & Row, 1964, 325–40.

Émile Durkheim, *Die elementaren Formen des religiösen Lebens*, trans. by Ludwig Schmidts, Frankfurt/Main, 2007.

Maurice Duverger (ed.), *Le concept d'empire*, Paris, 1980.

Florian Ebeling, *Catarino Mazzolàs Libretto 'Osiride' (Dresden 1781). Ein Beitrag zum kulturgeschichtlichen Umfeld des Librettos der 'Zauberflöte'*, in Mozart-Jahrbuch, 1999, 49–69.

Stephan Eberle, 'Lessing und Zarathustra', in *Rückert-Studien* 17 (2006/07) [Würzburg 2008]: 73–130.

Umberto Eco, *The Search for the Perfect Language*, Oxford, 1997.

Edrisi, *Geographia Nubiensis, id est accuratissima totius orbis in septem climata divisi descriptio <. . .> recens ex Arabico in latinam versa, übersetzt von Gabriele Sionita und Johannes Hesronita*, Rome, 1619; arabisch-französisch: Reinhart P. A. Dozy and Michael Jan de Goeje, *Description de l'Afrique et de l'Espagne par Edrîsî. Texte arabe publié pour la première fois d'après les ms. de Paris et d'Oxford avec une traduction, des notes et un glossaire*, 2 vols, Leiden: Brill, 1866.

Shmuel Noah Eisenstadt (ed.), *The Origins and Diversity of the Axial Age*, Albany, NY, 1986.

Shmuel Noah Eisenstadt (ed.), *Kulturen der Achsenzeit. Ihre Ursprünge und ihre Vielfalt*, 2 vols, Frankfurt/Main, 1987.

Shmuel Noah Eisenstadt (ed.), *Kulturen der Achsenzeit II. Ihre institutionelle und kulturelle Dynamik*, 3 vols, Frankfurt/Main, 1992.

Robert Eisler, *Platon und das ägyptische Alphabet*, in *Archiv für die Geschichte der Philosophie* 34 (1922): 3–13.

Erik H. Erikson, *Ontogeny of Ritualization in Man*, in *Philosophical Transactions of the Royal Society* 251 B, London, 1966: 337–49.

Eusebius von Caesarea, *Praeparatio Evangelica*: ed. by Karl Mras, *Eusebius Werke*, vol. 8: *Die Praeparatio Evangelica I*, Berlin, 1982.

Gerhard Fecht, *Der Vorwurf an Gott in den 'Mahnworten des Ipuwer'. Zur geistigen Krise der Ersten Zwischenzeit und ihrer Bewältigung*, AHAW 1972/1, Heidelberg, 1972.

Ernst Feil, 'Von der "Politischen Theologie" zur "Theologie der Revolution" '?, in E. Feil and Rudolf Weth (eds), *Diskussion zur Theologie der Revolution*, Munich and Mainz, 1969, 110–32.

Ernst Feil, *Religio*, vol. 3: *Die Geschichte eines neuzeitlichen Grundbegriffs im 17. und frühen 18. Jahrhundert*, Göttingen, 2001.

Ernst Feil, *Religio*, vol. 4: *Die Geschichte eines neuzeitlichen Grundbegriffs im 18. und frühen 19. Jahrhundert*, Göttingen, 2007.

André-Jean Festugière, *La révélation d'Hermès Trismégiste*, 4 vols, Paris, 1944–54.

Charles de Fieux de Mouhy, *Lamékis, ou les Voyages extraordinaires d'un Egyptien dans la terre intérieure*, Paris, 1734.

Hans Werner Fischer-Elfert, *Das verschwiegene Wissen des Irtisen*, in Jan Assmann, and Martin Bommas (eds), *Ägyptische Mysterien?*, Munich, 2002, 27–35.

Garth Fowden, *The Egyptian Hermes: A Historical Approach to the Late Pagan Mind*, Cambridge: Cambridge University Press, 1986.

Manfred Frank, *Der kommende Gott: Vorlesungen über die Neue Mythologie I*, Frankfurt/Main, 1982, 245.

Manfred Frank, *Gott im Exil: Vorlesungen über die Neue Mythologie II*, Frankfurt/Main, 1988.

Manfred Frank, *Unendliche Annäherung*, Frankfurt/Main: Suhrkamp, 1997.

David Frankfurter, *Religion in Roman Egypt: Assimilation and Resistance*, Princeton, NJ, 1988.

[M. Fréret], 'Recherches pour servir à l'histoire des Cyclopes, des Dactyles, des Telchines, des Curètes, des Corybantes & des Cabires', *Hist. de l'Acad. des Inscript. et Belles-Lettres* 27, Paris, undated.

Sigmund Freud, *Moses and Monotheism*, trans. K. Jones, New York, 1967.

Christiane Frey, 'Zeiten der Lektüre. Mosaisches und paulinisches Unterscheiden: Schiller, Herder, Mendelssohn' (unpublished ms.).

Freymäurer-Bibliothek, ed. v. Johann A. Hermann and Johann W. B. von Hymmen, Berlin, 1782.

Christian Froidefond, *Le mirage égyptien dans la littérature grècque d'Homère à Aristote*, Gap: Ophrys, 1971.

Amos Funkenstein, *Theology and the Scientific Imagination from the Middle Ages to the seventeenth century*, Princeton, NJ, 1986.

Amos Funkenstein, *Heilsplan und natürliche Entwicklung. Gegenwartsbestimmung im Geschichtsdenken des Mittelalters*, Munich, 1965.

Amos Funkenstein, 'Gesetz und Geschichte. Zur historisierenden Hermeneutik bei Moses Maimonides und Thomas von Aquin', in *Viator* 1 (1970): 147–78.

Alan H. Gardiner, 'The House of Life', in *JEA* 24 (1938): 157–79.

Peter D. A. Garnsey and Charles R. Whittaker (eds), *Imperialism in the Ancient World*, Cambridge, 1978.

Wilhelm Geerlings, 'Die theologia mythica des M. Terentius Varro', in Gerhard Binder and Bernd Effe (eds), *Mythos. Erzählende Weltdeutung im Spannungsfeld von Ritual, Geschichte und Rationalität*, Bochumer Altertumswissenschaftliches Colloquium 2, Trier, 1990, 205–22.

Alexander Giese, 'Freimaurerisches Geistesleben zur Zeit der Spätaufklärung am Beispiel des Journals für Freymaurer', in *Bibliotheca Masonica. Dokumente und Texte zur Freimaurerei*, ed. by Friedrich Gottschalk, Teil 2, Graz, 1988, 11–31.

Louis Ginzberg, *Legends of the Jews* (1909), vol. 1, Baltimore, MD: Johns Hopkins University Press, 1998.

Johann Wolfgang von Goethe, *Wilhelm Meisters Lehrjahre. Ein Roman*, 4 parts, Berlin: Unger, 1795.

Johann Wolfgang von Goethe, *Werke*, ed. on behalf of the Grand Duchess Sophie von Sachsen, Weimar 1887–1919, vol. IV/5.

Johann Wolfgang von Goethe, *Maximen und Reflexionen*, Hamburger Ausgabe, vol. 12.

Johann Wolfgang von Goethe, 'Aus Makariens Archiv', in Goethe, *Werke*, Hamburger Ausgabe, vol. 8, Munich, 1981, 460.

Arnold Goldberg, 'Der verschriftete Sprechakt als rabbinische Literatur', in A. and J. Assmann, Christof Hardmeier (eds), *Schrift und Gedächtnis*, Munich, 1983, 123–40.

Orly Goldwasser and Matthias Müller, 'The Determinative System as a Mirror of World Organization', in *Göttinger Miszellen* 170 (1999): 49–68.

Orly Goldwasser and Matthias Müller, 'The Building Blocks of a Conceptual Category: The Ancient Egyptian Evidence', in Bazzanella Morra (ed.), *Philosophers and Hieroglyphs*, 219–36.

Orly Goldwasser and Matthias Müller, *Lovers, Prophets and Giraffes: Wor(l)d Classification in Ancient Egypt*, Göttinger Orientforschungen, Wiesbaden, 2002.

Eveline Goodman-Thau, 'Sehen und Sagen in der jüdischen Tradition', in A. und J. Assmann (eds), *Geheimnis und Neugierde*, Munich, 1999, 99–120.

Friedrich Wilhelm Gotter, *Versuch über die N. N. oder die Unbekannten*, Berlin, 1780.

Koen Goudriaan, *Ethnicity in Ptolemaic Egypt*, Amsterdam, 1988.

Fritz Graf and Sarah Johnston, *Ritual Texts for the Afterlife: Orpheus and the Bacchic Gold Tablets*, London and New York, 2007.

Anthony Grafton, *Defenders of the Text: The Tradition of Scholarship in an Age of Science, 1450–1800*, Cambridge, MA, 1991.

Anthony Grafton, 'Gospel Secrets: The Biblical Controversies of Morton Smith', in *The Nation*, January, 2009.

John Gwyn Griffiths, *Plutarch. De Iside et Osiride*, [Cardiff] 1970.

John Gwyn Griffiths (ed.), *Apuleius of Madauros. The Isis-Book*. Edited with an introduction, translation and commentary, EPRO 39, Leiden: Brill, 1975.

Dieter Groh, 'Die Entstehung der Schöpfungstheologie oder der Lehre vom Buch der Natur bei den frühen Kirchenvätern in Ost und West bis zu Augustin', in Aleida Assmann, Ulrich Gaier and Gisela Trommsdorff (eds), *Zwischen Literatur und Anthropologie. Diskurse, Medien, Performanzen*, Tübingen, 2005, 147–60.

Dieter Groh, *Göttliche Weltökonomie. Perspektiven der Wissenschaftlichen Revolution vom 15. bis zum 17. Jahrhundert*, Frankfurt/Main, 2010.

Ruth Groh, 'Theologische und philosophische Voraussetzungen der Rede vom Buch der Natur', in Aleida Assmann, Ulrich Gaier and Gisela Trommsdorff (eds), *Zwischen Literatur und Anthopologie. Diskurse, Medien, Performanzen*, Tübingen, 2005, 139–46.

Hugo Grotius, *Annotationes in libros evangeliorum*, Amsterdam, 1641.

Karl Erich Grözinger, 'Reuchlin und die Kabbala', in *Reuchlin und die Juden*, ed. by Arno Herzig, Sigmaringen, 1993, 175–87.

Harald Haarmann, *Geschichte der Sintflut: Auf den Spuren der frühen Zivilisationen*, Munich, 2003.

Volkert Haas, 'Eine hethitische Weltreichsidee: Betrachtungen zum historischen Bewußtsein und politischen Denken in althethitischer Zeit', in Kurt A. Raaflaub (ed.), *Anfänge politischen Denkens in der Antike*, Munich, 1993, 135–44.

Pierre Hadot, *Le voile d'Isis*, Paris, 2004.

Pierre Hadot, *Zur Idee des Naturgeheimnisses: Beim Betrachten des Widmungsblattes in den Humboldtschen 'Ideen zu einer Geographie der Pflanzen'*, Abhandlungen der Akademie der Wissenschaften und der Literatur Mainz. Geistes- und sozialwissenschaftliche Klasse, Abh. 8, Wiesbaden: F. Steiner, 1982.

Karl Haidinger, 'Ueber die Magie', in *JF* 5 (1785): 29–56.

Moshe Halbertal, *People of the Book: Canon, Meaning, and Authority*, Cambridge, MA, 1997.

Johann Georg Hamann, *Hauptschriften erklärt*, ed. by Fritz Blanke and Karlfried Gründer, vol. 5: *Mysterienschriften*, Gütersloh, 1962.

John Hamill, *The Craft: A History of English Freemasonry*, Guildford, 1986.

Ludwig Hammermeyer, *Der Wilhelmsbader Freimaurerkonvent von 1782: Ein Höhe- und Wendepunkt in der Geschichte der deutschen und europäischen Geheimgesellschaften*, Wolfenbütteler Studien zur Aufklärung V,2, Heidelberg, 1980.

Christine Harrauer, ' "Ich bin, was da ist . . .". Die Göttin von Sais und ihre Deutung von Plutarch bis in die Goethezeit', in *Sphairos. Wiener Studien. Zeitschrift für Klassische Philologie und Patristik* 107/108, Vienna, 1994/95, 337–55.

François Hartog, 'Les Grecs égyptologues', in *Annales: Économies, Sociétés, Civilisations* 41 (1986): 953–67.

François Hartog, 'Voyages d'Egypte', in F. Hartog, *Mémoire d'Ulysse: Récits sur la frontière en Grèce ancienne*, Paris, 1996, 49–86.

Wolf-Daniel Hartwich, *Die Sendung Moses: Von der Aufklärung bis Thomas Mann*, Munich, 1997, 29–49.

Eric A. Havelock, *The Literate Revolution in Greece and its Cultural Consequences*, Princeton, 1981.

George D. Henderson, *Chevalier Ramsay*, London, 1952.

Martin Hengel, *Judentum und Hellenismus*, Tübingen 3rd edn, 1988 (1st edn, 1969).

Johann Gottfried Herder, 'Briefe zur Beförderung der Humanität', in *Werke in zehn Bänden*, ed. by Martin Bollacher, vol. 7, Frankfurt/Main, 1991, Zweite Sammlung, 26. Brief, 132–41.

Johann Gottfried Herder, *Briefe: Herders Briefe. Ausgewählt, eingeleitet und erläutert von Wilhelm Dobbek*, Weimar, 1959.

Johann Gottfried Herder, 'Historische Zweifel über F. Nicolai's Buch von den Beschuldigungen, welche den Tempelherren gemacht worden, von ihren Geheimnissen und dem Entstehen der Freimaurergesellschaft' (1782), in J. G. v.Herder, *Sämmtliche Werke, Zur Philosophie und Geschichte, Dreyzehnter Theil, Carlsruhe, im Bureau der deutschen Classiker 1820*, 266–360 = Sämmtliche Werke, Stuttgart, 1829, 258–345.

Carola Hilfrich, *'Lebendige Schrift'. Repräsentation und Idolatrie in Moses Mendelssohn's Philosophie und Exegese des Judentums*, Munich, 2000.

Otfried Höffe, *Koexistenz der Kulturen im Zeitalter der Globalisierung*, Munich, 2008.

Theodor Hopfner, *Fontes historiae religionis Aegyptiacae*, 5 vols, Bonn, 1922–5.

Horapollon: *Horapollinis Nilotici Hieroglyphica Libri II*, ed. by Francesco Sbordone, Neapel 1940; English: George Boas, *The Hieroglyphics of Horapollo*, Bollingen Series XXIII, Princeton, NJ, 1993; Greek-Italian: Horapollo, *I Geroglifici*. Introduzione, traduzione e note di Mario Andrea Regni e Elena Zanco, Mailand, 1996.

Pieter W. van der Horst, 'Chaeremon. Egyptian Priest and Stoic Philosopher. The fragments collected and translated with explanatory notes', *EPRO* 101, Leiden, 1984.

Pieter W. van der Horst, *The Secret Hieroglyphs in Classical Literature*, in Jan den Boeft, A. H. W. Kessels (eds), *Actus. Studies in Honour of H. L. W Nelson*, Utrecht, 1982, 115–23.

Pieter W. van der Horst, 'Hierogliefen in de ogen van Grieken en Romeinen', in *Phoenix ex Oriente Lux* 30 (1984): 44–53.

Matthias Hurst, *Im Spannungsfeld der Aufklärung: Von Schillers Geisterseher zur TV-Serie The X-Files: Rationalismus und Irrationalismus in Literatur und Fernsehen*, Heidelberg, 2001.

William Hutchinson, *The Spirit of Masonry in Moral and Elucidatory Lectures*, 2nd edn, Carlisle, 1795.

Sarah Hutton, 'Classicism and Baroque: A Note on Mosheim's Footnotes to Cudworth's *The True Intellectual System of the Universe*', in Martin Mulsow et al. (eds), *Johann Lorenz Mosheim (1693–1755): Theologie im*

Spannungsfeld von Philosophie, Philologie und Geschichte, Wolfenbütteler Forschungen 77, Wiesbaden, 1997, 211–27.

Moshe Idel, 'Deus sive Natura: Les metamorphoses d' une formule de Maïmonide à Spinoza', in M. Idel, *Maïmonide et la mystique juive*, Paris, 1991.

Moshe Idel, 'Reuchlin. Kabbalah, Pythagorean Philosophy and Modern Scholarship', in *Studia Universitatis Babes-Bolyai. Studia Judaica*, 2008, 30–55.

Hans-Josef Irmen, *Mozart: Mitglied geheimer Gesellschaften*, Mechernich: Prisca, 1988.

Hans-Josef Irmen, *Die Protokolle der Wiener Freimaurerloge 'Zur Wahren Eintracht' (1781–5)*, Frankfurt/Main et al., 1994.

Isidorus Orientalis [Otto Heinrich Graf von Loeben], *Guido*, Mannheim, 1808 (facsimile print, Bern et al.: Lang, 1979).

Paul Ernst Jablonski, *Pantheon Aegyptiorum sive de diis eorum commentarius cum prolegomenis de religione et theologia Aegyptiorum*, Frankfurt/Oder, 1750.

Margaret C. Jacob, *The Radical Enlightenment: Pantheists, Freemasons and Republicans*, London, 1981.

Friedrich Heinrich Jacobi, *Über die Lehre des Spinoza in Briefen an den Herrn Moses Mendelssohn*, Darmstadt and Hamburg, 2000.

Friedrich Heinrich Jacobi, Briefe über die Recherches philosophiques sur les Egyptiens et les Chinois par M. de Pauw (1773/74), in Jacobi, *Werke*, 6 vols, Leipzig, 1812–25 (reprint, Darmstadt, 1968), vol. 6, 265–344.

Jamblich, *De mysteriis Aegyptiorum: Jamblique, Les mystères d'Egypte*, ed. v. Edouard des Places, Paris 1989; *Iamblichus or The Mysteries*, trans. T. Taylor, London, 1821.

Karl Jaspers, *Vom Ursprung und Ziel der Geschichte*, Munich, 1949.

Peter Jeffery, *The Secret Gospel of Mark Unveiled*, New Haven, CT: Yale University Press, 2006.

Johann Friedrich Wilhelm Jerusalem, *Betrachtungen über die vornehmsten Wahrheiten der Religion*, Braunschweig, 1768.

Horace L. Jones, *The Geography of Strabo*, 8 vols, LCL, Cambridge, MA, and London: Harvard University Press, 1932–5.

Helge Jordheim, 'Die Hypokrisie der Aufklärer – oder: War Wieland ein Lügner? Eine Untersuchung zu Kosellecks Kritik und Krise', in Jussi Kurunmäki/Kari Palonen (ed.), *Time, History and Politics/ Zeit, Geschichte und Politik. Zum achtzigsten Geburtstag von Reinhart Koselleck*, Jyväskylä, 2003, 35–54.

Klaus-Peter Jörns, *Notwendige Abschiede*, Gütersloh, 2004.

Josephus Flavius, *Contra Apionem*, trans. John Barclay, Leiden, 2007.

Carl Gustav Jung, 'Die Persona als ein Ausschnitt aus der Kollektivpsyche', in C. G. Jung, *Die Beziehungen zwischen dem Ich und dem Unbewußten*, *Taschenbuchausgabe*, Munich, 4th edn, 1994 (1st edn, 1928).

Johann Heinrich Jung-Stilling, *Das Heimweh*, ed. Martina Maria Sam, Dornach, 1994.

Immanuel Kant, *Critique of the Power of Judgment*, trans. P. Guyer and E. Matthews, Cambridge, 2000.

Marc M. Kerling, 'O Wort, du Wort, das mir fehlt'. Die Gottesfrage in Arnold Schönbergs Oper 'Moses und Aron'. Zur Theologie eines musikalischen Kunst-Werkes im 20. Jahrhundert, Mainz: Grünewald, 2004.

Klaus H. Kiefer, *Die famose Hexen-Epoche: Sichtbares und Unsichtbares in der Aufklärung*, Munich, 2004.

Andreas B. Kilcher (ed.), *Die Kabbala Denudata. Text und Kontext.* Akten der 15. Tagung der Christian Knorr von Rosenroth-Gesellschaft, Morgen-Glantz 16/2006, Bern, 2006.

Athanasius Kircher, *Oedipus Aegyptiacus*, 3 vols, Rome, 1652–4.

[Johann Friedrich Kleuker], MAΓIKON *oder das geheime System einer Gesellschaft unbekannter Philosophen <. . .> und dessen Verwandtschaft mit ältern und neuern Mysteriologien gezeigt*, Frankfurt and Leipzig, 1784.

Adolph von Knigge, *Die Verirrungen des Philosophen oder Geschichte Ludwigs von Seelberg*, Frankfurt, 1787.

[Adolph von Knigge], *Illuminatus Dirigens oder Schottischer Ritter. Ein Pendant zu der nicht unwichtigen Schrift Die neuesten Arbeiten des Spartacus und Philo in den Illuminaten Orden* [Munich], 1794.

Klaus Koch, *Europa, Rom und der Kaiser vor dem Hintergrund von zwei Jahrtausenden Rezeption des Buches Daniel*, Hamburg, 1997.

[Carl Friedrich Köppen], *Crata Repoa, oder Einweihungen in der alten geheimen Gesellschaft der Egyptischen Priester*, Berlin: Stahlbaum, 1778.

Reinhart Koselleck, *Kritik und Krise: Eine Studie zur Pathogenese der bürgerlichen Welt*, Freiburg, 1959 (Frankfurt/Main, 1973).

Martin Krause, *Die Gnosis*, vol. 2, Zurich, 1971.

Anton Kreil, 'Ueber das Buch: Des erreurs et de la vérité' [Rez. St Martin], in *JF* 4 (1784): 55–164.

Anton Kreil, 'Geschichte des pythagoräischen Bundes', in *JF* 5 (1785): 3–28.

Anton Kreil, 'Geschichte der Neuplatoniker', in *JF* 6 (1785): 5–51.

[Anton Kreil], 'Ueber die wissenschaftliche Maurerey', in *JF* 7 (1985): 49–78.

Anton Kreil, 'Ueber die eleusinischen Mysterien', in *JF* 10 (1786): 5–42.

Ekkehard Krippendorff, *Die Kultur des Politischen: Wege aus den Diskursen der Macht*, Berlin, 2009.

Daniel Krochmalnik, 'Der Sinn der Opfer: Nach dem "Führer der Verirrten" III, 32', in *Der Landesverband der Israelitischen Kultusgemeinden in Bayern* 11/73 (June 1997): 21–4.

Karl-Josef Kuschel, *Vom Streit zum Wettstreit der Religionen: Lessing und die Herausforderung des Islam*, Dusseldorf, 1998.

Trolle Mogens Larsen (ed.), *Power and Propaganda: A Symposium on Ancient Empires*, Copenhagen, 1979.

Theodor Ludwig Lau, 'Meditationes, Theses, Dubia philosophico-theologica [Freistadt 1719]. Dokumente'. Ed. with an introduction by Martin Pott, *Philosophische Clandestina der deutschen Aufklärung* I.1, Stuttgart-Bad Cannstatt, 1992.

Gotthold Ephraim Lessing, 'Axiomata, wenn es deren in dergleichen Dingen gibt', in Lessing, *Werke*, vol. 8, 128–59.

Gotthold Ephraim Lessing, _Nathan der Weise: Ein dramatisches Gedicht in fünf Aufzügen_, Berlin: Voß, 1779.

Gotthold Ephraim Lessing, _Philosophical and Theological Writings_, ed. H. S. Nisbet, Cambridge, 2005.

Gotthold Ephraim Lessing, 'Rettung des Cardanus', in Lessing, _Werke_, vol. 7, 9–66.

Gotthold Ephraim Lessing, _Werke_, ed. v. Herbert G. Göpfert, Bände 1–8, Munich, 1970–9.

Bernard Lewis, Friedrich Niewöhner, _Religionsgespräche im Mittelalter_, Wiesbaden, 1992.

G. Chr. Lichtenberg, _Sudelbücher_, Heft H, Nr. 143, in _Schriften und Briefe_, vol. 2: _Sudelbücher II, Materialhefte, Tagebücher_, Munich and Vienna, 1971.

Godo Lieberg, _Die theologia tripertita als Formprinzip antiken Denkens_, in _Rheinisches Museum_ 125 (1982): 25–53.

Alexandra von Lieven, 'Im Schatten des Goldhauses. Berufsgeheimnis und Handwerkerinitiation im Alten Ägypten', in _Studien zur Altägyptischen Kultur_ 36 (2007): 147–55.

Wilgert te Lindert, _Aufklärung und Heilserwartung: Philosophische und religiöse Ideen. Wiener Freimaurer (1780–95)_, Frankfurt/Main et al., 1998.

Dolf Lindner, _Ignaz von Born, Meister der Wahren Eintracht: Wiener Freimaurerei im 18. Jahrhundert_, Vienna, 1986.

Paul Lucas, _Voyage du sieur Paul Lucas fait en MDCCIV par l'ordre de Louis XIV <. . .>_, nouvelle édition, vol. 3, Rouen, 1724.

Thomas Luckmann, _The Invisible Religion: The Problem of Religion in Modern Society_, New York, 1967.

Niklas Luhmann, 'Das Kunstwerk und die Selbstreproduktion der Kunst', in Hans Ulrich Gumbrecht and K. Ludwig Pfeiffer (eds), _Stil_, Frankfurt/Main, 1986, 620–62.

Niklas Luhmann, 'Form der Schrift', in Hans Ulrich Gumbrecht and K. Ludwig Pfeiffer (eds), _Schrift_, Munich, 1993, 348–66.

Ramon Llull, _Doctor Illuminatus: A Ramon Llull Reader_, ed. A Bonner, Princeton, NJ, 1985.

Jean-Pierre Mahé, _Hermès en Haute Égypte_, 2 vols, Quebec, 1978–82.

Scott Mandelbrote, 'Isaac Newton and Thomas Burnet. Biblical Criticism and the Crisis of Late Seventeenth Century England', in Richard H. Popkin and James E. Force (eds), _The Books of Nature and Scripture_, Dordrecht, 1994, 149–78.

Manetho, ed. and translated by William G. Waddell, _LCL 350_, Cambridge, MA, 1964.

Frank Manuel, _The Eighteenth Century Confronts the Gods_, Cambridge, MA: Harvard University Press, 1959 (reprint, New York, 1967).

Pierre Marestaing, _Les écritures égyptiennes et l'antiquité classique_, Paris, 1913.

Avishai Margalit, _The Ethics of Memory_, Cambridge, MA: Harvard University Press, 2003.

Douglas A. Marshall, *Durkheimian Dualism Redux. Homo Duplex and the Origin of Religion* (<http://www.allacademic.com/meta/p105188_index.html>).

Gerhard May, *Schöpfung aus dem Nichts: Die Entstehung der Lehre von der creatio ex nihilo, Arbeiten zur Kirchengeschichte 48*, Berlin and New York: Walter de Gruyter, 1978.

Christoph Meiners, *Über die Mysterien der Alten, besonders die Eleusinischen Geheimnisse. Vermischte philosophische Schriften III*, Göttingen, 1776.

Christoph Meiners, *Geschichte des Ursprungs, Fortgangs und Verfalls der Wissenschaften in Griechenland und Rom*, vol. 1, Lemgo, 1781.

Moses Mendelssohn, *Schriften über Religion und Aufklärung*, ed. by Martina Thom, Berlin: Union-Verlag, 1989.

Moses Mendelssohn, *Jerusalem: A Treatise on Ecclesiastical Authority and Judaism*, trans. M. Samuels, London, 1838.

Reinhold Merkelbach, *Isis Regina – Zeus Sarapis: Die griechisch-ägyptische Religion nach den Quellen dargestellt*, Stuttgart and Leipzig, 1995.

Reinhold Merkelbach and Maria Totti (eds), *Abrasax. Ausgewählte Papyri religiösen und magischen Inhalts*, 5 vols, Papyrologica Coloniensia 17/1–5, Opladen, 1990–2001; vols 1–2: *Gebete*, 1990–1; vol. 3: *Zwei griechisch-ägyptische Weihezeremonien (Die Leidener Weltschöpfung/Die Pschai-Aion-Liturgie)*, 1993; vol. 4: *Exorzismen und jüdisch/christlich beeinflußte Texte*, 1996; vol. 5: *Traumtexte*, 2001.

Dieter Metzler, 'A. H. Anquetil-Duperron (1731–1805) und das Konzept der Achsenzeit', in *Achaemenid History* 7 (1991): 123–33.

Markus Meumann, 'Zur Rezeption antiker Mysterien im Geheimbund der Illuminaten Ignaz von Born, Karl Leonhard Reinhold und die Wiener Freimaurerloge "Zur wahren Eintracht"', in Monika Neugebauer-Wölk (ed.), *Aufklärung und Esoterik, Studien zum achtzehnten Jahrhundert* 24, Hamburg, 1999: 288–304.

Matthias Meyer, 'Nachwort', in F. Schiller, *Der Geisterseher*, ed. by M. Meyer, Stuttgart, 1996, 219–42.

Wilhelm Friedrich Meyern, *Dya-Na-Sore, oder: Die Wanderer. Eine Geschichte aus dem Sam-skritt übersezt*, 3 vols, Vienna and Leipzig: Stahel, 1787–91.

[Karl Josef Michaeler], 'Ueber Analogie zwischen dem Christenthume der erstern Zeiten und der Freymaurerey', in *JF* 2 (1784): 5–63.

Karl Josef Michaeler, *Historisch-kritische Abhandlung über die phönicischen Mysterien*, Vienna, 1796.

Peter Michelsen, 'Die "wahren Taten" der Freimaurer. Lessings "Ernst und Falk"', in Peter Christian Ludz (ed.), *Geheime Gesellschaften*, Wolfenbütteler Studien zur Aufklärung V/1, Heidelberg, 1979, 293–324.

Walter Mignolo, 'The Many Faces of Cosmo-polis. Border Thinking and Critical Cosmopolitanism', in *Public Culture* 12/3 (2000): 721–48.

Peter N. Miller, 'Taking Paganism Seriously. Anthropology and Antiquarianism in Early Seventeenth-Century Histories of Religion', in *ARG* 3 (2001), 183–209.

Sigrid von Moisy, *Von der Aufklärung zur Romantik. Geistige Strömungen,* in München. Ausstellung Munich 2/6–24/8 (1984) (Exhibition catalogue).

Ludwig D. Morenz, 'Neohieroglyphs of the Italian Renaissance: Tradition and its Invention', in Bazzanella Morra, *Philosophers and Hieroglyphs,* 50–73.

Siegfried Morenz, 'Ptah-Hephaistos, der Zwerg. Beobachtungen zur Frage der interpretatio Graeca in der ägyptischen Religion', in *Festschrift für Friedrich Zucker zum 70.* Geburtstage, Berlin: Akademie-Verlag, 1954, 275–90.

Daniel Georg Morhof, *Theologiae gentium politicae dissertatio prima de Divinitate Principum,* Rostock, 1662.

Karl Philipp Moritz, *Andreas Hartknopf: Eine Allegorie,* Berlin: Unger, 1786; 1790.

Wolfgang Amadeus Mozart, *Briefe und Aufzeichnungen,* ed. by Wilhelm A. Bauer and Otto Erich Deutsch (eds), vol. 4, Kassel, 1963.

Wolfgang Amadeus Mozart, Franz Heinrich Ziegenhagen, *Eine kleine deutsche Kantate: 'Die ihr des unermesslichen Weltalls Schöpfer ehrt',* for voice and piano, ed. by Hiltrud M. Brinkschulte and Rainer Leptihn, Gauting, 2010.

[Johann Joachim Müller], *De imposturis religionum (De tribus impostoribus) – Von den Betrügereyen der Religionen.* Kritisch ed. and commentary by Winfried Schröder, *Philosophische Clandestina der deutschen Aufklärung,* Abt. I, vol. 6, Stuttgart-Bad Cannstatt: frommann-holzboog, 1999.

Klaus Müller, *Tora für die Völker: Die noachidischen Gebote und Ansätze zu ihrer Rezeption im Christentum,* Studien zu Kirche und Israel 15, Berlin: Inst. Kirche und Judentum, 1994 (2nd edn, 1998).

Klaus Müller, 'Die noachidische Tora. Ringen um ein Weltethos', in *Freiburger Rundbrief* 3 (1996) (<http://www.freiburger-rundbrief.de/de/?item=397>).

Klaus Müller, 'Über den monistischen Tiefenstrom der christlichen Gottrede', in K. Müller and Magnus Striet (eds), *Dogma und Denkform. Strittiges in der Grundlegung von Offenbarungsbegriff und Gottesgedanke,* Regensburg, 2005, 47–84.

Klaus Müller, *Streit um Gott. Politik, Poetik und Philosophie im Ringen um das wahre Gottesbild,* Regensburg, 2006.

Martin Mulsow and John Seldens, 'De Diis Syris. Idolatriekritik und vergleichende Religionsgeschichte im 17. Jahrhundert', in ARG 3 (2001), 1–24.

Martin Mulsow, *Die drei Ringe. Toleranz und clandestine Gelehrsamkeit bei Mathurin Veyssière La Croze (1661–1739),* Tübingen, 2001.

Martin Mulsow, *Moderne aus dem Untergrund: Radikale Frühaufklärung in Deutschland 1680–1720,* Hamburg 2002.

Martin Mulsow and Helmut Zedelmaier (eds), *Skepsis, Providenz, Polyhistorie: Jakob Friedrich Reimmann (1668–1743),* Tübingen, 1998.

Gabriel Naudé, *Considérations politiques sur les coups d'État,* Paris, 1667 (1st edn, Rome, 1639); New edition under the title: *Science des Princes, ou Considérations politiques sur les coups-d'état,* Strasbourg, 1673.

Birgitta Nedelmann, 'Geheimhaltung, Verheimlichung, Geheimnis – einige soziologische Vorüberlegungen', in H. G. Kippenberg and Guy G. Stroumsa (eds), *Secrecy and Concealment: Studies in the History of Mediterranean and Near Eastern Religions*, Leiden, 1995, 1–16.

Gérard de Nerval, *Le Voyage en Orient*, Oeuvres II, ed. by Albert Béguin and Jean Richer, Paris: Editions de la Pléiade, 1956.

Monika Neugebauer-Wölk, *Esoterische Bünde und bürgerliche Gesellschaft. Entwicklungslinien zur modernen Welt im Geheimbundwesen des 18. Jahrhunderts, Kleine Schriften zur Aufklärung 8*, Göttingen, 1995.

Monika Neugebauer-Wölk, 'Debatten im Geheimraum der Aufklärung. Konstellationen des Wissensgewinns im Orden der Illuminaten', in Wolfgang Hardtwig (ed.), *Die Aufklärung und ihre Weltwirkung, Geschichte und Gesellschaft Sonderheft 23*, Göttingen, 2010, 17–46.

[Isaac Newton], *Newton's Out of Cudworth*, in Richard H. Popkin and James E. Force, *Essays on the Context, Nature, and Influence of Isaac Newton's Theology*, Dordrecht, 1990, Appendix, 207–14.

Rosemarie Nicolai-Haas, *Die Anfänge des deutschen Geheimbundromans*, in Peter Christian Ludz (ed.), *Geheime Gesellschaften, Wolfenbütteler Studien zur Aufklärung V/1*, Heidelberg, 1979, 267–92.

Friedrich Niewöhner, *Veritas sive Varietas. Lessings Toleranzparabel und das Buch von den drei Betrügern*, Heidelberg, 1988.

Hugh Barr Nisbet, 'Zur Funktion des Geheimnisses in Lessing's "Ernst und Falk"', in Peter Freimark (ed.), *Lessing und die Toleranz*, Detroit: Wayne University Press, 1986, 291–309.

Hugh Barr Nisbet, *Lessing: Eine Biographie*, Munich, 2008.

Novalis, *Heinrich von Ofterdingen. Ein nachgelassener Roman*, 2 parts, Berlin: Buchhandlung der Realschule, 1802.

Origenes, *Against Celsus*, in J. Donaldson and A. Roberts (eds), *Anti-Nicene Christian Library*, vol. I, Edinburgh, 1869.

Eberhard Otto, *Der Vorwurf an Gott: Zur Entstehung der ägyptischen Auseinandersetzungsliteratur*, Hildesheim, 1951.

Jean Paul, *Die unsichtbare Loge. Eine Biographie*, 2 vols, Berlin: Matzdorff, 1793.

Cornelius de Pauw, *Recherches philosophiques sur les Egyptiens & Chinois*, London, Lausanne and Geneva, 1774.

Werner Peek, *Der Isishymnus von Andros und verwandte Texte*, Berlin, 1930.

Helmut Perl, *Der Fall Zauberflöte*, Darmstadt, 2000.

Plato, *Philebus*, trans. with commentary by R. Hackforth, Cambridge, 1972.

Friedrich Victor Leberecht Plessing, *Osiris und Sokrates*, Berlin and Stralsund, 1783.

Helmuth Plessner, 'Soziale Rolle und menschliche Natur', in H. Plessner, *Gesammelte Schriften*, vol. 10, Frankfurt/Main, 1985, 227–40.

Robert Plot, *The Natural History of Stafford-Shire*, Oxford, 1686.

Plotinus, *The Enneads*, trans. S. MacKenna, London, 1991.

Plutarch, *Religionsphilosophische Schriften*, ed. by Herwig Görgemanns, Düsseldorf, 2nd edn, 2009 (1st edn, 2003).

Plutarch's Moralia, vol. 15: *Fragments*, ed. by Francis H. Sandbach, Cambridge, 1969.

Richard H. Popkin, 'Newton and Maimonides', in James E. Force and R. H. Popkin, *The Third Force in Seventeenth-Century Thought*, Leiden, 1992, 189–202.

Porphyrios, *Epistola ad Anebonem*, ed. by A. R. Sodano, Naples, 1958.

Porphyrios, *De vita Pythagorae*: ed. and trans. by Édouard des Places, *Porphyre. Vie de Pythagore, lettre à Marcella*, Paris: Collection Budé, 1982.

Georges Posener, 'Sur le monothéisme dans l'ancienne Égypte', in *Mélanges Bibliques et orientaux en l'honneur de M. Henri Cazelles*, AOAT 212, Neukirchen-Vluyn, 1981, 347–51.

Karl Preisendanz and Albert Henrichs, *Papyri Graecae Magicae. Die Griechischen Zauberpapyri*, 2 vols, Stuttgart, 2nd edn, 1973–4 (1st edn, 1928–41).

Albert de Pury, 'Gottesname, Gottesbezeichnung und Gottesbegriff: "Elohim als Indiz zur Entstehungsgeschichte des Pentateuch"', in Jan-Christian Gertz, Konrad Schmid and Markus Witte (eds), *Abschied vom Jahwisten. Die Komposition des Hexateuch in der jungsten Diskussion*, BZAW 315, Berlin and New York: de Gruyter, 2002, 25–47.

Jan Quaegebeur, 'On the Egyptian Equivalent of Biblical Hartummim', in Sarah Israelit-Groll (ed.), *Pharaonic Egypt. The Bible and Christianity*, Jerusalem: The Magnes Press, 1985, 162–72.

Joachim F. Quack, *Die Lehre für Merikare*, Wiesbaden, 1992.

Jan Quaegebeur, 'La désignation (P3)Hry-tp: PHRITOB', in Jürgen Osing and Günter Dreyer (eds), *Form und Maß. Festschrift für Gerhard Fecht*, Wiesbaden, 1987, 368–94.

François Rabelais, *Gargantua and Pantagruel*, trans. M.A. Screech, London, 2006.

Michael Ramsay, *The Travels of Cyrus/Les Voyages de Cyrus*, 2 vols, Paris and London, 1727.

Donald B. Redford, *Pharaonic King-lists, Annals, and Yearbooks: A Contribution to the Study of the Egyptian Sense of History*, Mississauga, 1986.

Jacob Friedrich Reimmann, *Idea Systematis Antiquitatis Literariae Specialioris sive Aegyptiacae Adumbrati*, Hildesheim, 1718.

Helmut Reinalter, 'Ignaz von Born als Freimaurer und Illuminat', in H. Reinalter (ed.), *Die Aufklärung in Österreich. Ignaz von Born und seine Zeit*, Frankfurt et al. 1991, 33–67.

Carl Leonhard Reinhold, 'Ueber die kabirischen Mysterien', in *JF* 7 (1785): 5–48.

[Carl Leonhard Reinhold], 'Ueber die Mysterien der alten Hebräer', in *JF* 9 (1786): 5–79.

[Carl Leonhard Reinhold], 'Ueber die größern Mysterien der Hebräer', in *JF* 11 (1786): 5–98.

Carl Leonhard Reinhold, *Die hebräischen Mysterien oder die älteste religiöse Freymaurerey* (1787), ed. and introduced by J. Assmann, Neckargemünd, 2nd edn, 2006 (1st edn, 2001).

Johannes Reuchlin, *De Arte Cabbalistica – On the Art of the Kabbala*, trans. by Martin and Sarah Goodman, New York, 1983.

Christoph Riedweg, *Jüdisch-hellenistische Imitation eines orphischen hieros logos. Beobachtungen zu OF 245 und 247 (sog. Testament des Orpheus)*, Classica Monacensia 7, Tübingen, 1993.

Christina Riggs, *The Beautiful Burial in Roman Egypt: Art, Identity, and Funerary Religion*, Oxford, 2005.

[Abbé Claude Robin], *Recherches sur les initiations anciennes et modernes*, Paris, 1779.

Thomas Römer, 'Recherches actuelles sur le cycle d'Abraham', in André Wénin (ed.), *Studies in the Book of Genesis: Literature, Redaction and History*, Leuven, 2001, 179–211.

Edith Rosenstrauch-Königsberg, 'Ausstrahlungen des "Journals für Freimaurer"', in Beförderer der Aufklärung in Mittel- und Osteuropa. Freimaurer, Gesellschaften, Clubs', ed. by Éva H. Balasz et al., *Studien zur Geschichte der Kulturbeziehungen in Mittel- und Osteuropa 5*, Berlin, 1979, 103–17.

Edith Rosenstrauch-Königsberg, *Freimaurer, Illuminat, Weltbürger: Friedrich Münters Reisen und Briefe in ihren europäischen Bezügen*, Berlin, 1984.

Edith Rosenstrauch-Königsberg, 'Eine freimaurerische Akademie der Wissenschaften in Wien', in E. Rosenstrauch-Königsberg, *Zirkel und Zentren: Aufsätze zur Aufklärung in Österreich am Ende des 18. Jahrhunderts*, ed. by Gunnar Hering, Vienna, undated [1990], 67–87.

Edith Rosenstrauch-Königsberg, 'Zur Philosophie der österreichischen Freimaurer und Illuminaten mit Blick auf Mozart', in Gunda Barth-Scalmani, Brigitte Mazohl-Wallnig and Ernst Wangermann (eds), *Genie und Alltag. Bürgerliche Stadtkultur zur Mozartzeit*, Salzburg and Vienna, 1994, 317–50.

Alexander Ross, *Pansebeia, or, a View of all the Religions of the World*, London, 6th edn, 1696 (1st edn, 1652).

Paolo Rossi, 'La religione dei geroglifi e le origini della scrittura', in P. Rossi, *Le terminate antichità. Studi vichiani, Saggi di varia umanità 9*, Pisa, 1969, 81–131.

Rostorf [Karl Gottlob Albrecht von Hardenberg], *Pilgrimmschaft nach Eleusis*, Berlin: Unger, 1804.

Jean-Jacques Rousseau, *Émile ou de l'éducation* (1762), ed. with notes and index by François and Pierre Richard, Paris: Garnier 1999; *Emile, or, On Education*, trans. Allan Bloom, New York, 1979.

Michael Rowlands, Mogens Trolle Larsen and Kristian Kristiansen (eds), *Centre and Periphery in the Ancient World*, New Directions in Archaeology, Cambridge, 1987.

Ulrich Rudolph, 'Abu Bakr Ibn Tufail', in Friedrich Niewöhner (ed.), *Klassiker der Religionsphilosophie*, Munich, 1995, 126–41.

Jonathan Sacks, *The Dignity of Difference: How to avoid the Clash of Civilizations*, London, 2002.

Baron de Sainte-Croix, *Mémoires pour servir à l'histoire de la religion secrète des anciens peuples, ou Recherches historiques et critiques sur les mystères du paganisme*, Paris, 1784.

Elisabeth von Samsonow, *Giordano Bruno*, Cologne, 1995.

Paolo Scarpi (ed.), *Le religioni dei Misteri*, 2 vols, Milan, 2002.

Peter Schäfer, *Judeophobia. Attitudes Towards Jews in the Ancient World*, Cambridge, MA, 1997.

Friedrich Schiller, 'Die Sendung Moses', in Friedrich Schiller, *Werke und Briefe*, ed. by Otto Dann, vol. 6: *Historische Schriften und Erzählungen*, Frankfurt/Main: DKV, 2000, 451–74.

Friedrich Schiller, *Naïve and Sentimental Poetry, and, On the Sublime. Two Essays*, trans. J. Elias, New York, 1967.

Friedrich Schiller, *Essays*, ed. W. Hinderer and D. Dahlstrom, New York, 2005.

Hans Jürgen Schings, *Die Brüder des Marquis Posa. Schiller und der Geheimbund der Illuminaten*, Tübingen, 1996.

Norbert Schindler, 'Aufklärung und Geheimnis im Illuminatenorden', in Peter Christian Ludz (ed.), *Geheime Gesellschaften*, Wolfenbütteler Studien zur Aufklärung V/1, Heidelberg, 1979, 203–29.

Augustin Veit von Schittlersberg, 'Ueber den Einfluß der Mysterien der Alten auf den Flor der Nationen', in *JF* 9 (1786): S. 80–116.

Bernhard Joseph Schleiß von Löwenfeld [Pseudonym: Ketmia Vere], *Der Compaß der Weisen, von einem Mitverwandten der innern Verfassung der ächten und rechten Freymäurerey beschrieben*; herausgegeben mit Anmerkungen, einer Zueignungsschrift und Vorrede, in welcher die Geschichte dieses erlauchten Ordens, vom Anfang seiner Stiftung an, deutlich und treulich vorgetragen, und die Irrthümer einiger ausgearteter französischer Freymäurer-Logen entdeckt werden, von Ketmia Vere, Berlin and Leipzig: Christian Ulrich Ringmacher, 1779; 2nd edn, 1782.

Hermann A. Schlögl, *Der Sonnengott auf der Blüte: Eine ägyptische Kosmogonie des Neuen Reiches*, AH 5, Basel and Geneva, 1977.

Wilhelm Schmidt-Biggemann, *Das Geheimnis des Anfangs. Einige spekulative Betrachtungen im Hinblick auf Böhme*, in A. and J. Assmann (eds), *Schleier und Schwelle II: Geheimnis und Offenbarung*, Munich, 1998, 43–56.

Wilhelm Schmidt-Biggemann (ed.), *Christliche Kabbala*, Pforzheimer Reuchlinschriften 10, Sigmaringen, 2003.

Carl Schmitt, *Politische Theologie: Vier Kapitel zur Lehre von der Souveränität*, Berlin, 1922.

Carl Schmitt, *Der Leviathan in der Staatslehre des Thomas Hobbes*, Hamburg, 1938, reprint Cologne, 1982, 92

Heinrich Schneider, *Lessing: Zwölf biographische Studien*, Bern, 1951.

Winfried Schröder, *Ursprünge des Atheismus: Untersuchungen zur Metaphysik- und Religionskritik des 17. und 18. Jahrhunderts*, Quaestiones: Themen und Gestalten der Philosophie II, Stuttgart-Bad Cannstatt, 1998.

Benjamin Schwartz (ed.), *Wisdom, Revelation, and Doubt. Perspectives on the First Millennium B.C.*, Daedalus 104/2, Cambridge, MA, 1975.

John R. Searle, *Speech Acts. An Essay in the Philosophy of Language*, Cambridge, 1969.

Rolf Selbmann, *Der deutsche Bildungsroman*, Stuttgart, 1994.

John Selden, *De Diis Syris Syntagmata II*, London, 1617.

John Selden, *De iure naturali et gentium iuxta disciplinam Ebraeorum*, London, 1640.

Amartya Sen, *Identity and Violence: The Illusion of Destiny*, New York, 2006.

Amartya Sen, 'Humanity and Citizenship', in Joshua Cohen (ed.), *For Love of Country: Debating the Limits of Patriotism. Martha C. Nussbaum with Respondents*, Boston, MA, 1996, 111–18.

Georg Simmel, 'Das Geheimnis und die geheime Gesellschaft', in G. Simmel, *Soziologie: Untersuchungen über die Formen der Vergesellschaftung*, Frankfurt/Main, 1992, 383–455.

Linda Simonis, *Die Kunst des Geheimen: Esoterische Kommunikation und ästhetische Darstellung im 18. Jahrhundert*, Heidelberg, 2002.

Mark J. Smith, Article '*Sonnenauge*', in *Lexikon der Ägyptologie 5* (1984), Sp. 1082–7.

Jan A. M. Snoek, 'What does the word "religious" mean in Reinhold's "religious freemasonry"?', in Sibylle Appel (ed.), *Egypt – Temple of the Whole World*, Leiden and Cologne, 2003, 409–20.

Josef von Sonnenfels, 'Über den Einfluß der Maurerei auf die bürgerliche Gesellschaft', in *JF* 1 (1784): 135–64.

John Spencer, *De legibus Hebraeorum ritualibus et eadem rationibus libri tres*, London, 1685.

Hermann Spieckermann, ' "Ein Vater vieler Völker". Die Verheißungen an Abraham im Alten Testament', in *'Abraham unser Vater'. Die gemeinsamen Wurzeln von Judentum, Christentum und Islam*, ed. by Reinhard G. Kratz and Tilman Nagel, Göttingen: Wallstein-Verlag, 2003, 8–21.

Wilhelm Spiegelberg, *Der demotische Text der Priesterdekrete von Kanopus and Memphis*, Heidelberg, 1922.

Elisabeth Staehelin, 'Alma Mater Isis', in Elisabeth Staehelin and Bertrand Jaeger (eds), *Ägypten-Bilder*, Oriens Biblicus et Orientalis 150, Fribourg, 1997, 103–41.

[Johann August Starck], *Ueber die alten und neuen Mysterien*, no place of publication given, undated. [Berlin 1783].

Michael Stausberg, *Faszination Zarathustra: Zoroaster und die Europäische Religionsgeschichte der Frühen Neuzeit*, Religionsgeschichtliche Versuche und Vorarbeiten 42, Berlin and New York, 1998.

Daniel Stolzenberg, 'Lectio Idealis: Theory and Practice in Athanasius Kircher's Translations of the Hieroglyphs', in Lucia Morra and Carla Bazzanella (eds), *Philosophers and Hieroglyphs*, Turin, 2003, 74–97.

Harald Strebel, *Der Freimaurer Wolfgang Amadé Mozart*, Stäfa: Rothenhäusler, 1991.

Stefan Strecker, *Der Gott Arnold Schönbergs: Blicke durch die Oper Moses und Aron*, Münster, 1999.

Bruno H. Stricker, *De brief van Aristeas: De hellenistische codificaties der praehelleense godsdiensten*, Amsterdam, 1956.

Guy G. (Gedaliahu A. G.) Stroumsa, *Hidden Wisdom: Esoteric Traditions and the Roots of Christian Mysticism*, Leiden, 1996.

Guy G. (Gedaliahu A. G.) Stroumsa, 'Milk and Meat: Augustine and the End of Ancient Esotericism', in G. G. Stroumsa, *Hidden Wisdom*, Leiden, 1996, 132–46.

Guy G. (Gedaliahu A. G.) Stroumsa, 'John Spencer and the Roots of Idolatry', in *History of Religions* 40 (2001): 1–23.

Guy G. (Gedaliahu A. G.) Stroumsa, 'Comments on Charles Hedrick's Article. A Testimony', in *Journal of Early Christian Studies* 11/2 (2003): 147–53.

Guy G. (Gedaliahu A. G.) Stroumsa, Paula Fredriksen, 'The Two Souls and the Divided Will', in Albert I. Baumgarten, J. Assmann and G. G. Stroumsa (eds), *Self, Soul, and Body in Religious Experience*, Leiden, 1998, 198–217.

Sarah Stroumsa, 'Entre Harran et al-Maghreb. La théorie maïmonidienne de l'histoire des religions et ses sources arabes', in María Isabel Fierro (ed.), *Judíos y musulmanes en al-Andalus y el Magreb. Contactos intelectuales*, Madrid: Casa de Velazquez, 2002, 153–64.

Sarah Stroumsa, 'Sabéens de Harran et Sabéens de Maïmonide', in Tony Lévy and Roshdi Rashed (ed.), *Maïmonide. Philosophe et savant*, Leuven, 2004, 335–52.

Theo Sundermeier, Artikel 'Religion, Religionen', in Karl Müller and Th. Sundermeier (eds), *Lexikon missionstheologischer Grundbegriffe*, Berlin, 1987, 411–23.

Theo Sundermeier, *Was ist Religion? Religionswissenschaft im theologischen Kontext*, Gütersloh, 1999.

Jean Abbé Terrasson, *Séthos. Histoire ou vie, tirée des monuments, Anecdotes de l'ancienne Égypte; Ouvrage dans lequel on trouve la description des Initiations aux Mystères Égyptiens. Traduit d'un manuscrit Grec*, Paris, 1731.

Tzvetan Todorov, *Theories of the Symbol*, trans. Catherine Porter, Ithaca, NY, 1984.

John Toland, *Adeisidaemon sive Titus Livius a superstitione vindicatus <. . .> annexae sunt <. . .> Origines Judaicae ut* RELIGIO *propaganda etiam, quae est juncta cum cognitione Naturae; sic* SUPERSTITIONIS *stirpes omnes ejicendae annexae sunt Origines Judaicae sive,* STRABONIS, *de Moyse et Religione Judaica historia, Breviter Illustrata*, Hagae-Comitis [Den Haag]: Thomam Johnson, 1709.

John Toland, *Tetradymus*, London, 1720.

Karel van der Toorn, *Scribal Culture and the Making of the Hebrew Bible*, Cambridge, MA, 2007.

Maria Totti, *Ausgewählte Texte der Isis- und Serapis-Religion*, Subsidia Epigraphica 12, Hildesheim et al., 1985.

Victor Turner, *The Forest of Symbols. Aspects of Ndembu Ritual*, Ithaca, NY: Cornell University Press, 1967.

Victor Turner, Article 'Myth and Symbol', in *International Encyclopedia of the Social Sciences*, ed. by David L. Sills, vol. 10, New York: Macmillan and The Free Press 1968, 576–82.

Vera F. Vanderlip, *The Four Greek Hymns of Isidorus and the Cult of Isis*, American Studies in Papyrology XII, Toronto, 1972.

Jacques Vandier, *Le Papyrus Jumilhac*, Paris, 1960.

Herman te Velde, 'Some Remarks on the Mysterious Language of the Baboons', in J. H. Kamstra (ed.), *Funerary Symbols and Religion*, Kampen, 1988, 129–36.

Jean-Pierre Vernant, 'De la présentification de l'invisible à l'imitation de l'apparence', in J.-P. Vernant, *Entre mythe et politique*, Paris 1996, 359–77.

Giambattista Vico, *La Scienza Nuova Seconda*, Naples, 1744.

Erik Voegelin, *Die politischen Religionen*, ed. by Peter Opitz, Munich, 1996.

Eric Voegelin, *Order and History*, vol. 4: *The Ecumenic Age*, Baton Rouge, IN, 1974.

Michael Voges, *Aufklärung und Geheimnis. Untersuchungen zur Vermittlung von Literatur- und Sozialgeschichte am Beispiel der Aneignung des Geheimbundmaterials im Roman des späten 18. Jahrhunderts*, Tübingen, 1987.

Achille Vogliano, *Primo Rapporto degli scavi condotti dalla Missione archeologica d' Egitto della Regia Università di Milano nella zona di Madinet Madi*, Milan, 1936.

Aksel Volten, 'An "Alphabetical" Dictionary and Grammar in Demotic', in *Archiv Orientalní* 20 (1952): 496–508.

Wilhelm Voßkamp, 'Der Bildungsroman als literarisch-soziale Institution. Begriffs- und funktionsgeschichtliche Überlegungen zum deutschen Bildungsroman am Ende des 18. und Beginn des 19. Jahrhunderts', in Christian Wagenknecht (ed.), *Zur Terminologie der Literaturwissenschaft*, Stuttgart, 1989, 337–52.

Wilhelm Voßkamp, *'Ein anderes Selbst'. Bild und Bildung im deutschen Roman des 18. und 19. Jahrhunderts*, Göttingen, 2004.

Johann Georg Wachter, *Naturae et Scripturae Concordia*, Copenhagen, 1752.

Andreas Wagner (ed.), *Primäre und sekundäre Religion als Kategorie der Religionsgeschichte des Alten Testaments*, BZAW 364, Berlin and New York, 2006.

Guy Wagner, *Bruder Mozart. Freimaurer im Wien des 18. Jahrhunderts*, Vienna et al., 1996.

Baudouin van de Walle, 'Le Décret d'Horemheb', in *Chronique d'Égypte* 22 (1947): 230–8, 253f.

Michael Walzer, *Thick and Thin*, Notre Dame 1994.

Ernst Wangermann, *The Austrian Achievement 1700–1800*, London, 1973.

William Warburton, *The divine legation of Moses demonstrated on the principles of a religious deist, from the omission of the doctrine of a future state of reward and punishment in the Jewish dispensation*, London, 1738–41; London, 2nd edn, 1778.

Richard Weihe, *Die Paradoxie der Maske: Geschichte einer Form*, Munich, 2004.

Françoise Weil, 'Ramsay et la Franc-Maçonnerie', in *Revue d'histoire de la France* 63 (1963): 272–8.

Ernst-Peter Wieckenberg, *Johan Melchior Goeze*, Hamburg, 2007.

Christoph Martin Wieland, *Geschichte des Agathon. Roman.* Erstfassung von 1766/67, ed. and with an afterword by Rolf Vollmann, Zurich, 2001.

Christoph Martin Wieland, *Peregrinus Proteus,* 2 parts, Frankfurt and Leipzig, 1789–91.

Christoph Martin Wieland, 'Geschichte der Abderiten', in *C. M. Wielands sämmtliche Werke,* ed. by Johann Gottfried Gruber, vol. 18, Leipzig: Göschen, 1825.

Christoph Martin Wieland, 'Das Geheimniß des Kosmopolitenordens', in *C. M. Wielands sämmtliche Werke,* ed. by Johann Gottfried Gruber, vol. 40, Leipzig: Göschen, 1826, 441–78.

Christoph Martin Wieland, 'Reise des Priesters Abulfauaris ins innere Afrika', in *C. M. Wielands sämmtliche Werke,* ed. by Johann Gottfried Gruber, vol. 15: *Vermischte prosaische Aufsätze,* Leipzig: Göschen, 1795 (reprint Hamburg, 1984).

Erich Winter, Article 'Hieroglyphen', in *RAC* 15, Lieferung 113, Stuttgart, 1989, 83–103.

Chaim Wirszubski, *Pico della Mirandola's Encounter with Jewish Mysticism,* Cambridge, MA, and London, 1989.

Uwe Wirth (ed.), *Performanz: Zwischen Sprachphilosophie und Kulturwissenschaften,* Frankfurt/Main, 2002.

Karl H. Wörner, *Gotteswort und Magie: Die Oper Moses und Aron von Arnold Schönberg,* Heidelberg, 1959.

Frances Yates, *Giordano Bruno and the Hermetic Tradition,* Chicago, IL, 1964.

Jean Yoyotte, 'Les pèlerinages dans l'Égypte ancienne', in J. Yoyotte et al. (eds), *Les pèlerinages,* Sources orientales 3, Paris, 1960, 19–74.

Jean Yoyotte, 'Notes et documents pour servir à l'histoire de Tanis', in *Kêmi* 21 (1971): 40–2.

Jean Yoyotte, Pascal Charvet and Stéphane Gompertz, *Strabon: Le Voyage en Egypte. Un regard romain,* Paris: Nil éditions, 1997.

Louis V. Žabkar, *Hymns to Isis in her Temple at Philae,* Hanover et al., 1988.

Jan Zandee, *De Hymnen aan Amon van Pap. Leiden I 350,* OMRO 28, Leiden, 1947.

Index